# German Travel Cultures

# Leisure, Consumption and Culture

**General Editor:** Rudy Koshar, *University of Wisconsin-Madison*

Leisure regimes in Europe (and North America) in the last two centuries have brought about far-reaching changes in consumption patterns and consumer cultures. The past twenty years have seen the evolution of scholarship on consumption from a wide range of disciplines but historical research on the subject is unevenly developed for late modern Europe, just as the historiography of leisure practices is limited to certain periods and places. This series encourages scholarship on how leisure and consumer culture evolved with respect to an array of identities. It relates leisure and consumption to the symbolic systems with which tourists, shoppers, fans, spectators, and hobbyists have created meaning, and to the structures of power that have shaped such consumer behavior. It treats consumption in general and leisure practices in particular as complex processes involving knowledge, negotiation, and the active formation of individual and collective selves.

# German Travel Cultures

*Rudy Koshar*

Oxford • New York

First published in 2000 by
**Berg**
Editorial offices:
150 Cowley Road, Oxford, OX4 1JJ, UK
838 Broadway, Third Floor, New York, NY 10003-4812, USA

Berg is an imprint of Oxford International Publishers Ltd.

**Library of Congress Cataloging-in-Publication Data**
A catalogue record for this book is available from the Library of Congress.

**British Library Cataloguing-in-Publication Data**
A catalogue record for this book is available from the British Library.

ISBN  1 85973 446 4 (Cloth)
      1 85973 451 0 (Paper)

Typeset by JS Typesetting, Wellingborough, Northamptonshire
Printed in the United Kingdom by Biddles Ltd, Guildford and King's Lynn

# Contents

# List of Illustrations

# Preface

This book began with what appears to be a straightforward question: what is it that travel guidebooks have done in the history of modern tourism? The author was motivated to make this query after using tour books for many years as a traveler and researcher who relied on the more authoritative examples of the genre for background information on urban histories and monuments. But I was also interested in studying a popular cultural artifact that allowed me to ask how (or if) leisure practices gave rise to enduringly important conceptions of identity and the self in modernity. The history of tourism seemed an especially appropriate subject because, as both the travel industry and scholars tell us, tourism will be the biggest business in the world in the twenty-first century. What if one studied travel handbooks not only as data, not only as commodities, but also as 'texts' that had an important bearing on the cultural identity of their users?

The community in question is Germany, partly because for more than two decades my research specialty has been that country's modern history, but partly also because Germany matters in the history of leisure travel. The focus here will be on guidebooks to Germany as products of distinct yet overlapping 'travel cultures,' which were shaped in turn by liberal individualism, working-class socialism, modernist notions of sexuality and pleasure, Nazism, and American–German relations. I consider not only the origins and impact of the famous Baedeker guidebook, the first great Bible of the modern tourist experience, but also more specialized or competing guidebooks. In relation to the world according to Baedeker, these 'alternative' handbooks catered to marginalized groups, voiced repressed or overlooked historical memories, or re-mapped Germany to account for new political and cultural developments. It will be seen that German travel cultures both reflected and shaped the bitter political conflicts that marked twentieth-century European history. Whereas specialists will find useful information on German cultural history in the following pages, students and educated lay readers in other fields will also find something of interest because the book engages a broader scholarship on European leisure and tourism. What readers will not find is a comprehensive history of tourist handbooks or of German tourism domestically and internationally (an impossible task at this stage of research, in any case). Nor will they get a full analysis of the political context in which travel cultures emerged. Given the aims and length of this book, such political history must be kept to a minimum, providing essential background rather than exhaustive exposition. Throughout the study, I argue that travel guidebooks reinforced the individuating functions of tourism, even as leisure travel became more standardized, and even as dominant travel cultures and ideologies viewed individuals as only either victims or unthinking consumers.

If the emphasis is on individuation, the author nonetheless recognizes the collective efforts that have gone into tourist cultures, and that, not incidentally, make scholar/travelers' research possible. I want to thank the Department of History, the Institute for Research in the Humanities, the Research Committee of the Graduate School, the Center for German and European Studies, and the European Union Center at the University of Wisconsin in Madison; the Graduiertenkolleg of the University of Halle; and the Max-Planck Institut für Geschichte in Göttingen. These institutions and centers have given me both financial support and free time over several years to research and write this book. My thanks go also to the staffs of the Memorial Library and Department of Special Collections of the University of Wisconsin, Madison, the Deutsche Bücherei in Leipzig, and the Institut für Tourismus at the Freie Universität Berlin, for their expert help. Along the way, numerous people, including Johannes Elwardt, Heinz-Gerhard Haupt, Erik Jensen, Oliver Kersten, Christiane Klemm, Alf Lüdtke, Michael Müller, Lynn Nyhart, Sara Sewell, Hasso Spode, and James Steakley, facilitated my research. Colleagues, graduate students, and friends in Madison and elsewhere have commented on papers that emerged from this project or earlier versions of chapters; to list them would be to overlook someone. I would like to thank my editors, Maike Bohn and Kathryn Earle, for their strong interest in leisure as a subject worthy of serious historical scholarship. My thanks also to Sven Michael Wair for his careful copy-editing of the manuscript. As always, Judy, Drew, and Annie played an important role in the creation of this book, and it is not an exaggeration to state that we are what we are as a family in part because we gladly traveled together.

I dedicate this book to my mother and father.

# Introduction

As the American writer Bayard Taylor traveled on the Rhine River near Koblenz in the nineteenth-century, he marveled at how 'almost every mountain has a ruin and a legend.' 'One feels everywhere the spirit of the past,' he enthused, 'and its stirring recollections come back upon the mind with irresistible force.' Taylor noted that the English tourists on deck were equally enthusiastic, 'but in a different manner.' 'With Murray's Handbook open in their hands, they sat and read about the very towns and towers they were passing, scarcely lifting their eyes to the real scenes, except now and then to observe that it was "very nice"' (Taylor 1914, 5–6). Traveling and writing have always been closely associated, and travel accounts of the Rhineland have a long history going back to the time of Julius Caesar. Taylor's account suggests that in the modern age it is not only writing that is intimately linked with travel but also reading. And it is a kind of reading that, in Taylor's estimation, substituted for the experience of travel itself. The apparent paradox was not lost on the young American writer. In a time that could be described as the first great golden age of leisure travel, tourists were seemingly closing themselves off to the sites they came to see.

Murray's Handbook was one of the first modern tourist guidebooks. The Murray firm of London published a comprehensive guide to Europe and Germany in 1836, claiming to give the traveler a comprehensive picture not of what could be seen—this was the mistake of so much previous travel literature—but 'what ought to be seen' (Murray 1858, v–vi; Koshar 1998b, 323). Three years later a Koblenz book shop owner, Karl Baedeker, produced a handbook for the Rhineland that became the international standard, and soon Baedeker would become known throughout Europe as the publisher of highly reliable and comprehensive travel handbooks. What was said of Murray by a travel writer in 1855 could have been said of Baedeker by the last quarter of the nineteenth century: 'since Napoleon no man's empire has been so wide' (Gretton 1993, ii). The tourist guidebook has become ubiquitous in modern travel literature. But, as Taylor's observations indicate, the travel guidebook has always caused much hand wringing among critics, travel writers, and scholars (Boorstin 1961; Enzensberger 1964, 199; Fussell 1980).

From the critics' point of view, the travel guidebook's mere existence means that the pleasure of voluntarily moving between some form of sessility and an extended moment of leisured displacement—let this stand as a working definition of tourism—has been eviscerated. By what? By commodification and marketing, by materialism and the 'cash nexus,' and by a tourist industry that dilutes the discoveries of travel through predetermined itineraries and packaged experiences. The German writer Hans Magnus Enzensberger states the critique succinctly: 'Liberation from the industrial world has become an industry in its own right, the journey from the commodity world has itself become a commodity' (1964, 196). This statement may be seen in its connection to a larger criticism about the effects of commodification. Writing about the nineteenth century, historian Victoria de Grazia argues that 'at the moment people were recognized as having the right to demand necessities, the notion of the necessary was narrowed' (1996, 17). She makes this observation with reference to women, who paradoxically were most often responsible for getting the basic needs of the household, but whose ability to represent their interests in public life was occluded. But in modified form it could be extended to both men and women, and it applies as well to the critique of tourism. Enzensberger posits a great divide between the potential of modern tourism and the narrowed repertoire of needs and values to which commercial travel speaks. What was to have been a pleasurable or even emancipatory refuge was transformed into a commodified dead end, directions to which were given by the travelers' ever-present handbook. It should be noted that in de Grazia's study, there is ample evidence for how individuals—and once again women in particular—grapple with the simultaneous multiplication and narrowing of possibilities that late modern commercial society brings. In an analogous way, the reader of this book will find evidence for how the travel guidebook, in spite (or perhaps because) of its tightly woven itineraries, creates a space for significant individual practice.

The narrative from which Enzensberger's criticism of tourism stems takes in a long development, beginning as early as the seventeenth century. But it pinpoints the early nineteenth century, focusing in particular on Europe and North America, where the formation of industrial society and the evolution of tourism went hand in hand. The historical argument, accumulated through countless variations by individual authors, may be summarized: In the wake of the American and French revolutions—and despite the political reaction that followed these cataclysms—the Euro-American world saw the evolution of a new 'leisure regime.' Unleashed capitalism created extraordinary demands on the energies of those hard-driving, acquisitive spirits who nurtured it. Capital accumulation created both the necessity and the means for innovative leisure practices separated both emotionally and physically from the world of work, and for corresponding ways of seeing 'culture' and 'nature' as elemental forces untouched by factory, office, and city. At first, the new leisure regime benefited mainly the upper and middle strata of England and

North America, but it did not fail to touch the lives of Continental elites, the middle classes, and subsequently parts of the artisan and service classes as well.

The railroads were of course central to the evolution of pleasurable travel. It is no coincidence that the first modern travel guidebooks appeared in England and Germany in the 1830s, precisely the moment when an iron web slowly began to envelop these societies, transporting their inhabitants with unexampled speed and efficiency. But this development also had negative consequences, as rapid travel led to the annihilation of space and time. The well-off leisure traveler or commercial agent of the past may have gone by carriage or horseback, the pilgrim, artisan, or vagrant by foot. Their mode of transportation engaged them directly in the natural environment and the cultural rhythms of the places they visited. They experienced space and time as unfolding and sequential. Modern railways removed travelers from their immediate surrounding, creating a 'panoramic' mode of perception that took in landscapes not as tangible entities but as fleeting 'sights' (Schivelbusch 1986; Sternberger 1977). Space and time were to be conquered, not felt or experienced, and the process of travel itself was now diminished by the hegemony of the tourist destination.

The motivation for this act of conquest—so the critique goes—was not to be found in the love of travel, the pursuit of knowledge, or the social requirements of privileged belonging. This latter characteristic had regulated the activities of the sons of the European aristocracy and wealthier bourgeoisie, whose Grand Tour through Holland, the Rhineland, Switzerland, northern and central Italy, and Greece developed from a well-prescribed itinerary of country homes, spas, classical ruins, and political capitals. Leisure travel instead became 'tourism,' defined neither by the pursuit of individual betterment nor by tradition, but by pure enjoyment, and the getting and spending that modern recreation demanded. Commercial agents, railway timetables, hotel price lists, picture postcards, cheap souvenirs, and tourist guidebooks—these were the new accoutrements of travel. Travel had once been closely associated with 'culture,' in its double and often contradictory sense as individual self-fulfillment and the making of a whole way of life (Williams 1977, 11–20). But it was now pure consumption, or commercialized leisure—something reduced and enervated.

All historical arguments are caricatures, some more than others. But caricatures resonate, and the narrative of tourism as a diminished form of travel has had an extremely long half-life. The nineteenth century saw novelists, journalists, and scholars criticize the new age of travel in forms ranging from satirical scolding to harsh attack (Buzard 1993). English commentators worried aloud that tourism unleashed 'King Mob,' whose demands for social leveling found expression in the guise of middle-class tourists bustling through the itineraries set up for them by the first successful modern travel agency, Cook's Tours (Brendon 1991, 62). German writers at the turn of the century saw the entire sweep of commercial developments that spawned tourism as a direct threat to an 'organic' national community still uncertain of its power. Youth, artists, and workers on both sides of the Atlantic sought 'purer' forms of touristic experience as an antidote to travel governed by railways, ships, and (later) automobiles and airplanes. In the interwar period, travelers explored the more disreputable or titillating aspects of European cities invisible to Baedeker's ascetic eye. American tourists, and by no means only those writers and expatriates belonging to the 'lost generation,' meanwhile began to flock to the Continent. Although at times they embodied all the negative traits that the critique of tourism pinpointed, their presence in the streets of historic Paris, Rome, or Berlin suggested they too were looking for something more 'authentic' than the average tourist back home could grasp.

Political regimes likewise paid direct or indirect tribute to the critique of tourism. Mussolini and Hitler insisted that leisure travel was not merely commerce, and certainly not idle distraction, but something needed to mobilize the nation for political conquest (Baranowski and Furlough 2000; de Grazia 1981, 179–84). After World War II, the revival of industrial economies in Europe and North America depended in part on tourism. Leisure travel was now not only something people enjoyed; it also carried a heavy symbolic load, as the right to go on vacation was seen as an entitlement, as a sign that national economies could deliver the goods to demanding consumer-citizens. Precisely this notion made the critique of tourism more compelling for those who used it. They read the 'travel as a fundamental human right' argument as yet another sign of democratization gone out of control. On both the Right and the Left, they regarded the idea as typical of how capitalist societies offered superficial material compensation for deeper existential crises. They rued developments that turned potential citizens into passive consumers, who were nothing more than 'giant bacteria, called tourists,' in the hyperventilated words of the German writer Gerhard Nebel from 1950 (Bausinger 1991, 346). Yet political agents continued to use tourism, and in divided Germany, ground zero in the Cold War, capitalist and Communist regimes promoted travel as both ideology and social right.

Many scholars have grown weary of the critique, insisting that it rests on a false dichotomy between 'good' travel and 'bad' tourism, and that it cannot tell us why it is that so many people travel for leisure purposes (Confino 1998, 145; Levenstein 1998). Henry James' famous deprecation of the tourist—'vulgar, vulgar, vulgar'— will no longer do as a theoretical starting point or historical argument. But neither scholarship nor educated lay opinion, neither governments nor tourists themselves, have been freed from this persistent way of seeing the tourist experience. Meanwhile, the tourist industry cashes in on self-criticism: 'adventure tourism' and 'extreme sports' are only the most recent examples of the money to be made by selling alternatives to an allegedly stifling touristic norm. Travel guidebooks have in turn traced tourism's evolution, becoming the central 'printed medium of leisure migration' (Böröcz 1992, 716–17) and the 'devotional texts' of 'the main modern pilgrim' (Horne 1984, 10). Enzensberger regards the genre as an important motor in the regulation of tourism by capitalist values. The travel guidebook has the quality of a 'command,' writes Enzensberger, and those who are commanded find the guide no less useful because they pay for it (1964, 199). For Enzensberger, the travel guidebook reinforces a process whereby tourism's quest to get beyond the iron cage of the commodity world is constantly frustrated. Each alternative to commercialized travel becomes yet another instance of the process it condemns, each new tour book yet another artifact of the evaporation of tourism's potential.

Recent cultural history and theory hypothesize that neither culture in general nor leisure in particular can be treated as mere reflexes of politics, industry, and society. Leisure has its own history, neither wholly determined by the structures and constraints of the mode of production in which it develops, nor fully shaped by patterns of social power. Leisure is not intrinsically passive, as the critique of tourism so often insists, but potentially active and interpretive even when based on pure consumption. The exact nature of the relationship between leisure and society remains to be worked out, both in terms of its historical development and theoretical significance. One of the goals of my book is to concretize this relationship in a case study of a key tourist nation; to show that the travel guidebook, like 'the tourist,' has played a more proactive role than criticism suggests; and to show that travelers such as those that Bayard Taylor observed did more than substitute a fake 'tourist reality' for the 'real reality' that passed before their eyes.

## II

Aside from directing scholarly attention to the larger importance of popular culture, cultural studies offer the historian a crucial insight, namely that 'texts' of all kinds 'work' in particular and often contradictory or self-destructive ways (Barthes 1972; During 1999; Fiske 1989). Cultural productions ranging from books to automobile racing, from fashion to films, and from architecture to professional wrestling, do not just reflect larger political or social contexts. They also actively shape and re-shape such contexts, creating important webs of significance between the 'reader' and the text, and between the text and the larger community of readers. That community may be defined in terms of class, gender, ethnicity, nationality, sexual preference, historical destiny, religion, cultural style, regional identity, and political ideology. Its constituents undertake what French philosopher Michel de Certeau called the 'silent production' of reading, where reading does not refer to the reading of literature only but to talking, dwelling, walking, taking pictures, watching television and cinema, spectating, shopping, and cooking—in short, a whole, connected set of life practices. The reader 'inhabits' texts, spaces, and conversations, insinuating her meanings and interpretations into the productions of others. Through this process, wrote de Certeau, 'a different world (the reader's) slips into the author's place' (1984, xxi).

I am interested in how tourist handbooks potentially worked for their individual users and for the larger collective entities to which those users belonged. I cannot offer a comprehensive analysis of how guidebooks were interpreted in specific historical contexts. Not a transparent record of tourists' tactical operations, the guidebook may be read for the way in which it highlights the *conditions* of possibility for such operations. My goal is to pinpoint and explicate the parts of guidebooks that were open to certain uses and interpretations by tourist-readers. These uses and interpretations will be considered in relation to German 'travel cultures,' a term to be discussed shortly. My focus will be on how touristic information is conveyed as well as on content, on 'form' as well as on recurring themes, ideological motifs, and larger meanings. These larger meanings, seemingly buried in the tour book's practical tips and anodyne itineraries, have to do with questions of why tourists travel, what tourists see, and how leisure travel has become an existential necessity. They contribute to what may be called a 'hermeneutics' of tourism, a process of interpretation by which the individual tourist creates knowledge. Jonathan Culler (1981) writes that tourist readers are like semioticians, interpreters of signs, and guidebooks are among the 'markers' (along with travel brochures, 'on-site' plaques, and even souvenirs) that render tourist sights intelligible to visitors (MacCannell 1976, 110). What readings do guidebook-markers enable in different historical contexts? What 'mis-readings,' or even critical reinterpretations, are possible by tourists?

The question of how tourists interpret travel markers has everything to do with the nature of the world through which they move. Scholars now comprehend late modernity as an age of displacement and crossing borders. Immigrants, exiles, refugees, soldiers, students, scholars, artists, business travelers, and tourists have been the key actors in a global story of unremitting movement. Within nations, human travel creates new forms of community but also economic competition, cultural tension, and environmental destruction. Across the globe, the migration of people changes relations between states and cultures, generating new possibilities for multilateral cooperation as well as new divisions between governments, ethnic and religious groups, and producers and consumers. Social scientists argue that population movements develop in response to both 'push' and 'pull' factors. Labor migrants are literally pushed from their homelands because of tight job markets and economic shortages, but they are also lured by the promise of increased incomes and a better quality of life. Political exiles are forced from their homelands out of fear of persecution and death, but are also engaged by the freedom of the political culture to which they migrate. 'Leisure flows' (Böröcz 1996, 8) are stimulated mainly by pull factors, as tourists are attracted by the real and imagined pleasures

6

of distant or exotic destinations. Aside from rather extensive research on travel literature in early modern Europe, humanistic scholarship has done little to chart the history of tourism in general or to study wider relationships between tourism and political or cultural identities. The research that exists is open to much criticism, as noted later in this chapter. Some researchers have stressed that tourism did more to confirm the traveler's prejudices than to teach her about other cultures or classes. Separation from home and exposure to new experiences are said to promote a sense of difference, and representations of travel experiences reveal only the ideological dispositions of the observer rather than the nature of that being observed. Euro-American travel throughout the world is seen either in terms of a unidirectional and positive diffusion of Western values or, in a more critical reading, in terms of racism and imperialism. Travel within national borders is analyzed as a cognate of asymmetrical social relations; just as wealthy travelers from industrial nations exploit the people of poor countries, the well-heeled travelers of specific national societies are said to exploit their 'inferior' co-nationals.

Scholars from different disciplines are dissatisfied with this type of analysis. They neglect neither the ideological dimensions of travel nor the injuries of colonialism and class distinctions, but they ask if exposure to new experiences through travel has also produced novel forms of identity and novel ways of apprehending one's own or another culture. Travel accounts can no longer be read as one-way impositions of the viewer's ideology but rather must be seen in terms of an interactive process affecting both viewer and viewed. All cultures are 'traveling cultures,' writes anthropologist James Clifford (1997, 17–46), and cultural identity is the result of negotiation and intercultural transfer, for the powerful as well as the powerless, for 'natives' as well as strangers. Travelers move through 'intercultures' or 'contact zones' (Pratt 1992) where national, class, and gender identities are affirmed but potentially also destabilized or modified. Pratt argues that the expression '"contact zone" is an attempt to invoke the spatial and temporal copresence of subjects previously separated by geographic and historical disjunctures and whose trajectories now intersect' (ibid., 7). Meaningful interactions within various contact zones between traveler and 'host' (and between travelers themselves) are not prevented by unequal power relationships but rather constitute those relationships. This shift in emphasis may be described as a move from a 'diffusionist' to a 'contact' or 'interactive' perspective. Regardless of the label we give it, there can be little doubt it has important implications for understanding the lowly tourist guidebook as a significant cultural artifact, indeed as a product of, and a mediator in, such interactions.

My point of departure is that tourist handbooks, both symptoms and facilitators in the embrace of the world as a tourist destination, have also performed a kind of cultural labor that suggests the interpretive potential of 'displacement as leisure.' I take issue with those, such as Ursula Becher (1990, 197–8, 204–5), who argue that the central meaning of tourism was (and remains) a flight from everyday life, an attempt to use nature and history as 'pure' alternatives or 'counterworlds' to the social reality from which tourists escape. In making this criticism, I also revise my earlier analysis (1998b, 339), which posited tourism as an attempt to find meaning 'beyond' the everyday. Just as the critique of tourism has a long history, so too does the argument that work and leisure, the everyday and the extraordinary, are sealed off from one another in modern societies. But one does not have to accept either formulation. In the following analysis, tourism will be discussed as a form of leisure that potentially allows the individual to make sense of an existential fact of modern life: the consciousness of displacement. In other words, tourism may be a direct and tangible path to the feeling of being unsettled, but in a pleasurable manner, without the physical and psychological costs that displacement has for involuntary travelers. This does not mean that tourism is a form of commercialized voyeurism whereby privileged (social or colonial) classes delight in the plight of others. Leisure travel challenges even the most well-to-do tourist, who must make plane and train connections, deal with unpredictable hotels and travel agents, adjust to changes in diet and weather, negotiate cultural and linguistic barriers, endure family flare-ups, choose travel guides, and read the signs and images of tourist destinations.

It is worth remembering that the word 'travel' is derived from 'travail,' which meant suffering or labor, or both. Although we no longer inhabit the psychological world of the seventeenth century, when these terms were roughly equivalent (Wallace 1993, 18–19), tourism still demands risk and effort—and not a little anxiety. We know that in the course of the twentieth century, leisure travel has become equated with the vacation and 'getting away from it all.' (In my argument, in contrast to the work of sociologist Jean-Didier Urbain [1994], the vacation is subsumed in tourism, which I define as any practice arising from an individual's voluntary movement between relatively permanent 'settledness' and an extended moment of leisured displacement.) However, so my argument will go, traveling down the path to pleasure has neither excluded other motivations nor obliterated the traces of earlier historical moments of leisure travel in which the search for self-knowledge, the embrace of culture, and the positing of collective forms of belonging also played central roles. Tourism finds its meaning through effort, contact, and interaction, no matter how programmed or structured, and if something is learned through tourism, it reaffirms or alters the traveler's sense of self in unpredictable ways. 'I always returned from vacation as a homeless person [*Heimatloser*],' recalled Walter Benjamin of childhood excursions with his family (1992 [1950], 86). His parents' comfortable bourgeois apartment in Berlin had become a different—and less desirable—place after the experience of travel left its traces in memory. The muted tones and glancing images Benjamin used to describe his childhood recollection capture the subtlety with which leisure travel changes individual personalities.

In the following pages, tourist guidebooks are used to follow the traces of various tourist 'selves.' This individualizing perspective makes sense both analytically and practically because, despite the ubiquity of group tours throughout the world, modern tourism remains largely 'unorganized,' familial, or individual (Bausinger 1991, 348). I begin with the idea that the tourist was not only an individuated (and gendered) being, but also a producer and a consumer, the citizen of a national political community, and a person with experiences in common with travelers from other nations. Above all, the tourist was a reader—and a potentially very autonomous cultural 'producer'—in the sense that de Certeau used these terms. These and other roles could be used to form a relatively stable identity, a sense of one's consistent relationship with a larger community. But they could also be at odds with one another, especially at moments of societal conflict and cultural doubt, and their relationships could reveal meanings that were unintended by the reader-tourists who produced them. In Marshall Berman's classic analysis of cultural modernism (1988), literature and art are attempts to represent the central experience of modernity: having the ground cut from under one's self, the feeling that 'all that is solid melts into air.' In a similar fashion, the tourist responds to the sensation of displacement in which he has put himself by relating his various selves, by trying to make the parts add up to a whole, if only temporarily, by being a coherent reader. But she or he does so by traveling to particular sites deemed worthy of tourist attention, by voluntarily moving between physical and psychological states of 'home' and 'away.' (The issue of whether 'simulated mobility' through televisual images and computer technologies heralds an age of postmodern tourism or even the end of tourism in its present form must be left for another discussion [Urry 1995, 147–50].) Tourist guidebooks are formulas for travel, guides to the 'beaten track,' but they may also be read as distillations of the objects and routes of the tourist's cultural labor, and of the possibilities and diversity of experience.

The social medium through which the selves of the tourist were connected was the 'travel culture.' German scholars use the term 'travel culture' (*Reisekultur*) to refer generally to the practices and traditions of leisure travel (Bausinger et al. 1991). Towner (1996, 98–106) employs the concept to analyze a Renaissance-inspired impulse to travel on the part of British elites. When the term is used here it identifies a changing horizon of knowledge and expectation to which individuals were oriented as they traveled for pleasure and interacted with new peoples and environments. By focusing on representative guidebooks dealing with twentieth-century Germany, my book will demonstrate how the history and interaction of various travel cultures illuminated the multiple significations of modern tourism. It will treat the tourist guidebook as a text marked by travel cultures from which tourist-readers derived meaning and ideological orientation. In doing so, it will pay attention to how horizons of tourist knowledge, though based ultimately on individual experience, also related to the evolution of collective identity. Throughout the following pages, there will be much discussion of the relation between class (particularly middle-class) cultures and national identity. I regard national identity as a continuing though malleable source of linguistic elements and cultural symbols from which various travel cultures drew in their attempt to get tourist selves to cohere. But just as they drew from the existing stock of national orientations and symbols, travel cultures were also building blocks of national identity in their own right, in the same way trade unions, consumer cultures, generations, parties, associations, church communities, municipalities, and other sodalities were. That the search for national identity was an important element of German history over the last century requires little elaboration here. This search has been the subject of a large scholarly literature too complex to be given its due in this introduction. One could argue that the striving for national identity in German history was a kind of collective travel experience writ large, a violent, societal 'coming of age' through travel, or *Bildungsreise*, for which much of the world paid dearly.

Germans neither invented the modern tour guide nor created the first modern travel agency. They lagged behind both the English and the French early in the nineteenth century in developing a rail system and forming a tourist infrastructure. Yet even then patriots such as Friedrich Ludwig Jahn insisted that travel was a primordial characteristic of the Germans. Jahn wanted to revive the Germanic tribes' desire for travel with 'fatherland tours' that would get younger Germans to enthuse over the idea of a unified national state (Jahn 1991, 301-5). Not long after Jahn's reflections, 'the Baedeker' appeared, and the archetypal modern guidebook was born. English travelers, spurred by Romantic fantasies, had already turned the Rhineland into a favored destination. By the turn of the century, American travelers, influenced in part by the formative influence of German immigrant culture in the United States, also turned to 'romantic Germany.' Meanwhile, more and more Germans, buoyed by material growth and political mobilization, began to live up to their reputation as a peripatetic people. This reputation would only increase over the next half-century, as the German empire of travel grew and developed. The middle and upper strata had the greatest opportunity to go on tour, but the working class, particularly after World War I, also gained entry to the world of leisure travel. Germany was a much-traversed nation, and Germans created a true traveling culture.

Even so, German culture registered a deep anxiety about the effects of modern civilization, including commercialized leisure, on national life. Just as Germany became a traveling culture, it worried incessantly about the dissolution of its 'roots,' its sense of place, and its allegedly unique nationality. It was a country in which the tempo of change was rapid and the displacements of modernity were harsh, and where tourist selves were torn between different roles and meanings. And— so I will argue—it was a country in which a series of well-elaborated travel cultures evolved to adjudicate between the tensions and antinomies of the uncertainly traveling national culture. Germany has quite rightly been regarded as a country with rigidly defined *political* cultures out of which its main parties sprang in the nineteenth century: socialists (and later Communists), Catholics, liberals, democrats, and conservatives. Travel cultures should not be equated with political cultures or social classes in the following study. (Nor should the following be regarded as a comprehensive study of all German travel cultures.) But there is indeed a relationship between the idea of a rigid system of political 'camps' (or class identities) and the idea of relatively distinct travel cultures. Even so, it is difficult to claim that German travel cultures were impervious to one another or to international influences. The relationship between travel cultures is dynamic and historical, something that must be demonstrated in particular social contexts rather than defined *a priori*. The numerous crosscutting influences between German travel cultures and between German and foreign travel cultures in different historical periods are discussed throughout the book.

## III

Scholarly literature on tourism is best described as cluttered. Anthropological, ethnological, geographical, and sociological theories of tourism appear far more developed than historical scholarship is (Clifford 1997; Böröcz 1992, 1996; Enzensberger 1964; Horne 1984; Knebel 1960; Löfgren 1999; MacCannell 1976, 1992; Selwyn 1996; Smith 1977; Towner 1996; Urry 1990, 1995). Yet this activity is misleading. Whereas individual geographers have done much to promote scholarship on tourism (Towner 1996), the analysis of leisure travel within geography departments in Europe and North America is limited (Hall and Page 1999, 2–8). Urry argues 'there is really no sociology of tourism' (1995, 129–30). Maurer (1998) points out that gender analysis in tourist research is still relatively rare. Much of the literature does little to move away from some of the tried and true formulations sketched out earlier. From Daniel Boorstin's (1961) characterization of tourism as a typical product of Americans' need for 'pseudo-events,' to sociologist Jean Baudrillard's (1988, 9) argument that, in America, the land of the 'simulacrum,' 'nothing is further from pure travelling than tourism,' much scholarship explicitly or implicitly condemns tourism for its inauthenticity.

Anthropologist Dean MacCannell's scholarship (1976, 1992) is a notable counterpoint. Although critical of tourists and tourism, MacCannell maintains that 'tourism is a primary ground for the production of new cultural forms on a global base' (1992, 1). This point of view is taken up in an engagingly written book by ethnologist Orvar Löfgren, who sees tourism as a 'cultural laboratory' in which new leisure practices are tested (1999, 7). Urry's well-argued study *The Tourist Gaze* meanwhile makes the observation that, contrary to the implied meaning of the title, no single or essential tourist experience exists. Rather, tourism depends on a notion of multifaceted 'departure' from the everyday and a focus on the extraordinary. This is analogous to Löfgren's concept of 'elsewhereness,' which I take up in the conclusion. It should be pointed out that terms such as 'departure' and 'elsewhereness' make for a rather different view of tourism than that to be found in the following pages, in which leisure travel is seen as a process of interpreting the existential condition of displacement. Moreover, Urry, by emphasizing the tourist gaze, foregrounds the superficial and visual elements of leisure travel, a position very different from mine, which concentrates on the individual tourist's hermeneutical search for 'depth.' Nonetheless, both Urry and Löfgren correctly assume that tourism is associated with a multiplicity of forms and meanings, and may be apprehended only with a multiplicity of concepts that frustrate grand theories or all-embracing narratives.

Urry's sense of tourism as multifaceted and mutable lends itself well to historical study. As with the theoretical literature, however, the record of historical scholarship on tourism is mixed. As John Walton correctly states, 'tourism has not been accepted into the charmed circle of acceptable themes in European history' (1997, 563). Virtually in a category by itself, Eric Leed's study (1991) of the 'mind of the traveler' constructs a brilliant argument about the psychology of travel over the ages. But Leed does little to illuminate the everyday experiences of the traveler. In contrast, social history gives us finely grained accounts of the seaside and spas (Corbin 1994; Cross 1990; Mackaman 1998; Walton 1983), World War I battlefield tourism (Lloyd 1998; Mosse 1990, 30–1, 152–5), the 'tourist map' of early modern England (Ousby 1990), and the rise of Cook's travel agency (Brendon 1991). The origins of workers' tourism in Germany are discussed by Christine Keitz (1989, 1993, 1997), Shelley Baranowski (2000), and others (Erdmann and Lorenz 1985; Spode 1980, 1982). Keitz's work is the most detailed of these to date, but she pays too much attention to the social structures rather than the meanings, and to the 'hows' rather than the 'whys,' of tourist practice. We have scholarship on German regions and tourism (Applegate 1990, 63–5, 71–2, 213–15; Confino 1997; Lepovitz 1992); on 'heritage' tourism (Ashworth and Larkham 1994; Lowenthal 1985, 1996; Kirshenblatt-Gimblett 1998); on tourism and Euro-American relations (Dulles 1964; Endy 1998; Levenstein 1998; Pells 1997); and on Switzerland as a vacation destination (Bernard 1978; Tissot 1995). Significantly, there is little historical scholarship on leisure travel in socialist systems, which makes Böröcz's recent comparative study of Austria and Communist Hungary as tourist nations (1996) a useful contribution.

This literature reflects not only the rich mine of material available to the historian of tourism but also the tremendous gaps, the disparate and often unrelated foci, and the lack of a general framework. Bemoaning the lack of a general conceptual frame does not mean this author advocates a general theory or a grand narrative of tourism. Rather, it points to the need to offer a set of more general conceptual markers that will bring organization into a field that is at present dispersed and without direction. These markers do not (and could not) add up to a comprehensive and definitive history or a general explanatory model, but rather to a set of useful heuristic constellations, whose relationship with one another remains to be elucidated.

One possibility for focusing tourism research comes from the history of leisure and commercial culture, for which there is a developing scholarship on Europe (Baranowski and Furlough 2000; de Grazia and Furlough 1996). Although still in its infancy (compared to its more mature American sibling), this research helps us reflect on how leisure travel, usually regarded as a practice standing in opposition to everyday life, is itself woven into the history of commercial society. In the case of modern German historiography, scholarship on commercial society and the evolution of modern leisure regimes is especially spotty. Whereas Germans came to identify themselves in terms of not only industrial might but also high (even excessive) standards of consumption before World War I (Breckman 1990; James 1989), we still have little in the way of a developed scholarship on this topic. The Weimar Republic, Germany's first attempt at democracy from 1918 to 1933, was a crucible of modernist experiments in advertising, commercial culture, and leisure practices. Yet research on the effects and meanings of such activities in everyday life lags far behind scholarship on the more well-known aspects of Weimar culture such as film, avant-garde painting, literature, and architecture. Nazism evolved partly as a moralistic and nationalist protest against the cultural experimentation of the Weimar period. But it was in Hitler's time that the idea that all members of the nation had the right to vacation and travel became part of the general culture if not a matter of state policy. Even so, scholarship on consumption patterns and leisure activities under Nazism is dispersed and unfocused. Some historians have begun to turn their attention to the history of consumption in the postwar period (Wildt 1996), and analysis of gender relations has proved to be valuable for understanding the entanglement of social identity and commerce in this era (Carter 1997; Pence 1998). A social history of tourism exists in rather summary form for the first decade after World War II (Schildt 1995, 180–202), but scholars have little to go on for the period after the late 1950s. Here too, then, much remains to be done.

Another way of sharpening the research focus on German tourism is to refer to the scholarship on the *Bürgertum*, or middle strata. Trans-Atlantic debates among historians on the distinctiveness of the German national experience, the so-called *Sonderweg*, or 'special path' debate, have crystallized around the history of the middle strata. The debate hinges in part on the degree to which one can argue that German society was 'bourgeois,' or *bürgerlich*, and therefore to what degree German historical development was similar to that of French, English, and

American societies (Blackbourn and Eley 1984; Blackbourn and Evans 1991; Kocka 1988; Wehler 1995). The stakes of this debate are immense, for it speaks to the issue of how best to understand the roots of Nazism. The question of *Bürgerlichkeit* also has to do with leisure practices, since the German middle strata, like their counterparts in all societies with emergent commercial cultures, developed their own domestic architecture, reading habits, musical tastes, clothing, culinary traditions, and of course travel patterns. Wolfgang Kaschuba (1988) explores such facets of bourgeois life as part of a 'symbolic practice' for the early nineteenth century, and Bausinger (1987), Hein and Schulz (1996), and Nipperdey (1993, 1:125–91, 692–796) among others illuminate a number of cultural activities associated with bourgeois identity. Several collections and overviews (Bausinger et al. 1991; Kunsthistorisches Institut der Universität Tübingen 1981; Spode 1987) sketch the outlines of German and European leisure travel. We have studies of the cultural history of walking (König 1996), the rise of 'vacationing' (Prahl 1979), and German travel to the United States (Schmidt 1997). The automobile is central to the history of twentieth-century middle-class leisure, but there is little serious discussion of its daily use and cultural meaning in Germany (Haubner 1998; Möser 1998; Sachs 1984). Finally, several recent studies (Schildt 1995; Spode 1996) address the revival of tourism—a formerly bourgeois practice now available to more and more workers—in post-World War II German society. Significantly, the question of how middle-class identities related to the idea of nationality in various historical periods remains more implicit than explicit in tourism research on Germany. Little has been written on the issue of the tourist guidebook as an artifact of Bürgerlichkeit and national identity (Koshar 1998b).

Just as research on tourism is dispersed across a number of disparate subject areas, scholarly writing on travel guides presents a variegated though incomplete picture. There is abundant policy-oriented research from the field of tourism management. There are also scattered studies of the historical evolution of travel guidebooks as cultural artifacts (Allen 1996; Becker 1983; Böröcz 1992; 1996, 23–51; Koshar 1998b; Lauterbach 1989; Mendelson 1985; Moret 1992; Öhlberger 1987; Pretzel 1995), and of the tourist guidebook in relation to a larger theoretical or historical argument (Brenner 1990, 584–7; Barthes 1972, 74–7; Buzard 1993; Grewal 1996; Tissot 1995). Collectors and popular historians make available a large amount of bibliographical material on guidebooks (Hinrichsen 1988, 1991; Lister 1993; Vaughan 1974), and the Baedeker firm (whose valuable archive was destroyed in World War II) has been the subject of museum exhibits and collections (Frühauf 1992). For the most part, the bibliographical work has been uninformed by recent interdisciplinary discussions in cultural history. It is travel literature that has occupied the most serious scholarly attention, and although most of this work focuses on the eighteenth and nineteenth centuries (Brenner 1989, 1990; Krasnobaev et al. 1980; Liebersohn 1998; Pratt 1992), there is also scholarship on later periods (Schmidt 1997; Plonien 1995). Travel literature written by women has also come in for serious bibliographical and scholarly discussion in the last decade (Maurer 1998; Mills 1991; Morgan 1996; Pelz 1993; Siebert 1996). I draw on such research in the following pages to elaborate elements only hinted at in the guidebooks and to compare guidebook representations with travel accounts. But it is important to point out that arguments used to analyze the travel account are often not transferable to the travel guide. Whereas the former was written as a record of a journey already taken and digested, the latter anticipated future travel. Whereas the best travel accounts make no mistake of their status as works of interpretation, the travel guide represents itself as unmediated, 'transparent' communication.

Despite (or perhaps due to) the bad reputation travel guides have, there is no general history of this significant genre of tourist literature just as there is no general history of tourism as a cultural practice. I stake no claim to writing that history in the following pages. But given the unevenness of historical scholarship on tourism, given the lack of sustained analysis of travel handbooks as significant cultural artifacts, it is hoped that the approach offered here is a considerable step forward. It is my contention that a study of travel guidebooks enables one to explore the connections suggested by the foregoing discussion. That is, it facilitates thinking about how the broader evolution of leisure practices in commercial society related to the rise of tourism and the building of national and cultural (specifically though not exclusively middle-class) identities. Significantly, the emphasis on making bourgeois identities suggests the historical importance of notions of the individual self, a topic that will occupy much of the following narrative. Much recent historical research on tourism deals with collective identities—class, nation, region, gender, and so forth. These remain important to the study of tourism and social history, but my research does more to place the individual or, more accurately, the modern self, at the center of things. Travel cultures situate the tourist in historically specific social locations, I argue, but travel cultures are always mediated individually, and the travel guidebook is both a motor and a product of that mediation.

## IV

My aim is not to write a comprehensive history of the tourist guidebook in Germany. This, it seems to me, is an impossible task for a single nation, let alone for the Euro-American world. The problem is not only that the variability and constantly increasing number of guidebooks frustrate the researcher's attempt to grasp the genre as a conceptual whole. Anthropologist Hermann Bausinger (1991, 344) uses the term 'endlessness' to conceptualize modern tourism; one could easily apply this notion to the tourist handbook. But the guidebook's elusiveness also stems from its nature as a complex 'intertext' marked by traces of the travelogue, atlas, geographical survey, art-history guide, restaurant and hotel guide, tourist brochure, address book, and civic primer (Lauterbach 1989, 209–17). To list these genres is to gesture to the tour book's complex imbrication in leisure culture. Even so, it is possible to use a select number of guidebooks to illuminate broader themes. In the following pages, the plan is to examine several guidebooks that infer important trends and counter-trends in the history of tourism in Germany. In each chapter, the point of departure is to read the guidebook as a formal device embedded in a larger cultural matrix the traces of which may be found 'between the lines,' as it were.

Moving back and forth between text and context, my discussion elucidates some of the travel cultures to which tourist selves belonged in Germany over the past century. The existence of distinct travel cultures may be read from a guidebook's narrative style, its treatment of historical and political context, the content of its itineraries, and the tone and direction of its descriptions. The key issue is how these elements speak to larger cultural meanings, and how they evoke 'autoimages' and 'heteroimages,' or images of the Self and Other, in the process of negotiating a relationship between home and an extended moment of leisured displacement. The notion of the travel culture allows one to bring together the literary, social, cultural, and political dimensions of guidebook literature and relate them to wider societal processes. It also facilitates analysis of one of the central moments in the history of modern tourism, namely the tension between differentiation and homogenization of tourist markets. If a linchpin of my discussion is that German tourism was shaped by distinct travel cultures, then its corollary is that there were also significant areas of overlap and continuity between tourists as they can be located in history. Does tourism make the world more alike, or does it differentiate and segment? My argument results in a paradox: whereas it stresses the differentiation of travel cultures, it also puts the focus on the irreducibility of personal experience, and thus it sees a common thread of individuation running through the multiple readings tourists derive from their itineraries.

In the following pages, the emergence of five travel cultures in Germany is examined for the period from the decade before World War I to the first decade after World War II. The modus operandi is pointillist, and (in the first chapter in particular) the narrative relies on abundant material from the nineteenth century even though its focus is on the twentieth. It was in the last decades before World War I that a nascent 'mass tourism'—highly commercialized, promoted by a growing leisure infrastructure, and extended to ever larger groups of consumers—began to have effect in Germany. It is appropriate to write 'began' because, in contrast to England, German leisure travel still remained primarily a luxury good, and the Baedeker guidebook represented the canon of touristic literature for those who could afford to tour. Chapter One begins with a discussion of a 'national liberal' travel culture consisting largely of middle-class Germans, whose traditions of political liberality and classical learning were placed in the service of a rising superpower. My focus will be on the 1913 Baedeker to Germany, a publication that brought together previous guidebooks to German regions in a graspable synthesis. I argue that the Baedeker not only created a tangible image of German nationhood for the national liberal travel culture; it also created a self-image of cultured individuals consuming the nation in ways that reinforced existing hierarchies of social and gender difference.

The hegemony of Baedeker travel did not go unchallenged before 1914, but it was after the Great War that sporadic critique became a torrent of opposition. The Baedeker was too inattentive to social inequality, too prudish, too bourgeois, and too liberal in the eyes of its critics, who offered alternatives pulsating with the excitement and violence of interwar Germany. The next two chapters explore such alternative guidebooks as products of three distinct travel cultures promoting modernist sexuality, working-class identity, and bitter nationalist struggle respectively as the key to German identity. Chapter Two considers two guidebooks from the Weimar Republic, a 1931 guide to the sexual topography of Berlin, and a 1932 guide written for a socialist working-class audience. In Chapter Three, the focus is on the Nazi period. My main subject is a 1937 guide to Berlin produced by the *Sturmabteilung*, or SA, the National Socialist paramilitary group that fought the Communist party in the streets of the Weimar Republic. This guide takes the reader through the sites of that struggle, rendering the German capital as a web of 'realms of memory' (Nora 1996–8) for the Nazi movement. This chapter also analyzes a number of World War II guidebooks, exploring the relationship between seemingly antonymous terms: genocidal war and 'normal' tourism.

It has often been said that early modern English, French, and German travelers saw striking affinities between Rome, Milan, and Sicily before Italians themselves imagined they were a nation (De Seta 1997, 11). I argue that a similar process whereby the 'outsider' helped to define the national identity of the 'insider' was working in postwar Germany. Chapter Four uses the first comprehensive English-language guidebook to post-World War II Germany, Fodor's *Germany 1953*, to investigate how the German nation was imagined by non-German tourist literature. One might dispute the argument that a 'special relationship' between the US and Germany existed in the modern period. But there is little doubt that Americans were fascinated with Germany, just as Germans were fascinated with America's positive and negative qualities (Barclay and Glaser-Schmidt 1997; Gatzke 1980; Nolan 1994; Schmidt 1997). Building on information in previous chapters on American and other foreign travelers' impressions of Germany, this chapter uses the Fodor guide as a point of departure for examining a postwar American–German travel culture rooted in Cold War politics. The argument is that the Fodor, working much like the pre-World War I Baedeker, offered a 're-synthesis' of the German nation as a tourist whole that gave both Germans and Americans a measure of inter-societal understanding. Tourist Germany not only became a more integral part of Cold War America, but America brought its way of seeing into damaged Germany. An American travel culture, shaped by the political exigencies of the moment, thus became a German travel culture no less important to my story than the German-speaking travel cultures of previous decades.

The Conclusion steps back briefly from the evidence to consider some of the larger issues the book raises about relationships among leisure travel, identity, and the modern self.

# Chapter One

# Baedeker's Germany

## I

The history of German identity is a dialectical dance between dispersal and concentration, individualism and collectivism, 'the many' and 'the one.' The traces of this tension can be read in the opening lines of the first German-language Baedeker guidebook to unified Germany, published in 1906, more than thirty years after the founding of the Second Empire in 1871, and revised six times up to 1936. In the preface to the 1913 edition, one reads that *Germany in One Volume* (*Deutschland in einem Bande*) was a distillation of five previous guidebooks to German regions: the Northeast, the Northwest, the South, the Rhineland, and Berlin. These guidebooks had in turn grown out of a previous, single volume to Germany and the Austrian Empire, published in Koblenz, then the seat of the Baedeker firm, in 1842. By the time this volume appeared in a 15th revised edition in 1872, it had reached a size (961 pages plus introductory material and maps) and level of complexity that made it impractical for travelers. Each of the regional guides meanwhile developed, with multiple editions appearing every two or three years. A guide combining southern Germany and Austria persisted until 1884. The Berlin guide went through 21 editions from 1878 to 1936. In response to the 'often expressed wishes' of his readers, the editor stated, a new volume was now being published. It was designed for those 'who travel through great stretches, and who want to concentrate on the most important cities and most beautiful landscapes' (Baedeker 1913a, v). Those who wanted to explore individual regions more thoroughly were referred to the appropriate guidebooks. A single-volume guide to Germany had emerged from a proliferation of regional and 'cross-German' guides, which in turn issued from the single guide to Germany and Austria of 1842.

What did this act of condensation signify? It is my argument that the new single-volume guide was the product of a deeper process of nationalization. The tour book was mainly for German speakers; only one English-language Baedeker to Germany as a whole would appear, in 1936, and only two French-language editions were available from the Baedeker firm, appearing in 1914 and 1936. The Baedeker's international reach was indisputable, but *this* Baedeker was more insular by design. Not only out of practicality was the Austrian Empire dropped from the Baedeker's national focus well before 1913. It made sense that there should be a new guidebook to the German nation in an age when national identities became more exclusive. Austria was no longer part of Germany, even though just decades earlier many Germans could not conceive of a unified state without Austrian participation. But national exclusiveness was not easily achieved in the so-called Kaiserreich. There is a large scholarly literature examining the difficulty with which Germans imagined a positive national identity both broadly inclusive in terms of internal political culture and sufficiently self-confident to undertake a concerted line in foreign policy. As the newly unified Empire developed, the German Bürgertum's declining political fortunes exacerbated domestic tensions. A more intense nationalism was one result of the political fragmentation of the middle strata (Blackbourn 1998, 424–9). But so too was a more pointed cultural integralism that drew on the Bürgertum's identification with the art, literature, architecture, music, folklore, and natural landscapes of German tradition. To publish a single-volume guide to Germany in this context was to envision a nation whose political character and cultural boundaries still remained unclear. To grasp the 446-page volume as one traveled was thus potentially an act of national crystallization, at the least, a gesture of optimism.

The need for crystallization was simultaneously a response to the constant dispersal of national visions. The early history of the Baedeker guidebook and its creator, Karl Baedeker, is central to understanding this point, for the traces of the past, both biographical and political, were layered into the 1913 handbook at every point. The founder of the Baedeker travel empire lived from 1801 to 1859. Born in Essen to Gottschalk Diederich Baedeker, a well-to-do publisher and bookseller, his early life was typical of a young male from the cultured middle strata, or *Bildungsbürgertum*. He attended the classical high school (*Gymnasium*) in Essen and Hagen, immatriculating in the philosophy faculty at Heidelberg in 1819. His university study lasted for only one year, but he stayed long enough to be influenced by the progressive liberal ideas of historians Friedrich Christoph Schlosser and Georg Gottfried Gervinus. After moving to Bonn in 1820 he made the acquaintance of Ernst Wilhelm Hengstenberg, an ardent supporter of the nationalist, democratic student fraternity movement, which played an important role in early German nationalism. In 1824/5, Baedeker apprenticed with the Berlin book dealer Georg Andreas Reimer, also a proponent of liberal national ideals and a friend of the patriotic poet Ernst Moritz Arendt and the philosophers Johann Gottlieb Fichte and Friedrich Schleiermacher. The contacts he made from his father's acquaintances along with those he was making with publishers and intellectuals in Bonn and Berlin enabled Karl Baedeker to build a network on which he would draw both for inspiration and practical contributions to his later tour books (Frühauf 1992, 41–3).

Baedeker was a collector and a traveler. Having inherited his father's collection of autographs of famous people, he built up an impressive stock of more than 1,500 signatures of royalty, poets, scientists, and political figures. He published the result of his work in 1847 (Frühauf 1992, 43). Once the reserve of aristocratic enthusiasts, collecting worked its way down the social scale by the nineteenth century, when it was an important bourgeois leisure activity. Collecting and traveling were intimately related throughout the history of modern tourism. Whereas scientific travelers of the eighteenth century collected minerals and flowers, later tourists, more inclined to recreation, collected 'views and moods' (Löfgren 1999, 17). The link between collecting and traveling has a direct bearing on the Baedeker firm's later preeminence as tour guide to the German nation. Like traveling, collecting may be regarded as one of those modes of reading by which, as de Certeau (1984, xi–xxiv) maintained, individuals insert themselves into (and thereby change) environments others created.

Walter Benjamin once wrote that the art of collecting was shaped by 'a dialectical tension between the poles of disorder and order.' The objects of collecting (in Benjamin's case, rare books) are disorderly because they present a 'chaos of memories' to the collector, who like a tourist contemplating his travels, recalls the places where the items were found and purchased. The true collector values his collection because it has little utilitarian value. He or she revels in the individual details of each piece—where it originated, who wrote or manufactured it, who owned it, how and with what materials it was made. He draws these details into a 'magical circle' for which the 'thrill of acquisition' is the defining moment. Collectors are passionate owners, wrote Benjamin, and ownership is based on a tactical instinct through which 'the smallest antique shop can be a fortress, the most remote stationery store a key position.' A memory of the tactics of collecting results in a mental itinerary where the topography of purchases—Berlin, Dresden, Riga, Naples, Munich, Moscow, Florence, Basel, Paris, Danzig—becomes inscribed in the collection itself (Benjamin 1969 [1931], 60, 63, 67).

Karl Baedeker's skills as a collector were transferable to the emerging world of modern tourism. Just as the collector gloried in the details of his purchases, the tourist, as imagined by Baedeker, studied maps, itineraries, historical accounts, travel brochures, price lists, beautiful vistas, pictures of historical landmarks, and topographical descriptions. He collected information in his own circle of experience, crystallizing it into a workable whole oriented to future trips, or luxuriating in a nostalgic memory of places already seen. For a true collector, 'the whole background of an item adds up to a magic encyclopedia whose quintessence is the fate of his object' (Benjamin 1969 [1931], 60). The collector's mystical relationship with objects resulted in a highly individualized manner of appreciating the collection. For the traveler, the background of tourist sites adds up to a no less individualized magic encyclopedia whose quintessence is that sense of fate suggested by an important birthplace, a natural landscape, a historical battlefield. Even the latter-day vacationer uses his or her collection of photographs and mementos to evoke the emotions of trips taken and anticipated.

As he did with his autograph collection, Baedeker assembled tourist destinations, publishing the results in a way that enabled travelers to regard the national community as a tangible entity. But there was more than a metaphorical relationship at work here. Baedeker collected many of his autographs, and many of his friends as well, through a peripatetic existence that began as early as the age of 14, when he joined German troops fighting Napoleon's armies. He moved between Essen, Hagen, Heidelberg, Berlin, and Bonn. Such travels were by no means unusual for the sons of upper-middle-class families. Inspired in part by the publication of Goethe's *Italian Journey* in 1829, the German Bürgertum regarded travel in general and the Bildungsreise in particular as an important component of their identity and a necessary ritual in the transition from childhood to adulthood. Recent research argues for a differentiated picture of the social composition of early tourism that puts the focus not only on the aristocracy but on the bourgeoisie and artisans as well (Böröcz 1992, 710–12). In its itinerary and function the Bildungsreise was similar to the more elite Grand Tour, but the Bildungsreise also had a more modern ambience because it emphasized travel for travel's sake. At the same time, it was not identical to the mass tourism of the twentieth century, which put relaxation ahead of 'culture' (Wolbring 1996, 85–6, 94–5). Karl Baedeker's youthful travels were the functional equivalent of the middle-class Bildungsreise, a key early precedent for modern tourism. But his mode of travel was also not unconnected to the artisan tradition of 'tramping,' an important element of the craftsmen's training. Like so much of tourism, Baedeker's peripatetic drew on many traditions and experiences to create a hybrid, emergent practice.

Bourgeois travel had both collective (national, class) and individual dimensions. It was a symbolic practice through which the middle strata discovered and reinforced their membership in a tangible community bounded by shared rituals and self-images. At the same time, it contributed to personality development and a sense of individuality that found expression again and again in the travel accounts of the nineteenth and twentieth centuries. Baedeker's guidebook would address this sense of individualized tourism even when it laid out itineraries, lists of hotels, and train schedules. The dynamic of individualization through standardization should not be seen as peculiarly German but rather as an element of middle-class travel culture in all countries where tourism developed. Social theorists posit 'collective' and 'romantic' (or individual) moments as constitutive of the 'tourist gaze' throughout the Western world (Urry 1995, 129–40). The collection, the journey, the guidebook, and the nation shared a common goal: the resolution of a 'logic of contradiction' into a 'logic of sequence' (Leed 1991, 22). The nation would arouse emotional loyalties with the same intensity with which the collector regarded the objects of his desire. But just as collecting was ultimately an individualistic and quasi-mystical practice, touring could not be packaged or standardized but only experienced by each tourist, just as the citizen's sense of the nation finally came down to his or her perception of it.

Baedeker chose to move to Koblenz to begin his own bookstore in 1827 instead of taking over the family firm in Essen. The reason for his decision to go into business in this Rhenish city remains unclear; it is certain he had little intention at the time to go into the travel industry, and Koblenz was not yet the center of Rhenish tourism it would become. Among the items Baedeker's business published and sold were city maps, Rhine panoramas, local histories, and travelogues—all central to the emerging travel culture. Baedeker soon acquired the small Röhling publishing firm of Koblenz, which also gave him the right to publish a handbook of tourism from Koblenz to Mainz after the author J.A. Klein's death in 1832. Dissatisfied with this handbook, whose sales were marginal in comparison to German, French, and English guidebooks to the Rhine already on the market, Baedeker began working on revisions. He published a second edition in 1835 and a more thoroughly revised volume in 1839, which is regarded as the first of the Baedeker handbook line. In order to make his revisions, Baedeker traveled, and although he relied on the informed observations of scholars and officials, he prefaced the guide by insisting that all information contained therein rested 'exclusively on personal observation' (Baedeker [1849] 1978, n. p.). This tradition continued, and in the 1913 guide to Germany the preface claimed that all information on restaurants were based on the editor's gastronomic research (Baedeker 1913a, v). Like an ethnographer exploring distant lands, Baedeker and his successors in the family firm went collecting data, making notes on hotels and restaurants, railway and carriage routes, and numerous tourist sites. Baedeker acquired the talent to see the nation through the 'eyes of a tourist' (Kunsthistorisches Institut der Universität Tübingen 1981), and the leisure pursuits of the Bildungsbürgertum from which he came were the cultural foundations of this new practice.

Baedeker's Rhenish guide appeared at a propitious moment. Public interest in travel literature of all kinds was strong well before the 1830s. In the second half of the eighteenth century, travelogues and related literature grew from less than two percent of the German book market to more than four percent. In Baedeker's childhood some six thousand titles from the genre of travel literature were available to German readers. Early in the nineteenth century German children played board games such as 'A Day in Berlin' or 'A Day in Potsdam.' In these games players moved through a colorful panorama of landmarks on their way to the central sightseeing destination at the middle of the board, which for Berlin was the Brandenburg Gate. There was a strong interest in travel before transportation improvements brought the possibility of tourism into every bourgeois home (Bernard 1978, 95–6; Wolbring 1996, 88; Falkenberg 1991, 284–5). Travel was imagined before it was a concrete practice, a 'fiction' before it was a 'reality.' Imagination drove an important structural prerequisite for travel, namely the setting aside of economic resources for leisure activity beyond the reproduction of labor power. It is in my opinion inaccurate to argue, then, that tourism should be reconceptualized as 'travel capitalism,' as Böröcz maintains (1992, 736). The cultural prerequisites of mass leisure travel well preceded the structural supports needed to turn travel into a major capitalist industry.

As for the Rhineland, it had been a favored destination of well-to-do travelers since Roman times and a popular part of the Grand Tour of the eighteenth century. Böröcz himself concedes that an impressive continuity existed between the destinations of the Grand Tour and those of nineteenth-century travel (1992, 724) even though he maintains that the rise of industrial capitalism explains the spatial and temporal patterns of tourism. When regular steamship service began on the Rhine in 1827, a more middle-class clientele from England was drawn to the natural beauty, the castle ruins, and the Rhine trout and salmon served with generous amounts of local wine in Rhenish inns. Influenced by Rousseau, English Romantics such as William Wordsworth had already popularized a new way of imagining nature in the Lakes District of England and in the Rhineland in the late eighteenth century (Withey 1997, 32–57). Nature was no longer regarded indifferently or as something chaotic and threatening. Natural landscapes now embodied a wholeness supposedly lacking in commercial society or in the emergent industrial society of the turn of the century. At the same time, Romantic appropriation of both nature and culture depended as much on inner feelings as it did on the specific characteristics of what was being viewed. The heirs to the Roman tourists, the elite of the Grand Tour, and the English Romantics were the nearly half-million passengers booked on Rhineland steamers at the end of the 1830s (Lambert 1935, 129; Tümmers 1994, 198–9; Wolbring 1996, 88–9). They could embark on such tours because, just as the desire for travel drove the structural tendency to free up economic resources for leisure on the part of individuals, the 'hosts' of tourism—steamship operators, innkeepers, and purveyors of travel literature—devoted more resources to the travel infrastructure. Economic and cultural processes wove a web of influences shaping the early formation of modern leisure travel and situating the Rhineland at the center of things.

Political events also popularized the Rhineland in German culture. Annexed by Prussia after the Napoleonic Wars, the Rhineland was an important symbol of the emergent national community in the early nineteenth century. Rhineländer themselves felt uneasy about accepting Prussian hegemony until 1840, when French desires to recapture the region led to a war scare. The Rhenish population felt a strong identity with Prussia in resisting French claims. In 1848, the year of revolutions that began in Paris in February and soon spread to Germany and other lands, many Germans feared not only continued upheavals but also French invasion.

Baedeker himself wrote in 1848 in a letter to his cartographer of the 'growing danger of French inundation' of the Rhineland (cited in Baumgarten 1978, 379). The Rhineland was an important 'district of the fatherland,' as Baedeker averred in the preface to his 1849 guide to the region.

Even so, forces leading to a dispersal of the national vision were as strong in this period as those of centralization. The annexation of the Rhineland by Prussia also made it possible for inhabitants to regard themselves as a more cohesive region. The effects of French occupation and Rhenish Catholicism's sense of opposition to Protestant Berlin enhanced local people's sense of distinctiveness. They felt culturally German, but this did not always correspond to the desire to be part of a political entity dominated by Prussia. More generally, economic development reinforced the regional diversity of the country. Liberal nationalism, supported above all by the Protestant middle strata of the German states, also bore the traces of regional splintering. The fortunes of the liberal political movement often depended on balancing regional groups and interests, and on negotiating among political notables in the provinces (Sheehan 1978, 24–5, 98).

Tourism itself contributed to fractionalization. In the past, certain regions were favored tourist destinations while others lagged behind. Until late in the eighteenth century, Germany was less visited on the Grand Tour than were Italy and France, where the roads and inns were of higher quality (Lambert 1935, 119–200; Towner 1996, 106–28). In the nineteenth century, favored regions continued to develop— Switzerland, the spa towns of southwestern Germany, the Rhineland, and southern Bavaria and the Tyrol. By 1906 the Baedeker firm had produced 32 editions of a guidebook for the last-named region, more than for any other European area including Switzerland, for which 31 editions appeared (Knebel 1960, 25). Tourism also defined regions as quasi-independent entities irrespective of state boundaries. The Baedeker tradition of incorporating Austria and Germany in a single handbook drew on the tradition of regarding German nationhood in linguistic–cultural rather then territorial–political terms. Even when national unity of a kind was achieved, the physical form of the Baedeker guide to Germany reflected the potential fractionalization of the tourist's view. Users of the thick red handbook were given instructions in the preface for cutting the guide into six sections covering each of the geographical regions into which the presentation was divided (Baedeker 1913a, v). Parceled out in this way, the nation became a series of self-contained tours, artifacts of early 'niche' marketing, rather than the singular referent for an integrative national journey.

Internationalization also promoted the traversal of political boundaries. Böröcz's (1992, 714–15) linking of early tourism with the rise of industrial capitalism puts the focus on cross-national flows of resources. But there is a more specific story to be told with reference to the Baedeker guidebooks. Baedeker began producing his Rhineland guide partly in response to international competition, and he later admitted that he copied other guides, and most specifically the Murray guidebooks, in establishing his format (the red cover) and style. The canon of early tourist literature was very much a hybrid of transnational influences. Baedeker began producing French-language guides to the Rhineland in 1846 and soon other Francophone guides to many parts of Europe and the world were available from the Baedeker firm. The Rhineland was not only a cross-national tourist icon, but it also revealed the relatively undeveloped German market for tourism. In German speaking Europe, the first written record of the word 'tourist' appeared in 1834, four decades after its appearance in French and more than three decades after English (Böröcz 1992, 728). Baedeker was forced to go to an international market because the domestic culture of leisure travel was limited and belated. From the very beginning, then, the Baedeker was synonymous with international travel.

The touristic nation called 'Germany' was destabilized by internal regional differences, cultural definitions of nationhood straddling state boundaries, and patterns of trans-political traversal encouraged by an international tourist market. Yet tourism contained within itself the potential to counterbalance such forces. Even when the Baedeker became an artifact of international tourism, travelers themselves saw it as the export of a particular cultural community. 'The unfailing Baedeker,' always accurate and thorough to a fault, was 'the true product of the German mind,' wrote one American traveler (Temple 1898, 36). Reading the Baedeker, regardless of the language in which it was printed, was like reading a part of Germany. The secular trend of tourism also enhanced national identities. In Germany, the term *Fremdenverkehr*, which literally means 'travel by strangers,' became an alternative to the word 'tourism' as leisure travel became widespread. This usage signaled the importance of linguistic nationalism in the public understanding of the phenomenon (Böröcz 1992, 726). In addition, emergent transportation networks created resources for bringing together the nation. The young Karl Baedeker, after taking his first train ride in 1838, exclaimed in a letter to his father 'what fun traveling is now!' (Withey 1997, 99). One of the distinguishing features of the 1839 Baedeker guide was that it was oriented almost completely to the nascent rail network. Even the relatively slow-moving trains of this era were three times as fast as the stagecoaches that still carried many tourists. This was perceived as an extraordinary compression of time and space, both liberating and disturbing. In later pre-World War I Baedeker guides auto routes would also be introduced. This reflected the still class-bound character of the Baedeker readers, many of whom belonged to that small group of well-off consumers who could afford cars at this early moment in European automotive history. Yet the continued incorporation of the most up-to-date means of transportation in the guidebook reflected a process whereby Germans could be brought face-to-face far more rapidly than ever before. The great German exile poet Heinrich Heine, reacting to the expansion of the rail network in Europe at mid-century, wrote that he could smell German linden trees from Paris and hear the North Sea at his door (Wolbring 1996, 87–8). Rail and automobile travel could not transform metaphorical into substantive reality, but they made the metaphor all the more compelling. And although Heine himself was an exile who viewed his country from afar, the iron rails also linked him to the German homeland. The compression of time and space associated with rail travel was also, potentially and actually, a compression of one's political–cultural orientations.

The foregoing outlines an emergent national–liberal travel culture. I refer here not to a specific organization, a political party, or a well-defined social group, but rather to a horizon of expectations, experiences, and representations. This matrix was characterized in part by a commitment to German national identity that, in its state–political orientation, reflected the diversity of the national movement itself. 'National' suggested a set of possibilities for the future rather than a concrete idea of what the German nation was. Such possibilities were shaped by the constitutive tension between dispersal and concentration in German identities. The culture was liberal in the broad sense that travel, like many other aspects of contemporary liberal thought, was seen as a universal right no less important than the right to express political opinions, to run a business, to contest a legal ruling, and to assemble in voluntary groups. 'All people travel in order to better their personal life conditions,' wrote one observer (Dehn 1895, 54). Traveling in search of work and income remained the dominant form of individual travel, but in the modern era, one also improved one's 'life conditions' through leisure. Travel was central to those who asserted the *individual's* right to leisure beyond the straightforward reproduction of labor power or necessary consumption. Through much of the nineteenth century only the more affluent classes had the means to travel extensively for leisure. Given that German Catholics' socio-economic standing was generally lower than that of the Protestants throughout the nineteenth century, moreover, it was the Protestant upper and middle strata that benefited most from the new leisure travel culture. But tourism was becoming something that all social strata would have within their grasp on the way to the 'classless Bürger society,' the society of literate, aware citizens envisioned by so many in the middle strata. The individual members of the national–liberal travel culture therefore had important points of overlap with the Protestant Bürgertum in the National Liberal party, the party of German unification, but they were by no means coterminous with this constituency.

The national–liberal travel culture rested on the metaphorical figure of the collector/traveler, a specific kind of traveler who had a quasi-mystical relationship with the sites and objects encountered on tour. Traveling was an important source of collective identity, but even when leisure travel aided the individual's attachment to a social group or the nation, it always had a deeply personal character. This individualism was the emotional and cultural 'excess,' the part not entirely appropriated by group identities or by the processes of standardization that tourism

27

would undergo in the twentieth century. Like collecting, like effective reading, this orientation to travel also required knowledge and the acquisition of 'cultural capital' (Bourdieu 1984) consisting not only of the objects/sites to be 'collected,' but also of a developing expertise in travel. Leisure travel required training and application in a 'cultural laboratory' whose researchers were the tourists themselves (Löfgren 1999, 7). Critical reading took practice and experience. Such requirements worked against the more egalitarian aspects of the travel culture, putting a premium on specialized knowledge and social distinction. Just as the national vision of German tourism moved between the poles of dispersal and concentration, the metaphor of reader/traveler/collector ran the spectrum from egalitarian to elitist meanings. It will be shown later that leisure travel's moving back and forth between equality and hierarchy, between the popular and the elite, was not a singularly German phenomenon, even though the specific nature of national identity in Germany may have shaped German tourism in particular ways.

The first lines to the preface of *Germany in One Volume* pointed to an intricate web of biographical and social coordinates underlying the emergent culture of modern tourism. The principles on which these coordinates rested, outlined first by Karl Baedeker, were reinforced and elaborated by his sons, Ernst, Karl II, and especially Fritz, who directed the firm from 1878 to 1925, and who brought his own sons into leadership positions in the publishing house. But it is now time to focus the discussion more on the guidebook itself to understand the way in which it framed the tourist experience.

## II

1913

The central theme of the Baedeker guidebook was the freedom of the individual tourist. Tourists were not to act like the 'poor modern slaves and simpletons' John Ruskin made them out to be (Withey 1997, 102). Nor were they to be the butt of caricaturists' jokes in the magazine *Simplicissimus*, where travelers seeing 'Europe in Thirty Days' came in for much criticism. From the Baedeker view of things, the 'essence' of the travel industry was not to get 'control over the tourist experience,' as Böröcz claims (1992, 736). Rather, tourism was to be an act of liberation and self-control in which the Baedeker guidebook itself set a good example. It is true that the authority enjoyed by the tourist guidebook reinforced the tourist reader's dependence on it, as Gilbert argues (1991, 60). But given the fast-changing character of modern cities and the tourist's exposure to new environments, it is difficult to imagine that leisure travelers could do without some kind of guidebook. Guidebook literature in general—and the Baedeker in particular—promoted freedom and self-reliance, direction and focus. Using a terminology borrowed from contemporary tourism research, one could say that

*Figure 1    Europe in Thirty Days: 'Ma, are we in Munich today?'—'Is today the
fifteenth?'—'Yes, I think so.'—'Then today we're in Munich' (*Simplicissimus
19, 12 [22 June 1914]: 183).*

the modern guidebook's primary audience consisted of 'psychocentric' travelers—
individuals who were relatively anxious and inhibited in their wanderings. But
the guidebook also created resources for those 'allocentric' types who sought out
new adventures, and who looked for new places in which to exercise their
inquisitive spirit (Hall and Page 1999, 54).

In the 1913 preface, Baedeker editors took pains to stress that recommendations
on hotels were offered in full independence from innkeepers and restaurant owners.
Baedeker's advice was not 'for sale, *also not in the form of advertisements*' (1913a,
vi, italics in original). This statement belonged in a long Baedeker tradition of
giving the tourist resources to resist overbearing commercial influences. This
philosophy was stated in the 1896 edition for the Rhineland. The guide was

designed to 'supply the traveler with such information as will render him as nearly as possible independent of hotel-keepers, commissionaires, and guides, and thus enable him the more thoroughly to enjoy and appreciate the objects of interest he meets with on his tour' (Baedeker 1896, v). It appeared in even more explicit form in the English-language guidebooks to Italy, where the tourist could read that the Baedeker was there to 'protect him against extortion' (Baedeker 1895, x). In the 1913(a) Baedeker, 26 introductory pages gave the traveler the tools to deal with passport and visa regulations, money exchanges and shipping costs, transportation schedules and ticket prices, hotels and pension, cafes and restaurants (including the notation that good cigars were to be had in Germany at ten pfennig due to the absence of a tobacco monopoly in the country), communications (mail, telegraph, and telephone), sightseeing possibilities, and tips for bicycle and automobile travel.

Baedeker's goal of liberating the tourist from costly reliance on others was in fact being realized, at least for European travel. Professions such as Alpine guides or city guides for foreign visitors (*valets de place*) shrank to a tiny proportion of what they had been by the turn of the nineteenth century, partly as a consequence of the availability of guidebooks to the 'average' tourist. Since these local guides were so often a source of anxiety among tourists, who feared being cheated and overcharged, the availability of reliable guidebooks was indeed something that empowered the wary traveler (Knebel 1960, 27, 28). The little red handbook marked a larger sea change in the social organization of travel. In order for the tourist industry to become successful, it had to establish a relationship of trust with its customers, who did not have personal knowledge of the places they visited. These tourists were 'disembedded' from their local involvements, as all moderns are, and they needed reliable, risk-reducing stratagems to aid their journey beyond their immediate social horizons. Yet travelers' minds were not being 'colonized,' at least not entirely. No guarantee existed that tourists would use the guidebooks in prescribed ways. Moreover, tourists brought different levels of knowledge to their journeys, and different resources with which to confront the risks of leisure travel (Giddens 1991, 209; Simpson 1999, 690–1; Urry 1995, 143-4).

Beyond the practical goals of this act of liberation was a key moment of the Bürgertum's evolution as a force in the new public sphere of the nineteenth century. The elites of the Grand Tour traveled with a retinue of guides, tutors, and advisers—and with their own guidebooks (Towner 1996, 107–8). Touring was a 'corporate' undertaking with respect to both goals and social content. Even when the impatient sons of the well-to-do classes escaped the control of their overseers to go drinking, gambling, and whoring, they did so within a collective social tradition. For the middle-class tourist, the individual counted above all even if he or she was traveling with family or visiting sites that attracted huge crowds. Just as the individual needed to be freed from wasteful and immoral corporate restrictions imposed by tradition on politics and the economy, the tourist needed to be given the equipment to set out on his own, to explore the world from his point of view. It is common in cultural criticism and scholarship to distinguish between the individual traveler, ripe for unexpected adventure, and the 'mass tourist,' cowed by the triple hegemony of guidebook, itinerary, and travel agency. The Baedeker's goal—and the goal of many subsequent guidebooks—was to obliterate this distinction, to give every tourist the opportunity to become the traveler, to see the allocentric potential of even the most psychocentric voyager.

That the intended tourist of Baedeker's world was male is clear from the use of the pronoun 'him' in the passages quoted above. That he might have traveled with family in tow should not obfuscate the fact that the Baedeker addressed him as a *solitary* male. Leed (1991, 36) argues that the origins of modern travel, defined by choice rather than necessity, go back to the Middle Ages. It was at that time that the classical heroic journey became the 'individuating journey, one that defines the figure of the person undertaking it not as a member but as autonomous, separate, and detached.' The tradition of single male travelers was important to the Enlightenment-inspired scientific explorations of the early modern period. Much the same could be said for the Bildungsreise. Goethe took off on his famous Italian journey of 1786 alone, with no servant and only a single portmanteau and a valise for luggage. Thomas Jefferson preferred to travel alone in France, and early nineteenth-century American travelers to Europe thought solitary travel to be neither lonely nor unusual. Romanticism's adoration of nature was built largely on the figure of the 'lonely wanderer.' The solitude of travel was not denied a select group of women in the first half of the nineteenth century either. It is true that even when people moved about by themselves, almost all made acquaintances or undertook parts of their tours with companions. But single, unaccompanied males initially determined the norm of leisure travel, and they remained very much in the majority in the earliest decades of modern tourism (Levenstein 1998, 7, 27, 29; Frykman and Löfgren 1987, 51; Goethe 1982, 5). A chatty advice book on tourism from 1914 would still insist that 'wandering alone is the preferred way to travel for those who want to make observations and get to know the land and people' (Seelig-Stanton 1914, 40).

The male tourist of Baedeker's nation had a succinct idea of how costly his travel would be on the first page of the introduction to the 1913 guide. Here one reads: 'For a stay in the larger cities and spa resorts, the not too demanding traveler can reckon with fifteen marks daily' (Baedeker 1913a, xi). For British and American travelers, the Baedeker to Northern Germany was even more specific, suggesting that the 'modest pedestrian' who stays off the 'beaten track' could get by on 10–12 shillings a day. In contrast, those who preferred driving to walking, who stayed in more expensive hotels, and who employed guides and commissionnaires, would have to reckon with daily expenditures of 25–30 shillings (Baedeker 1913b, xi). It was clear from the tone and presentation of data which tourist the Baedeker respected more. Baedeker's ideal tourist embraced self-control, asceticism, and discipline—precisely the values that served the middle classes of Europe and North America in 'culture building' throughout the nineteenth century (Frykman and Löfgren 1987).

Even if he was a 'modest pedestrian' and 'not too demanding,' the Baedeker traveler belonged to the 'better' strata. *Deutschland in einem Bande* cost nine marks in 1913, when the average price of a guidebook was about six marks. Guidebooks in the popular Woerl's Reisehandbücher series, with more than 600 volumes, cost even less. Concentrating not only on the major Continental cities but also the less frequented middle-sized towns in Germany, these pocket-size guidebooks, usually around 100 pages in length, cost just 50 pfennig (Knebel 1960, 24; Woerl 1898). A single day's stay in a city or spa was reckoned by the Baedeker at 15 marks, a sum that did not take into account the cost of travel and many incidentals. By contrast, when a group of Berlin organizations tried to provide inexpensive summer outings for workers in 1904, their aim was to charge no more than 3 marks per day to prospective enrollees. A handful of metal workers, among the most handsomely paid of German workers, could take advantage of low-cost group tours of four to seven days in 1910 and 1914. Their maximum total cost, including hotels, food, travel, and all necessary fees, was between 8 and 13 marks per day (Keitz 1992, 43, 47). Young people traveled even more cheaply. Fourteen-year-old Albert Schramm, later a physician, departed with two school chums from his Swabian home on a three-week trip to Italy before World War I with just 30 marks for the entire journey (Schramm 1935, 21–2).

If we consider Baedeker's sum alone in relation to the possible length of time the 'average' tourist was away from home, we can see that extended leisure travel was by no means something available to the majority of Germans. The Baedeker guidebook recommended that a fast tour of the main attractions in western and central Germany would take four weeks (not counting railway travel time), for eastern Germany one week, and for southern Germany two weeks (Baedeker 1913a, xxiii). If the two-week tour is considered, maintenance costs alone for a single person would total more than 200 marks. In 1912, more than half of all employed Germans made less than 900 marks annually (Hohorst et al. 1975, 106). But even if the Baedeker user belonged to the relatively comfortable socio-economic classes, he was not a person of unlimited resources, but rather the member of the middle and upper-middle Bürgertum who needed to be aware of his investment (Knebel 1960, 24). He was the German schoolteacher who on average made a little less than 3,300 marks annually in 1909, or the mid-level civil servant with annual pay of 2,800 marks. Already before World War I, the holders of such civil service occupations had gained the legal right to a paid vacation (Hohorst et al. 1975, 112; Keitz 1997, 33).

How did the Baedeker tourist travel? In answering the question, one should not overestimate the importance of rail travel, at least for the middle two thirds of the nineteenth century. It would take the improved *social* organization of rail travel, not only the realization of its technological possibilities, before the railroad became indispensable to tourist markets (Urry 1995, 142–5). Between 1831, when the first German railway opened up between Nuremberg and Fürth, and 1873, the number of passengers on stagecoaches was still on the increase, growing by fifteen times. Coach travel would be romanticized in the twentieth century, but many contemporaries criticized it for its many discomforts even though travelers used it enthusiastically because it was cheap. For at least one American traveler, the economic advantage of touring by *droschke*, a light landau, failed to compensate for the discomfort of seeing German drivers' cruelty toward their horses (Pitman [Deane] 1883, 37).

Soon rail would be king, in any case. In the quarter century before World War I, the number of person-kilometers registered by railway travel quadrupled (Knebel 1960, 19; Hohorst et al. 1975, 82). Baedeker tourists were informed that in northern Germany they could travel in four classes, the first- and second-class compartments with upholstered seats, and in southern Germany except for Alsace-Lorraine and Württemberg, three classes. Separate compartments for nonsmokers and women were available. The guidebook made no comment on the relative merits of traveling in each class, unlike the Satchel guide, which was happy about both first- and second-class travel on Continental railways, but not the third class, which was described as 'not so good, especially in Italy.' An American guidebook for women traveling in Europe recommended that third class would do for those who needed economical travel but warned that only a first-class ticket was acceptable for overnight trips (Baedeker 1913a, xii; Rolfe 1899, 10; Levenstein 1998, 158).

Both contemporaries and later critics bemoaned the effects rail travel had on people's ability to appreciate the landscape unfurling before their eyes (Schivelbusch 1986). There was not a hint of such cultural criticism in the Baedeker, which after all could attribute much of its success to the existence of the railways. But there was more here than crass 'bottom line' thinking. In the touristic perception of things, the railways could be as much a part of the travel experience as the scenery of natural settings and cityscapes could. This argument inspired a series of more than 70 tour guides entitled *Right and Left of the Railway!* (Fischer 1914, 3). Getting from one location to another was by no means discredited as ancillary to sightseeing in Baedeker's Germany. In the scenic Black Forest area of Höllental, Hinterzarten, and the Titisee, beautiful forests, lovely mountain villages, and glowing streams could be seen from a winding rail line that sliced through tunnels and cliffs. The Baedeker alerted the traveler where the 'grandest' stretch began in the Höllental, and noted the many tunnels, the iron bridges, and the bronze stag that could be glimpsed high above the passage between the upper and lower Hirschsprung tunnels (Baedeker 1913a, 316). One could argue that the Baedeker in effect legislated how tourists should view this violation of natural landscapes by an iron modernity. Yet travelers genuinely embraced the railway for bringing such sites to them. Writing a short poem in a hotel guest book, a Black Forest traveler enthused over the scenic Titisee: 'You achieved your destiny of gladdening the heart once the powerful iron ruler of our century forged a path to you through the mountains—the locomotive' (Zimmermann 1889, 143).

Eric Leed's (1991, 75–7, 129) discussion of the 'passage' as a key element of the structure of travel is relevant here. Leed argues that 'the world is objectified and made fluid through motion' during the traveler's passage. The passage places the traveler in a 'flow state' that creates a pleasing sense of 'autotelic motion' and transforms both the sites being seen and the means of transportation into a seamless web. Although the traveler enters a train, ship, or car voluntarily, the inertia induced by the 'perceptual envelope' of motion creates order and sequence, having a therapeutic effect that is finally independent of the travel destination or the motivations for undertaking the trip. The argument that train travel debilitated the tourist's perception of the landscape ignores the fact that the experiential flow of travel itself has a self-contained and independent status. Baedeker's uncritical acceptance of the train had an important role to play in modern tourism's embrace of new modes of passage and new flow states for a distinctively modern psychology of travel.

As we might expect given the reference to the 'modest pedestrian,' the Baedeker incorporated walking tours as well. Walking had always been part of the autotelic motion so pleasurable to the traveler, but the meaning of walking also changed over time, especially with the transportation revolution beginning in the eighteenth century (Wallace 1993). Walking now became an antidote to the disorienting— and increasingly popular—rapidity of mechanized transportation, a goal in itself rather than a means to an end, a 'cult' rather than a formerly plebeian mode of getting around (Löfgren 1999, 48–56). Even when the Baedeker incorporated the most up-to-date means of transportation, it also left room for such traditional practices. But this was not only a function of the guidebook's psychological orientation or of its focus on economical travel. Walking had its democratic element, either in the form of vigorous 'wandering,' which evoked the traditions of medieval scholars and tramping artisans, or the measured 'stroll,' which was thought to be more appropriate for women because of its pace and local orientation. Both forms of walking appeared as distinct cultural practices of the Bürgertum in the late eighteenth and early nineteenth centuries. Later, members of the Wandervogel youth groups, the offspring of the Bürgertum, would adopt wandering as a form of romantic (and elitist) social protest (Bausinger 1991, 347–8; Kaschuba 1991; König 1996). Guides for the traveler on foot existed early in the nineteenth century

(Becher 1990, 206). But it was at the end of this century that the genre became prominent. Ambitious hiking tours as well as strolls undertaken as part of a leisurely weekend of relaxation were part of the menu of possibilities. Walkers could buy booklets with titles such as *Where should We Go Next Sunday?* to help them choose routes (Knyrim 1900). The evening promenade or Sunday-afternoon walk allowed the Bürger to see and to be seen as he occupied a position in the growing public sphere of leisure. The product of a new bourgeois sensibility toward both nature and the city, leisure walking was incorporated in Baedeker discourse as a fundamental element of the national–liberal travel culture.

Walking also corresponded to the idea of taking one's time. In part due to the success of Thomas Cook's excursion tours to the Continent, the pace of leisure travel accelerated by the late nineteenth century, as middle-class tourists, anxious about squeezing as much out of their limited resources as possible, were rushed from monument to city hall to museum. Baedeker walking created the possibility of putting the brakes on such radically ambulant tourism and taking a few minutes to inspect an interesting fresco or painting, or an intricately shaped design on a Rathaus gable. It distinguished the Baedeker tourist from the 'Cookies,' as they were so derisively called, who were criticized for their superficial understanding of the sights they took in on their breathless roundtrips. The Cook's agency even lost business due to tourists' fear that their health would be endangered by enrolling in the fast-paced regimen of its Continental excursions (Levenstein 1998, 160–2). Some guidebooks, most notably the English-language *Walks in London* (1894), stressed a moderate and high-bourgeois pace for cultural tourism by lacing the text with literary references and numerous *bon mots*, virtually requiring its users to take their time and consider the reactions previous travelers had to the sites being viewed. The 'modest pedestrian' embodied both the democratic impulse of the nineteenth-century Bürger on foot and the elitism of those who derided the 'mass tourist' of Cook's and his ilk. It is possible to separate these moments analytically, but they remained firmly intertwined in the practice of the national–liberal travel culture in Germany.

The Baedeker also took account of the fact that automobile travel was on the horizon, if mainly for the well-to-do strata, who often used this mode of transportation as a way of separating themselves from the 'lesser' classes in the relatively egalitarian trains. Motoring therefore had a point of connection with the elitist side of the cult of walking. But the desire for social distinction was not the only motivation for becoming an 'automobilist,' to use the term popular before the Great War. For the writer Otto Julius Bierbaum, the slow but steady automobile travel still prevalent on the nation's uncertain roads was superior to train travel because it allowed one to see that modernity's 'great cultural upheavals had not yet leveled out all differences between regions.' The popular embrace of railway travel was unfortunate, from Bierbaum's perspective, because it homogenized landscapes and destroyed local subtlety. This was not an original critique, as we have seen, but it was compelling to many. Bierbaum wrote an account of his travels by auto (an Adler Phaêton), train, and ship in Germany, Europe, and the Middle East, with Baedeker constantly at hand (Bierbaum 1903, 93, 261, 271).

Auto travel and walking tours rested on the same logic of giving the traveler more time to learn and explore on his own. But it is important not to overestimate the importance of the automotive perspective in the Baedeker experience for most German cities. Auto travel in Germany was generally less developed than in France, the European leader in roads and automotive production and design in this era. French guidebooks to Paris emphasized the possibilities of auto travel—and sang the praises of French cars—much more than the German-language guidebooks to Germany did (Levenstein 1998, 134). Even so, as the first decade of the twentieth century wore on, it was common to see omnibus tour groups advertise trips in various German regions, as in the Harz mountains, where the Bissing travel firm of Braunschweig hawked its wares in 1910. This firm argued that the 'inexhaustible beauties' of the rugged Harz were inaccessible to those who were not 'good on their feet.' Those who could not pay the price of a private car, as well as those limited to rail travel, were similarly disadvantaged. The solution was precisely the kind of bus tour the Bissing company sold (Bissing 1910, 3). Here the pleasures of automobile tourism were marketed to less cosmopolitan types than those for whom Bierbaum wrote, and to less financially armored people than those who toured the countryside in their own Brennabors, Mercedes, and Adlers.

The Baedeker traveler on the eve of World War I was often a first-time tourist (Knebel 1960, 24–5). This meant he needed instruction of the kind the Baedeker asterisk system offered. Adopted first from the Murray handbook by Karl Baedeker in 1844, the asterisk led tourists to notable sites. Later a double asterisk was included to single out 'especially stellar attractions' and then extended to hotels and restaurants (Lauterbach 1989, 217; Mendelson 1985, 391). Variations on this system occurred throughout the literature. By the second half of the nineteenth century, the Murray system used two stars for inns the editor knew from personal experience, one star for those recommended to him. Following on the tradition of the Grand Tour, Baedeker's itineraries established a canon of important destinations for the tourist in need of organization and planning. Notions of 'proper' leisure travel were discussed widely already in the middle of the nineteenth century (Wolbring 1996), and Baedeker's accomplishment was to crystallize such notions in a readily usable form. It may be true that guidebooks are by nature 'democratic' because they 'equalize all points of interest and all events,' as David Sears (1989, 24) argues with respect to Niagara Falls and other US tourist sites. Yet the Baedeker qualifies this statement because it used not only the asterisk but also alternating font sizes to denote relative importance, thereby creating a hierarchy of sites and markers.

The asterisk system came in for much criticism. One travel writer wrote in 1873 that it eliminated the need to 'look' because 'thanks to the double and single stars, we already know if we will enjoy ourselves a lot, or just enjoy ourselves' (Vorsteher 1991, 311). Even so, it is my argument that this system was still based on experimentation and individual taste. Planning and systematization by no means precluded the satisfaction of personal tastes and idiosyncratic wishes. The Baedeker would never have contemplated the kind of detailed 'skeleton tours' that an American guidebook to Europe written by Henry Winthrop Sargent did. Intended 'to assist those who have not time or interest enough to work out their own journey' (Sargent 1870, 6), this book mapped out the tourist's entire itinerary, from meals to arrival and departure times at various landmarks. On the right side of the page, the price of each activity was toted up. In contrast, the Baedeker was there to offer as much detailed information as needed to let the tourist go out on his own. This also put it at odds with the philosophy of the 'excursion tours' invented by Thomas Cook and imitated by Henry Gaze & Son in England and the Stangen firm in Germany. Although only a small percentage of Cook's business consisted of personally conducted group tours, the firm was established in the public mind as the provider of collective tourism. In contrast, Baedeker might well have subscribed to the terse statement made by a contemporary guide to the Hessian city Kassel, the preface to which read: 'The tourist should not be deprived of the pleasure to find his way himself' (Werner n.d.). And indeed there were defenders of the Baedeker asterisk, even in the 1920s, when a high tide of criticism undermined the red book's legitimacy. The asterisk 'hindered no one from making his own discoveries,' wrote Franz Hessel, the author of a flaneur's guide to Berlin (1984 [1929], 95).

Baedeker maps did much to enable the tourist as well, but in a particular way. The 1913 guide was a cornucopia of cartographic representation, including 19 maps or plans of various regions and another 68 city maps or ground plans of museums. Maps play an important role in allowing people to imagine themselves as a community. They collapse space and time, framing complex relationships in tangible wholes. Maps belong to a broad category of pictorial and graphic representations of physical spaces whereby the borders of a collectivity are established and a citizen-traveler's place within it is located. Boyer (1994, 204–23) avers that even as maps became more exact in the modern age, they always mixed fantasy with precision. Maps had aesthetic appeal and 'romance' even when they laid out the world in ever more scientific dimensions. This point is quite clear in the Baedeker handbooks. The firm gained a well-deserved reputation for the high quality of its maps. But anyone conversant with Baedeker guidebooks before World War I must note that some of the maps were not easily usable. The city maps were usually presented not as part of the text but separately, often in a foldout format, and their use in windy or rainy conditions must certainly have tried the patience of the most dedicated Baedekerite. One could of course remove the maps, but anyone wishing to leave the handbook intact would not accept this solution. Yet the maps were also undeniably beautiful in their use of detail and color, and the floor plans of buildings such as the Kaiser-Friedrich-Museum in Berlin enlivened the text even as they offered guidance. Maps and plans were utilitarian, but they were also part of the same aesthetic experience, the same geometric sensuality, which framed modern cities as landscapes of cultural achievement.

Reading his maps and asterisks, the Baedeker tourist engaged in a cultural pursuit now available to the middle Bürgertum. His tourism could not be planned in isolation from economic limits, just as it was not undertaken without an eye to the status it brought in the marketplace of cultural values in which the entire Bürgertum invested. Economy and commerce were themselves on parade in the panorama of destinations the leisure traveler took in, Baedeker in hand. The notion of 'proper' tourism also bore the stamp of economic life, but in a particular sense. The 'not too demanding' tourist of Baedeker vintage was not only aware of the practical exigencies of travel but also a responsible consumer in a society that was engaged in an intense debate over 'luxury.' Consumption threatened to become excessive, in the eyes of many German critics, who worried aloud about the Janus-faced influence of capitalism on public mores. A higher level of consumption betokened spreading prosperity, but it could also weaken and 'feminize' society, making clear the need for discipline if Germany was not to lose its distinctive culture or its historical traditions (Breckman 1990). By properly organizing his consumption, by seeing the connection between the sites he visited and the wider cultural implications of his leisure practice, the Baedeker tourist not only aided German material advance. He also 'lived' the qualities of balance, profundity, and bürgerlich austerity that were deeply rooted in a notionally unique *Kultur*. It is not quite accurate in this light to regard tourism as 'a form of anti-consumption,' as Löfgren (1999, 5) puts it. Rather, tourism, in its Baedeker variety, presented a model of proper consumption that mediated between excess and grudging parsimoniousness, between conspicuous display and suffocating stinginess.

This position could put the Baedeker at odds with the elites of Wilhelmine public culture. Although the Baedeker guidebooks embraced the symbols of monarchical power in Imperial Germany, there was a significant difference between the Baedeker and the royal house on issues of consumption. That both Kaiser Wilhelm II, who rose to power in 1888, and his wife had become consumer 'brands' is clear from travel accounts of the period. The queen's visage appeared in shop windows throughout German cities, and the Kaiser and his family were on display in Berlin's famous wax museum, the 'Castan'sche Panopticon' (Zimmermann 1889, 167, 176). Wilhelm II himself was a willing participant in the selling of the Kaiser. He adored lavish historical restorations of medieval castles and other landmarks, events that were celebrated in public ceremonies and marketed as tourist attractions. Army maneuvers and parades in Berlin and other German cities where the Kaiser reviewed the troops were major events, and hotel, bar, and restaurant owners counted heavily on the income they generated (Vogel 1997). Wilhelm II was famous for his showy visits to such pageants and his wearing of colorful military uniforms and other symbols of martial pomp. So extensive were his highly visible public appearances and international tours that the monarch was nicknamed the *Reisekaiser*, or 'traveling Kaiser' (Koshar 2000, 25; Kohut 1991, 164–7).

Historians of consumption have distinguished between a tradition of 'courtly consumption,' practiced by the early modern aristocracy and based on the notion of the civilizing effects of possessing material objects, and a conspicuous form of consumption based not on the aristocracy of birth but of 'spirit.' This latter form of consumption was associated in the late nineteenth century with the 'dandy,' who embraced material display in a way that distanced him from both the old aristocracy and the new middle strata (Williams 1982). Wilhelm II's love of material excess was a hybrid of aristocratic consumption and 'dandyism,' and therefore quite different from the sober approach to leisure practiced by a middle-class head of household and his family using a Baedeker guidebook for a two-week tour of Berlin or Dresden. Admirers of Bismarck praised the Iron Chancellor, the scion of Junker country living who ruled the Empire from its founding until 1890, for the simplicity and unpretentiousness of his furnishings and clothes (Kessler 1935, I:204–5). Bismarck's differences with the Kaiser had to do not only with policies but also with the style and ambience of rule. Baedeker travel embraced Bismarckian asceticism in its approach to consumption, thereby creating an important social analogue to the National Liberal party's support for Bismarck, the unifier of Germany, in the political sphere. When that political support dissolved in the late 1870s, the tradition of balanced consumption persisted, coloring the Baedeker's approach to leisure travel even when parts of the Bürgertum adopted more lavish spending habits.

The gender dimensions of this cultural matrix should not go unnoticed. Baedeker asceticism intersected with the culture of bourgeois domesticity, which embraced thriftiness and avoidance of excess as Christian values, and which often assigned to women the function of incorporating these values in household life. Yet women were also both the symbols and practical agents of undisciplined consumption in the eyes of many critics. The famous political economist Werner Sombart tied the historical origins of modern luxury to illicit love in general and to early modern French courtesans in particular, whose material wants and sensual excesses were said to have corrupted the aristocracy and middle strata alike (1967 [1913]). Tourism seemed to reinforce this connection. Internationally more and more women were becoming tourists, and their interests and tastes were reflected in travel industry advertisements (Levenstein 1998, 177–95; Löfgren 1999, 100–101).

Whereas the 'feminization' of tourism applied most centrally to the middle class, it did not fail to include parts of the working class as well (Keitz 1992, 44). Cook's tours had more women than men, the spinster schoolteacher or governess becoming a symbol for the firm's business. More than half of all US tourists registered in Paris hotels in summer 1888 were women (Brendon 1991, 52–3; Levenstein 1998, 185). Even so, an advice book on tourism published just before the war still asked 'Should one tour with women?' The answer was revealing: 'Yes, if the women can step out smartly and are of a cheerful disposition—why not? But don't expect the trip to be inexpensive' (Seelig-Stanton 1914, 39).

One effect of this transformation was that shopping, the 'most alluring of feminine pastimes' according to one tour book, was now a well-established theme of tourism (Waxman 1912, 7). Shopping had of course not always been seen as a typically female activity; it was common for men to make the bulk of purchases outside the home until well into the nineteenth century. Moreover, bourgeois women were closely associated with cultural tourism, with its visits to museums and art galleries, the seeming antipode to shopping tourism. But leisure travel now did much to increase the identity of women as shoppers, and Paris' many fine clothing stores in particular became magnets for English and American women travelers. The importance of shopping also gave rise to an 'anti-tourist' critique that targeted women for their alleged shallowness and materialism—the popular analogue to Sombart's academic discourse. In this critique, all of the negative traits associated with the burgeoning world of tourism were laid at the door of the women becoming increasingly visible on the radar screen of the tourist industry (Levenstein 1998, 117–21, 149–52, 189).

The Baedeker tradition's point of departure was the male traveler/collector, but women were not ignored. In some guidebooks they were treated as a burden, as in the case of a prewar Baedeker to Italy, where one reads that 'when ladies are of the party, the expenses are generally greater' (1895, xi). This was all the more reason for advising women in the spirit of the 'not too demanding' traveler in the same way men were. Although the 1913 guide's itineraries concentrated on art and monuments, it did not overlook shopping, directing visitors to Berlin to the Wertheim's department store, built between 1897 and 1904 by modernist Alfred Messel, and noting Düsseldorf's reputation as a commercial center. Its tips on housing reflected an interest in women travelers as well, as it counseled single females to stay in the evangelical pensions and hospices, inexpensive dwellings more conducive to the morals of young unmarried women (Baedeker 1913a, xiv, 19, 286). Eating and drinking establishments also deserved attention in this context, as the Baedeker guide to Berlin cautioned that women stay away from the city's many beerhouses because of the 'strong tobacco smoke' (1889, 18). The guidebook was here responding to prevalent notions at least among American women travelers, who, like Margery Deane, felt that 'Europe must be a paradise to gentlemen; for

40

in no place on the Continent, save in the church, is it forbidden to smoke' (Pitman 1883, 40). The responsible tourist also had to look after the aesthetic economy of tourism, and activities which resulted in unpleasant or even morally questionable experiences were to be avoided just as carefully as overspending was. Baedeker's Germany subsumed women in a discourse shaped by the male head of the household, and to the considerable degree they were treated as ancillaries to the male cultural experience, their 'typical' propensity to over-consume required discipline.

Not just reflected in advice given the traveler, the economy of tourism was also enacted in guidebook syntax. The Baedeker refined a radically sparse grammatical style consisting of partial sentences and abbreviations punctuated with the famous 'Baedeker parenthesis,' which inserted practical information throughout the itineraries. The reader perusing the section on the Thuringian forest in the 1913 guide (1913a, 222) found the following terse statement: '*Blankenburg* (225m), small town with 3,450 inhabs., is dominated in the north by the remains of *Greifenstein* castle (400m; 20 min.; restaurant).' The Murray handbooks from the same period appear impossibly verbose when compared to the compressed style of the Baedeker. Baedeker discourse aimed for transparency and an unmediated presentation in which 'referential proliferation' was minimized (Grewal 1996, 85, 103–4). This necessitated a great deal of complexity and textual density. The Baedeker text was an intricate web of sentences and part-sentences, names of important sites in either italics or boldface (the latter with one or two asterisks if appropriate), smaller print for less essential background, references to maps and ground plans, vital dates, and historical figures. All tourist destinations found their place in a complex hierarchy of description, annotation, and meaning.

The editors of a popular American guide to Europe wrote of the 'bewilderment' experienced by some travelers as they waded through this information (Rolfe 1899, v). The idea was not to bewilder the traveler, however, but to avoid the possibility that too many meanings might adhere to tourist destinations. The uncertainty of travel and the potential for semiotic static were to be met with a guidebook language noted for extreme economy, precision, and comprehensiveness. The linguistic style of the handbook reflected and shaped the tourist's balanced and moderate approach to leisure travel; precision of language recapitulated economy of practice. Even so, the Baedeker was not concise enough for some. American editors of *The Complete Pocket Guide to Europe* maintained that, unlike the 'larger and more cumbrous handbooks,' *their* pocket guide would live up to its name. They offered a product the brief descriptions of which were marked by an impressive 'editorial diligence,' and which was so compact as to be carried 'in a man's coat or hip pocket, or in a woman's dress-pocket or muff' (Stedman and Stedman 1909, 1). This disagreement over how much detail was needed suggested that the Baedeker guide, despite heroic efforts to minimize semiotic proliferation, in fact opened the door to reinterpretation, critique, and even confusion.

14 *Route 1.*        BERLIN. *Kaiser-Friedrich-Museum.*

in den Kuppelsaal und 1. durch den I. Saal in den Seitenkorridor: Düssel-
dorfer. II. Saal: Münchner, Düsseldorfer u. a. 1. Kabinett: Dresdener.
2. Kab.: Münchner. 3. Kab.: Wiener. 4. Kab.: *Karl Becken.* 5. Kab.:
Berliner. III. Saal: Berliner. — DRITTES GESCHOSS. Vorraum: Bilder und
Skulpturen vom Anf. des XIX. Jahrh. II. Eeksaal: Fresken aus der Ge-
schichte Josephs von Ägypten, von *P. v. Cornelius, Fr. Overbeck, Ph. Veit,
W. v. Schadow* (die Übertragung in den VI. Saal ist geplant). III. Saal:
Franzosen. IV. Korridor, V. Saal: Sammlung B. Grönvold. 1. u. 2. Kab.:
Ausländer. 3. Kab.: *Prellers* Zeichnungen zur Odyssee. 4. Kab.: *E. Hilde-
brauds* Aquarelle von seiner Weltreise. 5. Kab.: Handzeichnungen. VIII.
Saal: Sammlung F. Koenigs. VII. Korridor: dekorative Malereien von
*M. Klinger.*

Auf der NW.-Spitze der Museumsinsel liegt jenseit der Stadt-
bahn das **Kaiser-Friedrich-Museum** (Pl. H 5), im italienischen Barockstil von *v. Ihne* 1897-1904 erbaut. Vor dem kuppelge-
krönten Haupteingang an der NW.-Ecke ein Reiterbild des Kaisers,
von *Maison.* Das Innere enthält christl. Bildwerke, Erzeugnisse
koptischer und vorderasiatischer Kunst, Gemälde älterer Meister und
das Münzkabinett. Eintritt s. S. 6; amtl. Führer 2¹/₂, kl. Ausg. ¹/₂ℳ.

ERDGESCHOSS. — Aus dem Vorderen Treppenhaus (Pl.), in dem ein
Bronzeabguß des S. 12 gen. Reiterbildes des Großen Kurfürsten aufgestellt
ist, gelangt man geradeaus durch einen Gang in die Basilika (Pl. 3),
mit größeren Altarwerken von *Fra Bartolomeo, Francia, Andrea della
Robbia, L. Vivarini, Paris Bordone* u. a. — L. vom Hinteren Treppenhaus (Pl. 27) ist Saal 11, mit der *Palastfassade* von *Machadra* (Syrien;
Anfang des VIII. Jahrh. nach Chr.). — L. Saal 9 u. 10: persisch-isla-
mische Kunst. — Saal 4-8: koptische, byzantinische, altchrist-
liche und ältere italienische Bildwerke (an der Schmalwand von
Saal 7 ein Mosaik aus S. Michele in Affricisco zu Ravenna aus dem J. 545).
— Aus Saal 4 wendet man sich durch die Basilika in die Säle 17-26. Zu-
nächst Saal 23 u. 24: deutsche Bildwerke aus romanischer und go-
tischer Zeit, ältere deutsche Gemälde. Saal 20: deutsche Klein-
plastik der Renaissance. Saal 21: deutsche Bildwerke der Renaissance,
des Barock und des Rokoko. In den Sälen 17, 19, 22, 25, 26 Abgüsse
italienischer Bildwerke. — Saal 15, 16: Münzen und Medaillen.

Aus dem Vorderen Treppenhaus (Pl. 1) hinauf in das

OBERGESCHOSS, mit der **Gemäldegalerie:** l. die niederländischen
und deutschen, r. die italienischen Schulen und italienische Bildwerke in
Marmor und Bronze. Steht auch die Galerie in der Anzahl der Hauptwerke
erster Meister hinter den Sammlungen von Florenz, Paris, Dresden, Madrid
zurück, so kommt ihr an Vollzähligkeit der Künstler der verschiedenen
Schulen und Zeiten nur die National Gallery zu London gleich. Die
vornehme Ausschmückung vieler Räume mit alten Türen (meist aus Genua,
Venedig und Florenz), Kaminen, Möbeln und Altären ist zu beachten. —
L. in Kab. 73: 884. *J. van Ruisdael,* Seestück; 223. *Adr. v. Ostade,* Dorf-
kirmes. — Kab. 72: *512-523. *Hubert* und *Jan van Eyck,* zwölf Tafeln
vom Genter Altar, dem Hauptwerk der altniederländischen Malerei, 1432
vollendet. — Kab. 70: 533, 539. *Dierick Bouts,* Elias in der Wüste, Passah-
fest; 523a, 525g, *525a. *Jan van Eyck,* Bildnisse; 538a. *Meister von Flé-
malle,* Christus am Kreuz; 1617. *Jean Fouquet,* Estienne Chevalier mit dem
h. Stephan. — Kab. 68 und Saal 69. Niederländische Meister des XV. u.
XVI. Jahrh.; 535. *Roger v. d. Weyden,* Flügelaltar; 561. *Quinten Matsys,*
thronende Madonna; *1622a. *Hugo v. d. Goes,* Anbetung der Hirten. —
Kab. 67: 586d, *586, *H. Holbein d. J.,* Bildnisse; 1629. *M. Schongauer,*
Anbetung der Hirten; *557c. Bildnis des Nürnberger Ratsherrn
Hieron. Holzschuher, 557 f. Madonna mit dem Zeisig, 557 d. Bildnis des
Nürnberger Ratsherrn Jak. Muffel, 557g. kleines Bildnis einer Frau; 564a.

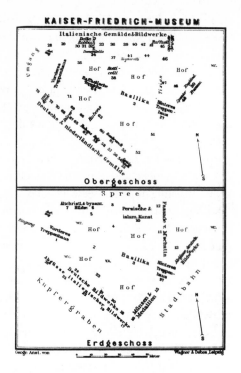

*Figure 2*    *Baedeker textual density (Baedeker 1913a, 14–15).*

In general, the grammar of prudent tourism was a feature of the Euro-American world more than it was a specifically German phenomenon. It was an aspect of the Atlantic culture of pleasure travel that developed with greater intensity than ever before at the time Baedeker's guide to Germany appeared. To the degree that industrial societies in Europe and North America saw the middle strata enter the tourist market in the late nineteenth and early twentieth centuries, the emphasis on careful planning and judicious marshalling of economic resources became a watchword for bourgeois leisure. The Baedeker was rather understated on this matter compared to the manic approach taken by some American contemporaries, more steeped in a tradition of materialism than Germans were, and more inclined to transform tourist destinations into pure commodities (Gilbert 1991, 73). One journalist from the United States took account of just about everything a traveler would spend money on, from transportation to medicine and 'cathedral fees,' as he budgeted a three months' stay abroad for $430 (Hemstreet 1875). American tourists were highly self-conscious about such matters, their familiarity with a materialist culture notwithstanding. The popular Harper's guide to Europe put the point directly: 'We, as a nation, have unfortunately acquired a reputation abroad of great prodigality in our expenditures . . . it is an unhappy feeling to think that we must always be on our guard' (Fetridge 1884, xiii). Because Americans acquired a reputation for overspending, they needed to embrace the ideas of prudence and moderation whenever they toured.

On balance, Baedeker's Germany gave relatively little space to commercial and industrial society, a function of its grammar of economy. In some cases the difference between the Baedeker and other guides is a matter of ambience, in others a question of actual content. The Stangen travel agency's German-language illustrated guide to Berlin also put emphasis on cultural and art history. Yet it was very much unlike the Baedeker because it was full of advertisements for hotels, pharmacies, and beer halls (Stangen 1888/9). The combination of cultural tourism and open reference to local business created a different tone than is found in the more 'scholarly' Baedeker. The Bible of American cultural travel in Europe, the Satchel Guide, also featured advertisements, but only in the front and back of the volume. Readers would find ads on steamship companies, custom house brokers, travelers' 'letters of credit,' and 'Horsford's Acid Phospate' for seasickness, a malady from which as many as 80 percent of Atlantic tourists suffered (Levenstein 1998, 128; Rolfe 1899). Even more commercially minded because of its large business clientele from England and America was the North German Lloyd's guide to Europe. Quasi-luxury tourist cruises between Europe and North America had become big business as shipping lines developed new markets after German emigration to the United States declined by the end of the century. Improvements in transportation made such travel feasible, and one of the fastest passenger ships carried as many as 2,000 people in Atlantic crossings of six days or less. Full- and half-page ads appeared throughout the North German Lloyd guide as tourists were invited to visit not only museums and landmarks but also businesses and factories (North German Lloyd 1898). None of these guides could match the *Pharus-Buch* to Berlin (1906, pt. 2:1–51) which included a step-by-step guide through major streets listing not only monuments and other sights but also businesses and hotels at each stop along the way. To the degree that these guides opened themselves to the blandishments and cultural forms of commercial society, they departed from the Baedeker's bourgeois austerity.

The figure of the modest pedestrian avoiding the seductions of over-consumption also had a connection to the national–liberal travel culture's reticence to discuss sexuality, either as an experience associated with travel or as a commodity. Corbin (1994, 77) writes of a developing 'eroticization' of travel as young men and women had increased chances to meet and observe one another at the beach or the resort. One might also mention a latent 'homoeroticization' within groups such as the German Wandervogel. These mostly male bourgeois youth groups originated in the pre-World War I era as alternatives to the staid tourism of the middle class. An intense and emotional group-life developed, often with distinct homoerotic undercurrents, as boys and young men took long hikes in the forests and country-sides singing folk songs, sitting around camp fires, and decrying their parents' stifling bourgeois existence (Heineman 1989). Among the German upper middle classes, meanwhile, leisure travel at home and abroad signified the opportunity for (mainly) heterosexual adventure, as depicted in the many satirical drawings in the magazine *Simplicissimus*. Here one found images of attractive, usually well-to-do women and men cheating on their spouses while at the beach, the spa, or on vacation in Italy or Greece.

If tourism now carried stronger erotic overtones, it found uneven expression in the guidebook literature as a whole and almost none at all in the Baedeker. Paris was already known for its prostitution and its display of female flesh in art museums, ballet, and opera. The perceived licentiousness of the French capital was a common, if understated, theme of guidebook literature relatively early in the nineteenth century. By the eve of World War I, however, sexual motivations for tourism were more openly acknowledged, at least for men (Levenstein 1998, 198, 209). Berlin nightlife was a central motif of bourgeois tourism only in the interwar period in Germany, but the more ribald aspects of the city had already received specialized attention in travel accounts and tourist literature, to say nothing of serious social analyses like Hans Ostwald's study of prostitution. Ostwald made the point that in no German city was prostitution as widespread or as flagrantly practiced in public as in Berlin (1905/07, 2:3). Remembering his first impressions of the great city in the Second Empire, the painter Rudolf Schlichter wrote of its 'dark, secret depravities' (Spode and Gutbier 1987, 33). A guide to the city's bars, cabarets, and restaurants used satirical articles and poems to highlight an 'amusing Berlin' marked by heavy drinking, smoking, and sex. The guide's drawings of young women lounging in lingerie or fending off overzealous suitors in Berlin dancehalls suggested the joys of excess and sexual dalliance to a mainly male readership (Schloemp 1913, 5, 33).

The Baedeker would have none of this. For Berlin it only hinted at the 'traffic' to be encountered in 'evening hours' on certain streets. Visitors to St. Pauli in Hamburg were told that the area was the 'showplace of the sailors' life' and, without attracting undue attention to the more titillating aspects of the great city's night life, that the Spielbudenplatz featured 'many music-halls' (1913a, 8, 36). Hamburg guidebooks did not go into much more detail either. The guidebook put out by the Hamburg tourist agency, the Verein zur Förderung des Fremden-Verkehrs, noted that St. Pauli featured a 'diverse and agitated' street scene 'unlike any other in Germany,' and that 'every kind of entertainment appropriate to any taste or need' was available (1903, 116). But such comments did little to expose the illicit pleasures of the district. Of course, such restraint was perfectly compatible with how many middle-class tourists themselves responded to real or imagined licentiousness. Peter Gay writes persuasively of how the nineteenth-century city encouraged a 'Platonic libertinism'—'erotic information on which [the bourgeoisie] might act or not as the opportunity presented itself.' For many, such libertinism was based purely on 'looking' rather than 'touching' (1984, 334). Whether it was Montmartre in Paris or St. Pauli in Hamburg, it is possible that most male tourists preferred merely to be able to see prostitutes rather than to employ them, or, in the case of women, to see rough sailors or bohemian artists rather than to take up with them in passionate liaisons. Titillation at a distance, at a minimum (economic and moral) cost, was the goal, and in this context the Baedeker's mere mentioning of such sights was adequate to the task.

It is not quite accurate to argue that 'bourgeois culture was like an organism with a hidden body,' as Frykman and Löfgren write (1987, 223). Rather, bourgeois culture in its Baedeker mode treated open recognition of the physicality of the body as an *option* rather than something to be entirely hidden or repressed. Those travelers who picked up the Baedeker's hints, or were ready to move beyond Platonic libertinism, were free to do as they pleased. Nor should it be overlooked that a degree of erotic pleasure was already implied in the Baedeker cultural itinerary. Sculpture, painting, opera, and theater were after all never without direct and indirect sexual overtones, for men as well as women. Romanticism had put a premium on the deeply subjective and emotional elements of cultural consumption. Male and female travelers reacted to art and natural beauty with outpourings of emotion that bordered on the orgasmic. It is therefore unconvincing to characterize more sexually explicit tourism as a new form of 'recreational tourism' that undermined older forms of cultural travel, as Levenstein does (1998, 209). The possibility of sexual pleasure, whether directly experienced or sublimated, was never absent from the high-cultural pursuits of the Bildungsreise. The sexual economy of travel was assuming a different shape at the turn of the century rather than appearing as a distinct departure.

The Baedeker's prudence with respect to advertising or urban vices reinforced the image of propriety, balanced consumerism, and bürgerlich austerity that the firm conveyed from the beginning of its existence. This too was a constitutive element of the national–liberal travel culture, which shared a general nineteenth-century liberal inclination throughout Europe and parts of North America to favor the delay of material and physical gratification. Yet as before, contemporaries often regarded disciplined consumption and the condemnation of unbridled luxury to be German traits. Indeed, Americans regarded 'frugality' as the product of an allegedly typical German propensity for orderliness, an image Germans were more than willing to reinforce in representations of their own culture (Freese 1990). A similar remark could be made for the thoroughness and precision with which the Baedeker went about representing the judicious tourist. These qualities recommended it as something distinctively German to European and American travelers (Temple 1898, 36).

## III

*Germany in One Volume* organized the country into six regions, which in turn were divided into 99 separate routes. Piers Brendon (1991, 63) argues that tourism is the 'discovery of the well-known' whereas travel is the discovery of the ill-known and exploration of the unknown. This distinction is too rigid, but it does highlight how, more than other forms of travel, tourism foregrounds that which is already famous. But if one uses these criteria, then the Baedeker encompassed sites for not just the tourist but the traveler as well. The reader following the Baedeker national itinerary described a backward 'S' through the country's well-known and not-so-well-known destinations. Starting with the German capital and Potsdam in the first region, he then took in the great northern region of the country, moving between Hamburg and Schleswig-Holstein in the west and East Prussia in the east. He continued in a clockwise direction, encompassing Silesia and Saxony in the southeast and central Germany in the third region, then moving westward through Thuringia, Hessen-Nassau, and Westphalia in the fourth. In the fifth region, the tourist moved counterclockwise as he swung through the Rhineland and southwestern Germany on the left bank of the Rhine including the provinces of Alsace and Lorraine, wrested from the French in the Franco-Prussian War of 1870/ 1. Finally, in the sixth region the traveler headed east, taking in the remaining parts of southern Germany from Württemberg to Bavaria.

Train lines linking key cities determined the routes. In each region, most of the suggested routes took the traveler from a major urban center to other communities or regions, but did not prescribe a roundtrip. The Satchel Guide criticized this guidebook convention of giving only detached routes, offering instead a continuous journey designed to eliminate superfluous and costly travel (Rolfe 1899). The Satchel Guides's approach was closer to the original definition of the word 'tour,' which in the French referred to circular movement, and which retained this sense in the English adaptation (Böröcz 1992, 726). In the Baedeker, major cities had a single route devoted to them, and for travel within these communities or for other regions and towns, additional information on walking tours, carriages, steamboats, and trolleys was given.

Users of the 1913 guide could orient themselves to the itineraries by reading a nine-page introductory section entitled 'Main Points of Interest in Germany.' This gave the traveler 148 cities and towns worth visiting and mentioned 229 key attractions that could be explored in the itineraries along with additional destinations. These sightseeing and vacationing opportunities can be grouped into six broad categories, pertaining to monuments and history, industry and commerce, the military and politics, museums and the arts, nature, and resorts and spas (Koshar 1998b, 332–3). A strong cultural emphasis emerges in this categorization: nearly one-third of the sites of interest belonged to the category of history and monuments while 12 percent pertained to art galleries and museums. This impression is reinforced if one considers the key attractions listed for Berlin, for which the handbook distributed 55 single or double asterisks. Twenty-two of these were given for individual paintings alone, and another 13 referred to sculpture and monuments. Only one of the 14 buildings given an asterisk dealt with commercial activity, the Wertheim's department store, but this building may have been singled out more for its iconic status in architectural modernism than for the buying and selling that went on inside it.

All this reflected the Baedeker's close relationship with that stratum of educated consumers who referred to themselves as 'the cultured' (*Gebildeten*), the educated middle strata. Like the Murrays, the Baedeker family was itself a product of this milieu, keeping up a lively correspondence with the nation's leading philosophers, novelists, and art historians and relying on such intellectuals to write pithy introductory essays for the guides. Among those who wrote for the Baedeker were the Dresden art historian Cornelius Gurlitt, one of the most prolific scholars of his time, the Bonn art historian Anton Springer, and the revered historian of the ancient world, Theodor Mommsen. The German-language Baedeker adored German *Kultur*, the painting, philosophy, music, poetry, architecture, monuments, and scholarship, which could potentially be seen as superior to the less authentic 'civilization' of other nations, particularly though not exclusively that of France. Many within the German middle classes believed they had a profound relationship with art and culture, a relationship crystallized in the Bildungsreise of the nineteenth century (Schmidt 1997, 58–63; Wolbring 1996). This autoimage found explicit reinforcement in the separate indexes for artists and other cultural figures found in some of the Baedeker guides. Scholars of German history have often regarded bürgerlich adoration of culture as evidence for the 'aping' of aristocratic styles and values by an insecure and politically enervated middle stratum. Yet it is my contention that the embrace of high culture did more to strengthen German middle-class self-awareness than to increase dependence on the aristocracy. In the eyes of the Bürgertum, the Bildungsreise was not an exercise in learning courtly etiquette, but a well-organized tour designed to foster the self-confidence and knowledge of the individuated traveler. The Baedeker was a key primer in this learning process.

It is important nonetheless to point out that the Baedeker's linking of tourism and culture was not unique to Germany. Cultural tourism, increasingly based on an internationally recognized canon of sites and objects, made the German middle classes more like their counterparts in England, France, and the United States (Levenstein 1998). The first half of the nineteenth century saw well-off American travelers, anxious to soak up Old World culture, embrace their own version of the aristocratic Grand Tour just as it 'dissolved into a dissolute parody of itself' on the Continent, as Harvey Levenstein observes. Levenstein (1998, 27, 139) also makes the point that cultural tourism in Europe corresponded to the growing importance for American elites of 'conspicuous consumption' and its close relation, 'conspicuous leisure,' as analyzed famously by the Norwegian-American economist Thorstein Veblen (1953 [1899]). But cultural tourism was not only for the most affluent US traveler. From 1872, the Satchel Guide to Europe was published in the United States for 'cultivated Americans' (Rolfe 1899, I). Like the Baedeker, it concentrated on art galleries, museums, and historical churches, and it was perhaps even less aware of the sites of industry and technology than the Baedeker was. The Satchel Guide made an explicit attempt to be more portable than Baedeker or Murray guides, and this may have explained some of its inattention to economic life; there was simply not enough room for the factories once one had 'done' the monuments. It also targeted the short-term vacation traveler, not the person with many months and unlimited financial means available to study the cultural treasures of Europe with Murray or Baedeker in hand. Nonetheless, it approached leisure travel as a form of cultural labor, recommending US scholar James M. Hoppin's advice to youthful travelers visiting Gothic landmarks. 'For an educated American youth to have no knowledge at all of architecture,' wrote Hoppin, 'this would deprive him of a species of sharpened culture that is not dreamy or vague, but is as scientific and harmonious as the laws of music' (ibid., 6). 'Sharpened culture' operated here as a kind of watchword for an American Bildungsreise.

Cultural emphases notwithstanding, the 1913 Baedeker also appreciated modern industrial life. Its second largest category of sightseeing opportunities comprised industry and commerce, with nearly one-quarter of the total. If the self-definition of the cultured Bürger depended heavily on the consumption of art and history, it also depended on the love of technology, consumption, and material advance. It is not entirely true therefore that 'two types of landscape,' one based on industrial production, the other on romance and recreation, were strictly separated in bourgeois tourism, as Frykman and Löfgren argue (1987, 51). But the idea of two landscapes does point to a contradictory element of Baedeker discourse. The themes of technology and material life were less developed (though by no means absent) in all of the itineraries than one would expect given the introductory information. Even this observation needs to be qualified. Baedeker guides from the middle of the nineteenth century had done quite a lot to identify commercial and industrial patterns, and pre-Baedeker guidebooks from the late eighteenth and early nineteenth centuries were fascinated with factories, dams, roadways, artisan shops, businesses, and harbors (Becker 1983; Huck and Reulecke 1978). Such information was a signature element of travel writing influenced by Enlightenment ideas of progress and fascination with technological mastery of nature. In the decades before World War I, moreover, travel writers such as the Frenchman Jules Huret (1908, 335–6) were impressed by German industrial advances and the general prosperity of German cities.

48

It may be that by the turn of the century, the novelty of great industry had worn off for many Germans, or that the Bürgertum's diminishing political fortunes vis-à-vis the growing working-class movement lessened middle-class identification with industrial sites. But even if industrial culture was now a diminished element in the Baedeker itineraries, it should not be forgotten that when the Baedeker of 1913 led its readers to key art galleries and monuments, it remained firmly focused on German urban centers. The cumulative impression is that Baedeker's nation was very modern, indeed that the act of viewing national heritage in the form of great monuments or art works was itself made possible by a highly modern mode of leisure of which the Baedeker was a key part. The road to modernity led through the picture galleries and museum collections that the Baedeker traveler admired. And were not these museums part of that 'reassuring accumulation of goods,' the 'riches' and 'treasures' of a history of art, to use Roland Barthes' words (1972, 76), that the modern bourgeoisie saw as its cultural savings account? The 'two landscapes' of bourgeois tourism continued to have a reciprocal effect on one another even when they appeared to overlap only rarely.

Despite many German intellectuals' skepticism about industrial civilization (Mosse 1964), the Baedeker not only gave anti-modern pessimism little room; it also lauded an economic system whose pinnacle was Berlin, 'one of Germany's most important commercial centers and perhaps the foremost industrial city of the Continent' (1913a, 8). By comparison with turn-of-the-century guidebooks to Chicago, in which an 'aggressive modernity' set the tone, the Baedeker was ambivalent, to be sure. But Chicago at this time presents the strongest contrast possible with Berlin, even though the cities were thought to be alike in their go-for-broke mentality. Chicago's sights were set wholly on the future; the past belonged to a now outdated 'Currier and Ives' sentimentality that dressed the city in old-fashioned garb (Gilbert 1991, 47). For many American travelers to Europe, meanwhile, evidence of modernity was cause for chagrin, as the Old World was supposed to look old. Berlin was one of the sources of irritation, and American travel writers took it to task for its wide streets and impressive new buildings (Endy 1998, 572, 588). Such views reflected a binary distinction between a Europe of the past and an America of the future, a binarism that did not exist in Baedekerian discourse. It should not be forgotten in any case that ambivalence consists of the positive and the negative, acceptance and doubt. In addition to cultural venues, the German speaking Baedeker tourist was encouraged to visit Berlin commercial and industrial settings such as the Wertheim and Tietz department stores or the royal manufactory of porcelain. He or she could visit the AEG firm with its 33,000 employees, and in Essen, the great Krupp steel works, with more than 37,000 employees and 'exemplary' facilities for workers' welfare, was highlighted in the 1913 guide (Baedeker 1910, 160, 162; 1913a, 295).

But modernism was tempered by a significant demurral. The Berlin section ignored the working-class neighborhoods to the north and east of the city center.

This was not only a function of reduced space, as shown by the 1910 Baedeker to Berlin, which potentially had more room for social description. This guide advised the tourist that 'the parts of the city laying to the east of Old Berlin offer the visitor little' (1910, 162). And despite Essen's status as the center of one of the world's richest coal-mining districts, a fact duly noted in the 1913 guide, the city's churches, museums, and monuments came in for more discussion than did industry or workers. Some Baedeker guides of the period did better than others when it came to representing the social ambience of a place, notably the guide to Austria–Hungary, which directed the tourist to the nobles, Jews, workers, and bohemian artists of Vienna (1911, 20–2). One is nonetheless tempted to take an anachronistic view of Baedeker's perspective. If the careful reader envisioned German cities and landscapes solely on the basis of Baedeker descriptions, then the image of a society depopulated by the neutron bomb comes to mind. The monuments, churches, and great factories still stood, but most inhabitants had made a mysterious exit, leaving an eerily 'post-human' world behind.

A broader point may be made about the Baedeker's simultaneous embrace of modernity and inattention to social patterns. With little exception, the Baedeker ignored the people who worked the foundries and assembly lines, the individuals driving the carriages and omnibusses, and the people behind the counters of the new department stores. More than a reticence to confront industrial life, this perspective stemmed from a deeper impulse, constitutive of the guidebook genre as Baedeker formed it, to ignore or caricature human interactions. Consider for a moment an example far removed from the great cities and industrial heartlands of the country. It was significant that the 1913 guide made only passing reference to the Wends, or Sorbs, the Slavic minority of the Spree forest areas, about 100 kilometers southeast of Berlin, where natural and man-made tributaries of the Spree created a web of riparian landscapes, fields, and isolated villages. In the 1910 guide to Berlin and its environs (207), the Sorbs came in for slightly more attention: 'Here the Wend inhabitants, who live from growing vegetables and animal husbandry, have preserved their language and customs, and the women their traditional dress.' But such descriptions merely dispensed with the Sorbs in the same way the French Blue Guides, famously critiqued by Roland Barthes (1972, 75), turned Spaniards into 'a vast classical ballet.' 'They are a mere introduction,' wrote Barthes, 'they constitute a charming and fanciful décor, meant to surround the essential part of the country: its collection of monuments.' The Baedeker thus reinforced the 'disease of thinking in essences,' which Barthes insisted was 'at the bottom of every bourgeois ideology of man' (ibid.). This disease either tucked individuals away, as if the vast machinery of society ran of its own accord, or it reduced workers, prostitutes, and 'scenic' ethnic groups to caricatures. Much of the subsequent critique of Baedeker tourism in Germany made its start by offering antidotes to the disease of thinking in essences.

Places pertaining to political and military functions constituted a little more than 13 percent of the total number of sightseeing opportunities sketched out in the Baedeker introduction. These sites consisted not only of the German capital but also provincial capitals and militarily important sites such as the fortified cities of Strassburg and Metz in the West and Kiel, the Germany navy's most important harbor, in the north. Within the itineraries, the traveler was led to the most important public buildings and installations relevant to these functions. If Germany's political and military life seemed to get relatively short shrift, it should not be forgotten that the handbook paid due attention to Germany's many memorials and national monuments, which also referred to a long history of war and political struggle (Koshar 2000, 29–52). Yet this too needs to be regarded carefully, for military and national symbolism could often be viewed through cultural lenses.

We may concretize the point by considering the Berlin material more closely. The fulcrum of Baedeker's backward 'S' was no idle matter. The first Murray guidebook to England and Wales as a whole appeared in 1878; its principle of organization was an alphabetical listing of all cities and counties. In contrast, the 1913 Baedeker itinerary not only radiated out from Berlin, but also devoted more than 6 percent of the guidebook's space to the great conurbation, more than twice the amount reserved for the city in the first guide to Germany and Austria, published in 1842 (Öhlberger 1987, 287). Berlin's centrality was of course a function of the city's growth into a metropolis and geographical point of departure to the country, with major train lines running to Hamburg, Cologne, Munich, Danzig, Breslau, and other towns. Lying at the hub of this network, Berlin attracted people from all over Germany, who settled down to work and establish families. During the Empire, more than 60 percent of the city's population consisted of people who were not born there, in some districts as much as 80 percent (Spode and Gutbier 1987, 33). Tourists came as well, of course, and the flow of leisure travel to the capital reinforces the idea that tourism was an attempt to experience the thrill of displacement—which after all had made Berlin what it was—without paying its full physical and mental costs. But putting Berlin at the center of things was also part of the Baedeker guide's tendency to concentrate the national image. Of great importance in this context was the monarchical presence, which made the city a 'showplace of festive processions of the royal house and the victorious military as well as of many other festivities and events' (Baedeker 1913a, 7–8), and which condensed the unified Empire into a single figure.

Baedeker's Berlin was a city of grand official buildings, museums, and monuments. The tourist could find 42 monuments listed, more than 20 museums and galleries, 8 notable government ministries, and 9 historical churches. The monarchy and Prussian military tradition were well-represented in this canon. Of the 42 monuments given in the index, 24 represented either Prussian royalty, military heroes such as von Moltke and Wrangel, or political icons like Bismarck.

Architectural sites such as the Brandenburg Gate, the Berlin royal castle, the Avenue of Victory, Frederick the Great's Sanssouci palace in Potsdam, added to a web of monuments and landmarks revolving around monarchical history and Prussian military prowess. An Italian traveler attested to the importance of such sites to Germans, who regarded the palace of Wilhelm I, built between 1834 and 1836, as a 'place of patriotic pilgrimage.' There was little doubt in the eyes of this traveler that Berlin, replete in its Prussian ambience, was 'la capitale germanica' (Yorickson [Ferigni] 1909, 255).

Festival life and street scenes created a related image. The Baedeker was enthusiastic in recommending the 'incomparable military show' that occurred in Berlin in May and September as Wilhelm II led the marching Gardekorps from its maneuvers on the Tempelhof Field back into the city. Tribune seating could be had for anywhere from 3 to 10 marks. One of the few occasions on which Baedeker guides focused on people as a part of the tourist experience was when the presence of 'many soldiers, particularly the handpicked troops of the Garde' was noted in Potsdam (1910, 188; 1913a, 5, 25). Even so, the Baedeker was silent about the overall effect of such events, preferring not to speculate about their political implications. It never made claims of the kind one found in the popular Richter tour guide, which upon noting the spectacle of the Kaiser's entry into the city, averred: 'All political disagreements are silenced, for Berlin loves the Kaiser with the entirety of its critical love' (1915, 5). Such images were also part of an indelible impression of the city noted by non-German tourists. The American Minerva Brace Norton (1889, 10) was taken by the 'number of striking military uniforms mingled with the more sober garb of civilians,' 'officers of fine form and gentlemanly bearing, in uniforms of dark blue with scarlet trimmings and long, dragging, rattling swords . . .' and 'frequent glimpses of gold-laced light blue or scarlet jackets or of plumed and helmeted hussars.' Norton was no exception, for many American travelers to Europe gained a well-deserved reputation for chasing after every trace of royal or feudal pomp they could find. Their enthusiasm for such symbols bordered on 'aristo-mania,' as the romantic Old World of Europe was contrasted (nostalgically or critically) with the American New World of gleaming modernity (Levenstein 1998, 143; Buzard 1993, 71–81). Umberto Ferigni also stressed the sheer variety of uniforms and colors to be seen, but he noted that the tourist could be disappointed when the Kaiser was absent from the capital and the military presence was correspondingly less pronounced (Yorickson [Ferigni] 1909, 289–90).

Such accounts left little doubt as to the centrality of Berlin to German identity. In the years immediately after the formation of the Second Reich, Bismarck stressed the Prussian rather than German symbolism of the city. He was happy to allow the national parliament to meet in temporary quarters, which it did until the opening of a monumental new building in 1894, duly recognized in the Baedeker with (only) a single star and two fairly lengthy paragraphs on its design and symbolism. In contrast, Wilhelm II wanted to make of Berlin the capital of Reich nationalism grounded by the Hohenzollern monarchy. The signature element here was the broad Avenue of Victory (*Siegesallee*), inspired by the Kaiser himself, completed in 1901, and consisting of 32 massive marble statues of monarchs from Prussian and Brandenburg history (Lehnert 1998). Considered impossibly ugly by architectural critics as well as opponents of the Kaiser, the avenue nonetheless also rated a star in the Baedeker canon, and numerous tourists walked along it observing one statue after another as they enjoyed the manicured grounds of the site. An official and inexpensive (50 pfennig) guidebook to the avenue published by the educational ministry provided historical cues, photographs, and a ground plan (Königliches Unterrichtsministerium, n.d.).

Disagreements over the Avenue of Victory revealed how different Wilhelm II's image of Berlin was compared to that of the city administration and its middle-class supporters. For the Kaiser, Berlin meant the central district of museums and monuments, which were sites of representation of kingly power. Everything else was *terra incognita*. Rejecting the city magistrate's efforts to host a world exhibit, the Kaiser remarked: 'In Berlin nothing more draws the visitor than a pair of museums, palaces and the soldiers; in six days with the little red book in hand he can see everything' (Mommsen 1993, 189). For much of the liberal Berlin Bürgertum, however, the city meant not only Hohenzollern equestrian statues and palaces but also modern thoroughfares, factories, and entertainment. For them, the Baedeker passage about Berlin's status as 'the third city of Europe behind London and Paris' (1913a, 7) was at least as important as references to royal pomp were. A world's fair would have drawn attention to the capital's global status, city leaders thought, but it was not to be.

Two points are relevant here. First, popular military pageantry was a key part of the national–liberal travel culture, as it was of German culture more generally. There was significant overlap between micro- and macro-structures in this instance. Jakob Vogel (1997, 277) argues that 'folkore militarism,' which gloried in military symbols and festivals as popular entertainments, should not be equated with nationalist or militarist political views that supported the Kaiser and his allies. Folklore militarism may have provided a fundament for German nationalism— perhaps all political conflicts were indeed silenced when the Kaiser made his entrance—but it was less easily manipulated for this purpose than was the popular militarism of the major war veterans' associations or radical national groups like the Pan-German League. One might nonetheless attribute the popular embrace of military festivals to the 'feudalization' of the German Bürgertum were it not for the fact that one can detect an international trend here. Vogel finds deep popular attachments to military symbols in both France and Germany before World War I, though he is cautious to point out differences between the societies as well. He insists, however, that there was no German 'special path' in this case, and thereby challenges a long tradition of scholarship that sees Germany as a nation in which military symbolism had a unique and unhealthy hold on popular loyalties.

My second point is that this argument may be broadened beyond Vogel's perspective. Many scholars, from sober German historians to radical French social theorists, argue that culture was becoming 'spectacle' by the early twentieth century (Debord 1973; Mommsen 1995, 139). The idea of the spectacle, in Guy Debord's theory, was that capital accumulated until it became an image expressed in advertisements, urban landscapes, historic restorations, popular festivals, sports events, and theme parks. Associated with the coming of the spectacle was the gradual replacement of aural by visual stimuli. This process picked up speed by 1900 but it was present earlier in the nineteenth century, when travel photography, to take a key example, became a 'fundamental binomial of Modernity,' in the words of Italo Zannier (1997, 15). A society shaped by visual stimuli represented reality 'as a dancing of the stars, something to see, an exciting drama' (MacCannell 1976, 64). German tourists, impressed by the military pomp of Berlin and Potsdam, were no doubt influenced by their national history and the founding of the first modern German nation-state, the child of three wars of unification. Yet like their French contemporaries who flocked to military parades on Bastille Day, they participated in an international phenomenon, as tourists from all European nations reveled in military festival life much like the German speaking Baedeker tourist did.

Military spectacle takes us into the world of 'post-tourism' (Feifer 1985, 259–68). Urry (1990, 11) argues that post-tourists 'almost delight in the inauthenticity of the normal tourist experience.' One may question what the 'normal' tourist experience is and why post-tourists 'almost' delight in inauthenticity. Nonetheless, Urry is correct to point to a phenomenon of modern sightseeing in which tourists take pleasure in the 'multiplicity of tourist games' and see their leisure as 'a series of games or texts that can be played.' But scholars who link this tendency solely with postmodernism, usually regarded as a product of the 1960s or 1970s, fail to recognize its deeper historical roots. If the society of the spectacle was on the horizon already before the Great War, then so too was its playful denizen, the post-tourist. It would be incautious to argue that viewers of Berlin militarism were unaffected by nationalistic appeals and patriotic pride. But the distinction made above must once again be drawn between the core of militaristic or radical nationalist culture and the tourists who thought little about the political drama in which they had become actors. For the latter, the appeal of folklore militarism may have been its obviously 'artificial' and 'constructed' character, its status as a brilliant dance of Prussian stars whose substance was enjoyment of the moment.

Even so, Baedeker's Berlin was more Athens than Sparta, more a site of cultural distinction and picturesque aspect than martial conquest. Sixteen of the listed monuments for the city represented intellectuals, poets, philosophers, and architects.

The descriptions of monuments and buildings rarely failed to mention key sculptors and architects. And of course, even when the great museums and galleries carried the name of royal figures, the art-historical descriptions focused on the cultural capital to be consumed at these impressive sites. Berlin had been a center of a kind of 'bildungsbürgerlich tourism' well before this time, as philosophers, poets, and artists were attracted to the city's famous salons, the university, and academies (Spode and Gutbier 1987, 30). Fin-de-siècle tourism now picked up on this tradition, stressing not only cultural achievements but the 'romantic' aspects of the Hohenzollern capital and it surroundings. For the intrepid Marie von Bunsen, who toured Germany in a sailboat, the Garrison Church of Potsdam, famous as the burial site of Frederick the Great, was memorable above all for the 'light, old-fashioned chimes' of its carillon. These same chimes were mentioned as a tourist attraction in the Baedeker guidebook, which noted that the bells could be heard every quarter hour (von Bunsen 1914, 13; Baedeker 1913a, 26). Berlin 'fairly bristles with weapons and militancy,' wrote the American Robert Haven Schauffler, but it also had surprisingly picturesque vistas. A sunset on the Spree River seen from one of its upper bridges bathed the surrounding museums and churches in a rosy half-light, creating 'a picture containing more of the elements of romance than one had dreamed that the city possessed' (Schauffler 1910, 71).

At first glance, such cultural readings of preeminently political sites suggest a key difference between Baedeker tourism and the Grand Tour. The Grand Tour's sites were determined in large part by the political interests of the European aristocracy and the 'managerial classes' of the developing national states. Diplomatic and official relationships often decided where the scion of an aristocratic family would tour, or whom the aspiring state official would meet. Even when the cultural pull of Italy or Greece shaped itineraries, participants in the Grand Tour understood that their activity prepared them for later diplomatic or political service. In the seventeenth and eighteenth centuries, Venice was the ideal destination for the English Grand Tour, but not only for its picturesque architecture and canals. The aristocracy also regarded it as an efficient and powerful oligarchy whose policies were to be emulated (Knebel 1960, 13–14; De Seta 1997, 7–9; Treue 1953, 332). In the interwar era there emerged another form of political tourism, but it was based on the ideologies of Marxist and fascist movements. By contrast, was Baedeker tourism a form of depoliticization?

The answer must be guardedly negative. Baedeker tourism may be regarded as 'political' if we remember that its favoring of Berlin as the centerpiece of the tourist experience derived from the city's status as national capital. It was political in a broader sense because cultural tourism corresponded to a secular process whereby the German Bürgertum was 'becoming public,' to borrow MacCannell's phrase (1976, 49–50). It is true that the late Empire saw the decline of middle-class political fortunes in the Reichstag. But if we consider politics in its connection to culture and society, then Baedeker tourism must be seen as a component of the continued political maturation of the German middle classes, whose ability to shape the leisure regime of late Imperial Germany signaled their growing self-confidence and material power. This is not to deny that there was something of the 'unpolitical German' in the romanticization of Berlin sites. But it is doubtful that this rested on peculiarly German foundations. If one considers the Satchel Guide's approach to Germany, it was the American guidebook that was far more depoliticized. The Satchel Guide passed right through Potsdam without saying anything more about the history enshrined in the local architecture than that the city was the 'Versailles of Prussia' (Rolfe 1899, 123). American guidebooks to the sites of the Franco-Prussian War or to landmarks of the bloody Paris Commune of 1871 were similarly bereft of accurate details about political history (Levenstein 1998, 139–42). For many affluent Americans, European travel nurtured 'implicit or explicit visions for the international position of the United States,' as Christopher Endy argues (1998, 565). The guidebooks' unpolitical gaze suggests there was a contradiction between how Americans experienced the Continent and how they defined the larger purpose of their travels. More broadly, the evidence indicates that the reluctance to consider direct political implications at tourist sites emerged at least as much from the secular and transnational thrust of commercial culture as it did from the peculiar circumstances of German party politics.

A little more than one-tenth of the sightseeing destinations mentioned in the Baedeker introduction consisted of natural sites. The three most important areas were the Prussian Rhine province, the Harz mountains, and the Bavarian Alps. Already a popular tourist attraction for Germans and an international clientele, the Rhineland was said to be better known than the Hudson River to American travelers in the 1880s (Pitman [Deane] 1882, 59). The Baedeker lauded it for its natural beauty, its many small towns and vineyards, the scenic castle ruins and cliffs, national monuments such as the Niederwald Monument near Rüdesheim, and architectural treasures such as the Cologne cathedral. The Baedeker described the Harz as 'the northernmost important elevation in Germany' and 'a fully isolated forested mountain eyrie towering up from the plain, from which it is segregated and detached' (1913a, 193). The wildly shaped Brocken was the nucleas of the Harz, the highest mountain in central Germany, and the scene of tales of witches' meetings on St. Walpurgis' Night, the eve of May Day, a tradition Goethe adapted famously in *Faust*. Travel reports on the Harz were popular among the literate classes in the eighteenth and early nineteenth centuries (Hermand 1983, 179). But on the eve of World War I, the southern parts of the Harz were still considered to be off the beaten track in relation to the northern Harz, the Rhine valley, or other very popular spots (Seelig-Stanton 1914, 31).

The 1913 Baedeker failed to go into the folkloristic aspect of the Harz, no doubt for reasons of space, although the English-language Baedeker to northern Germany included such information in smaller print designating a secondary importance. In contrast, the contemporary German-language guide to Northern Germany took full account of regional legend in a paragraph using standard-size print. That same guide noted the fine view to be had from a tower on the Brocken but also warned the tourist that a fully unobstructed and cloudless view was rare from the often mist-enshrouded heights (Baedeker 1913b, 338; Baedeker 1883, 388). The Baedeker's approach was more sober than one finds among Harz boosters. They, viewing the expanse of Germany from the top of the Brocken, expressed both a feeling of release and mountain asceticism, and a desire for 'freedom and lightness, of forgetting all the bourgeois and languid ease of cities and houses' (Ernst 1907, 88). Such vistas made the Harz mountain area an especially favored destination for German artists and literati (Dawson 1901, 230).

From the Rhineland to the Harz, the Baedeker's focus on nature is connected to a much broader development in German and European cultural history. At the origin of modern tourism one finds not only new ways of appropriating culture but new orientations to nature. In a long transformation of sentiment and perspective, nature became not a demonic and threatening force, but, particularly by the turn of the eighteenth century, an inspiration and an alternative to the depravations of 'civilized' society. An important transmission belt of this new perspective was the history of the middle-class 'stroll.' Although strolling was often done in urban settings where green space could be found, it was also related to the new form of appreciation of nature. At the turn of the twentieth century, the 'summer vacationer,' or *Sommerfrischler*, also appeared. Often seeking the 'tonic' qualities of fresh country air, they were middle-class individuals and families staying several weeks in rental houses or hotels in scenic rural areas, often in rather sparse quarters. Although the vacationers wanted to 'get away from it all,' their appearances at the beach, on evening walks, in restaurants, and other public spaces reflected the strong social element of what amounted to a kind of nature tourism. And even when hiking occurred on the highest peaks of European mountain ranges, it shared with the stroller, the Rhineland tourist, and the Sommerfrischler the desire to be seen, and to see others relating to nature. For such tourists, nature had the status of a work of art, something to be admired and discerned, a 'view' to be had from the terrace of a comfortable lodge or while strolling slowly along a forest lane, but not something to be engaged directly. The guestbooks of middle-class tourist hotels reflect both this sense of nature as 'spectacle' and a belief in the therapeutic need for viewing nature, for feeling its cool breezes or summer rains, as an antidote to urban life (Sauermann 1992, 89–92). Barthes' analysis (1972, 74) of this phenomenon was deeply critical. He considered the guidebook-enhanced adoration of nature to be a 'labor-saving adjustment' for the bourgeoisie, who saw in 'mountains, gorges, defiles, and torrents' scenes that encouraged 'a morality of effort and solitude.' These were

*Figure 3    Constantin cigarettes on summer vacation (*Simplicissimus *19, 14 [6 July 1914]: 219).*

precisely the values with which the middle classes approached work life. In Barthes' view, the middle-class stroll in nature becomes a routinized adjunct to the staccato rhythms of the office, the classroom, and the courts.

Just as the mountain vacation was slowly turned into 'a copy and evocation of urban life' (Bernard 1978, 178), tourism's nature as a whole began to take on the characteristics of the city. Intrepid French and English mountain climbers in Switzerland had done much to popularize Alpine lore by the time of the French Revolution, and by the 1830s Alpine regions were attracting climbers as well as artists, botanists, mineralogists, and tourists. Gottfried Ebel wrote the first comprehensive guide to the Swiss Alps early in the nineteenth century, a work that has been seen by some as the true forerunner to the Baedeker. Other guidebooks followed, including, in the 1830s, a guidebook for women climbers. Such tourism became more organized as the century progressed. Paradoxically, the trend toward organization stemmed initially from a sense that Alpine tourism had become too routinized. The first members of the Alpine Club, formed in 1856 in London, were mainly English upper-class gentlemen who dreaded the 'cocknification' of the mountains and thought of themselves as rugged individualists. They set themselves apart from the growing masses of tourists clamoring over the hotel-bedecked slopes of the great Alps (Knebel 1960, 24, 29; Schama 1995, 494–5, 502–6).

German-language Alpine organizations followed, first in Vienna in 1862 and then in Munich seven years later. The two organizations combined in 1873 to become the German–Austrian Alpine Club, and by the first decade of the twentieth century more than 300 sections with 50,000 members existed. The Alpenverein wanted to advance the cause of mountaineering but also to promote scientific study of the Alps and make tourism easier. It blanketed the mountains with kilometer markers, paths, and shelters, inspiring previously isolated mountain outposts to become comfortable hotels. Tourist guidebooks were an integral part of the opening of the Alps to tourist culture, which amounted to an 'urbanization' of the region. By 1906 the Baedeker firm produced its 31st edition of a guide to Switzerland and the 32nd to southern Bavaria and the Tyrol. The Meyer firm emulated its more upscale rival, producing 21 editions of its handbook to Switzerland by 1906 and its tenth edition of a southern Bavarian guide (Knebel 1960, 25). All this led the Englishman William Harbutt Dawson to write of Alpine Germany: 'There is probably no district frequented to any degree which has not been made so easy of access that wayfaring men, even fools (which, alas, many are) need not err therein' (Dawson 1901, 224).

As might be expected in the tradition of German 'associational mania' (*Vereinsmeierei*), organized Alpine tourism fragmented into numerous special interests and competitors. The Alpine clubs had considerable room for maneuver in their local sections, and as the century developed groups for mineralogy, botany, zoology, geography, cartography, folk songs and folk dance, mountaineering, hiking, gymnastics, bicycling, skiing, and photography formed. Older members still serious about the 'asceticism' and nature worship of the Alpine ideal often looked askance at younger generations interested in the social life and consumerism of comfortable ski resorts and hotels (Knebel 1960, 29–31). The grassroots tourist clubs unaffiliated with the Alpenverein in Germany and Austria had both a more restricted gaze and a less ambitious set of goals. For some, mere 'pedestrianism,' as the English phrased it, was the motivation.

Opposed to the Alpenverein on ideological grounds were the 'Friends of Nature,' or *Naturfreunde*, initially formed in Vienna in 1895 by skilled laborers and intellectuals in the Social Democratic movement, then extended to Germany a decade later. German membership in the association was over 10,000 on the eve of the Great War (Keitz 1992, 45). Convinced that workers needed their own form of leisure activity, the Friends of Nature organized a type of 'social traveling' that consisted of weekend nature hikes, group tours, and youth group hikes in the countryside. They marked nature paths and built shelters, and by the eve of World War I they had constructed 30 Naturfreunde clubhouses (Zimmer 1984, 14). They nurtured a 'proletarian' travel culture that had connections to the 'everyday

Alpinism' of shepherds, smugglers, mineral collectors, hunters, and many others who set out into the mountains to enjoy nature outside the constricted cultural and physical paths of the Alpenverein. Not to be forgotten is the correspondence between working-class tourism in the Empire and the artisan journeymen's 'travel years,' or *Wanderjahre*, undertaken by select apprentices as an initiation into the guild. A travel guide oriented directly to workers, *Scherm's Reise-Handbuch für wandernde Arbeiter*, had gone through a third edition by 1889. Its entry for the scenic university town Marburg did not mention the elegant Gothic Church of St. Elizabeth, a perennial in guidebook literature, but rather brought attention to the town's machine-building and surgical instrument firms. But it was not only a matter of focusing on alternative sites. The skilled metalworker Fritz Kummer, who spent three years traveling the world, read the standard tour guides as a provocation. In 1913 he wrote that the Baedeker star on a hotel name was a 'warning' to workers. What was 'economical' for the bourgeois tourist was 'unpayable' for the ordinary traveler: 'The travel routes of the well-to-do are not those of the proletariat' (Kramer 1984, 43–4). The formation of working-class travel as a distinct alternative to the national–liberal travel culture would await further significant development between the wars, but its roots go back to the historical moment when Baedeker was king. Even so, proletarian leisure was not wholly immune to the seductions of the bourgeois travel culture either: already before 1914 some Friends of Nature groups organized winter sports and skiing departments just as their middle-class opposites did (Keitz 1992, 45–6).

The final category comprised resorts and spas, amounting to less than one-tenth of the sightseeing opportunities mentioned in the introductory material. Dating back at least to Greek and Roman civilizations, the complicated history of spas may be understood only with reference to the interaction of numerous environmental, cultural, economic, and political processes (Towner 1996, 53–95). The Baedeker offered detailed information on popular spa towns such as Baden-Baden, Bad Ems, Bad Homburg, and Wiesbaden. In addition, the Bavarian resort towns of Bad Reichenhall, Berchtesgaden, Mittenwald, and Oberammergau received due attention. Bad Ems was favored for bronchial weaknesses, Wiesbaden for patients with gout or rheumatism as well as those who wanted a 'general bracing up,' and Bad Homburg for much the same (Dawson 1901, 226–7). Wiesbaden was the biggest of the spas, with 200,000 visitors annually, according to the Baedeker, almost twice the local population. Bad Ems was much smaller but also more venerable, and at one corner of its scenic Kurgarten the Benedettistein commemorated the diplomatic negotiations that served as the prelude to the Franco-Prussian War of 1870. The guidebook noted that Baden-Baden, a town of just over 20,000, 'competed with Freiburg and Heidelberg for the honor of being the most beautiful city in Baden and after Wiesbaden is the most visited German health resort.' Copious information followed on hotels, the price of the thermal baths, and 'the life of the resort,' which consisted of a full round of concerts, eating, outings to the countryside, and promenading on the elegant Lichtentaler Allee ('especially lively on afternoons'), designated with one star (Baedeker 1913a, 248–9, 252, 306–7). Wiesbaden and Baden-Baden were once known worldwide as much for their gambling casinos, especially favored by the aristocracy and upper bourgeoisie, as for their curative powers. When the city of Monte Carlo in the principality of Monaco tried to attract a rich spa clientele in the early 1860s, it boasted of a 'Casino rivaling the most glittering ones in Germany' (Levenstein 1998, 146). But gambling was forbidden in 1872, and by the end of the century, the thermal spas drew visitors because of the hygienic facilities, family vacations, balls, musical concerts, and parties the resort towns offered.

The German aristocrat Harry Graf Kessler recalled with pleasure his childhood memories of spending the summer months with his parents in the spas of Bad Ems, Baden-Baden, and Kissingen. Men and women of high birth or substantial pocketbooks would meet regularly at the resorts from summer to summer, often angling to be included in the social circle of the Kaiser if he was present. Kaiser Wilhelm I himself made no unusual demands on resort staffs when he took his annual cure. Even so, every morning when he turned to leave the thermal spring after finishing his drink of spa water, the assembled crowd would 'bow in long rows before him like a cornfield in the wind' (Kessler 1935, I:39–43, 55). The spas were also favored by the less exalted strata, and by American and English travelers as well. Indeed, Bad Homburg had been so popular among English tourists that the presence of 'foreigners' was considered by some to be intrusive. At Baden-Baden meanwhile, Americans were the dominant foreign group. The main promenade, the Lichtentaler Allee, lined with beautiful trees and flower gardens, caused one German-American journalist to observe that by comparison America's boulevards resembled 'desert paths strewn with telegraph posts' (Dawson 1901, 233; Zimmermann 1889, 146). The Satchel guide praised Baden-Baden as 'one of the most fashionable resorts in Europe' and gave it an inordinate amount of space, devoting 24 lines to the town while giving the metropolis of Frankfurt am Main just 14 (Rolfe 1899, 111, 115).

The American Margery Deane found both Wiesbaden and Homburg to her liking. In the former she recalled that 'ladies sit all day knitting in the open air, and families take their meals out of doors' and in the latter she found that 'all the German ladies I knew . . . regretted that they were no longer permitted to gamble.' For Deane, Wiesbaden was surprisingly inexpensive, costing a single tourist less than 3 dollars a day, which included the *table d'hôte* dinner of nine courses. Deane was shocked by how much there was to eat at German spas, and how much the Germans themselves whiled away their time at Homburg eating. 'One never ceases to wonder,' she wrote as her last lines on German spas, 'that such music and such poetry come from such a nation of eaters, drinkers, and smokers' (Pitman [Deane] 1882, 62, 94, 100).

Deane was responding to a broader development in spa tourism. As the clientele of the thermal baths became more solidly middle class in the first half of the 1800s, the spas emphasized the health benefits and scientific basis of hydrotherapy. Therapy was in the hands of medical experts, who organized patients' visits, from the early-morning drinking of the waters (preferably on an empty stomach) to bathing and dining. Regimentation did not exclude bountiful meals of the German resorts, which were also available in French resorts, or socializing. But it did impose a degree of discipline on the consumption habits and schedules of spa visitors, who often needed a doctor's permission to receive hydrotherapy. In the second half of the century, this regime of 'medicalized leisure' became less stringent, often to the dismay of the experts and spa administrators. It was still the case that 'during the rush of the season, long columns of shivering people, each with glass in hand, [were to] be seen as early as six o'clock, slowly filing past the favorite springs which pour forth their unsavory hot water and health' (Dawson 1901, 229). But spas throughout Europe began to have large numbers of guests that did not 'take the waters' at all. Rules for drinking and bathing in the waters that had been applied uniformly to all guests were relaxed and sometimes tailored to the individual constitutions and maladies of visitors (Weber and Weber 1898, 52–3). Guidebooks reflected and directed this development. One guide, the *Reisealmanach* (Kunter 1910), claimed to be the most comprehensive handbook available for Germany's many spas and health resorts. It included plenty of information on taking the waters at various sites, but it also gave copious detail on hiking paths, scenic natural sites, monuments, shooting ranges, and breweries. Reflecting the broadening social composition of spa clientele, it also mentioned the less well-known and smaller resorts off the beaten path of the more luxurious or visible watering holes of the day.

Douglas Mackaman (1998) attributes the loosening of the balneological regime to bourgeois tourists' growing sophistication in the 'tactics of leisure.' Over the course of the century, middle-class spa visitors felt less compelled to follow the dictates of medical experts, relying more on their own sense of proper leisure-time behavior. Mackaman's point could be extended to the phenomenon of beach going. Sea bathing began as an extension of water cures, but by the end of the nineteenth century pleasure rather than medical cosmology determined behavior, dress, and fantasy at the beach. Even so, not everyone was happy about the new leisure regime at the seashore, and women in particular were warned about the dangers of exposing themselves too boldly in revealing bathing suits or stepping into the waters to swim (Löfgren 1999, 116–20). Whether referring to spas or beach resorts, the argument coincides with my emphasis on how the national–liberal travel culture promoted the freedom and individual decision-making of the responsible tourist. Once again, the Baedeker is at the center of this shift; more than any other guidebook, it epitomized the liberating and self-organizing aspect of the new tourist culture.

*Figure 4*   Simplicissimus *goes to the beach. The satirical magazine devotes an issue to the latest tourist craze (12, 19 [5 August 1907]).*

## IV

The Baedeker guide to Germany was an impressive act of synthesis at a moment when the still-young German Empire had a bright future. An industrial superpower ready to assume European economic leadership, Germany had a standard of living, an urban infrastructure, a transportation network, and an educational system that were the envy of citizens in all the advanced nations. It is true that the political situation was uncertain: externally, because of a constantly frustrated desire to be a world-class imperial power, and internally because of the German elites' adamant opposition to parliamentary reform and the Bürgertum's political splintering. Yet the real and potential political instability of the situation made little impact on

Baedeker's Germany, where a degree of optimism reigned. And why not? From the perspective of the Baedeker traveler, the German nation was within reach as an advanced, prospering community anchored by an impressive cultural tradition and enabled by modern technologies that allowed the individual to get around as never before. The world of leisurely displacement was a world of individual discovery, balanced consumption, learning, culture, and spectacle. The traveler-collector from the Bürgertum regarded this world with a mix of desire and awe as he or she used the Baedeker to transform its many pleasures into a logic of sequential experiences that modeled modernity's ceaseless movement. It would be inaccurate to say that this world of pleasurable displacement was unrealistic. But Baedeker's representation of Germany was partial—not the least because it was so individual—as all tourist realities are. Its partiality not only made it blind to the troubling political developments that would plunge Europe into an unprecedented war of mass slaughter, but it also stimulated alternative touristic appropriations of Germany oriented to identities and emotions left out of the Baedeker's singularizing perspective. Each new alternative tried to re-frame Germany in a new synthesis. But each new alternative only continued a downward spiral, as the relationship between dispersal and concentration, mediated so skillfully through the prewar Baedeker guide's focus on the individual bourgeois traveler, was broken.

# Chapter Two

# Sex and Class

## I

The Bible of tourism was the Baedeker guidebook, a synonym for leisure travel itself. The writer and Social Democratic Reichstag deputy Anna Siemsen (1927/ 8, 249–52) made a prescient comment on the Baedeker guides a decade after the war, arguing they 'are the books of the bourgeois world of today, how it lives, develops, and relaxes when it finishes its work.' But well before the Great War, the limits of the Baedeker public were clear, and by the 1920s they were widely recognized. 'It is taken for granted,' wrote Siemsen, 'that the darker side of bourgeois leisure is only intimated. The books are so respectable, so correct that only hints to "interesting popular traditions" or "nightlife" must suffice for the initiated. Every young girl can read them. They report only that which one can discuss in the company of ladies.' Siemsen's reference to the 'darker side' of bourgeois travel suggested that there was something else, something less polite and possibly more salacious, going on within bourgeois travel that the Baedeker public failed to recognize or even purposely suppressed. In this 'something else,' this chapter argues, there is evidence for the formation of a modernist travel culture that, among other things, put sexuality at the center of its leisure pursuits.

But Siemsen also wanted to make the German culture of travel more accessible to a new public, the articulate, politically conscious, and economically stable working class. Perhaps 10 percent of the working class had both the economic wherewithal and political power to claim the right to leisure travel on a par with members of the middle strata (Keitz 1997, 41). But many others either traveled for leisure only infrequently, or they were too culturally inexperienced to take full advantage of their free time. What should these workers—as workers—see and do on their travels? What should they learn? Siemsen's complaint on this score was clear: 'Of economic life and the economic development of a country, of the occupational structure, of the construction and relations of its industry and agriculture, the Baedeker knows little.' The Baedeker guide to Switzerland contained no more than a half dozen sentences on economic life, in Siemsen's estimation. Even more seriously, the national–liberal travel culture forgot workers. 'That the Baedeker tells nothing of the workers' movement and its history,' wrote Siemsen, 'that [for the Baedeker] trade union halls do not exist, is self-evident.'

This led to a paradox. Although the industrial working class was a product of the most advanced technological and economic developments, the worker who traveled did so 'as in the Middle Ages.' Like the medieval apprentice, he moved about by word of mouth, relying on colleagues or the pre-existing contacts of masters and shops, without the kind of detailed instructions and information open to the Bürgertum on tour. Of the Baedeker, Siemsen argued: 'Let us leave it to the bourgeoisie.' The 'traveling proletariat' required his own tour book, one that told of 'his work in society and his struggles, his culture and history,' and one that would become 'as comprehensive a document of the developing culture of the working class as the Baedeker is for the Bürgertum.' The worker's vision needed to be modernized, in other words, so that his leisure-time pursuits could be brought into congruence with the advanced technological status of his work life. This was the second pillar of Siemsen's critique, which pointed to a socialist travel culture shaped by the histories, expectations, and work experiences of manual laborers.

Siemsen's focus was not limited to Germany. The Baedeker was a symbol of the bourgeois world, an international phenomenon, just as the desire to open up leisure travel to workers was part of an international movement of liberation. Nor did Siemsen's criticism indicate that the Baedeker had lost its legitimacy altogether. Even Franz Hessel, iconoclastic author of a flaneur's guide to 1920s Berlin, regarded Baedeker description of tourist sites to be 'better, more pregnant, and more knowledgeable' than that which could be had from live tour guides (1984 [1929], 92). But the tide had turned, and the nationalism of the time also worked against the Baedeker's international reach. It was with the little red books in mind that the Touring Club Italiano, promoting a new series of guides to the peninsula, stated it wanted to free its readers from the travel literature 'imposed' on Italians in the past (Bertarelli 1924, 5; Podic 1986, 6; Bosworth 1997, 382, 390). As before the war, Baedeker discourse could not be easily divorced from German culture, and Siemsen's critique of Baedeker began on German soil.

World War I had done much to make Siemsen's criticisms more timely. The English writer Robert Roberts (1971, 186) recalled that 'the first world war cracked the form of English lower-class life,' bringing about 'basic alterations in certain habits and customs.' Such changes were not confined to the English class structure, though. They were part of a broader transformation of European society that convinced many that prewar relations could never be rehabilitated. Roberts titled his chapter on the effects of the war 'The Great Release.' And indeed, for many, the war did more than permanently disable older social forms. It liberated energies that had been percolating more than a decade before the bloodletting began. Modris Eksteins (1989, xv) notes that many Germans went into the Great War with the idea it would be a 'war of liberation,' a *Befreiungskrieg*. But Germans were only the most advanced of the European peoples in terms of their 'obsession with emancipation' and preoccupation with 'becoming,' both definitive moments of modernism for Eksteins. Whereas the desire for movement and 'becoming' characterized many corners of European culture before 1914, World War I widened the possibilities of its expression. Leisure pursuits would not be unaffected.

Writing during the Weimar Republic, the incisive cultural critic Siegfried Kracauer opined that travel had taken on a 'theological' significance. Movement from one place to another no longer had a 'self-contained' meaning, but rather 'granted access to the Beyond.' Even though travel was an effect of the technological mastery of the world, it also promised redemption from the machine-world and a sense of meaning beyond spatio-temporal reality. Kracauer's argument was compatible with the sense of modernism as 'becoming,' as emancipation and movement. The last lines of Kracauer's essay put it well. He wrote that travel and dance potentially 'become filled with meaning once people extend themselves from the newly won regions of this life here to the infinite and the eternal, which can never be contained in any life here' (1995, 65–73). It is true that the national–liberal travel culture emphasized emancipation as well, and to the degree it did it may be seen as a precursor to the tourism of the era of the wars. Yet Baedeker tourism envisioned emancipation within the coordinates of a bourgeois world. Travel pointed to meaning within the social matrix. The new, more 'theological' travel Kracauer saw pointed beyond the present, suggesting a form of emancipation *from* Baedeker's universe. Even so, in seeking release and emancipation, the new travel culture burrowed into everyday life as never before, just as Kracauer himself analyzed the theology of the time by studying how commercial culture permeated experience. The argument of the following is that access to this realm of emancipation was thought to be gained through liberated (though 'rational') sex and the pleasures of the body, or alternatively, through the modernized vision of a socialist working class shaped by daily rhythms of labor and leisure.

## II

World War I caused a sharp drop in tourism, but it stimulated new forms of leisure travel and was at the root of yet greater structural changes that would facilitate tourism in the interwar years. War has been a major stimulus to travel since ancient times, when warriors plundered foreign lands and acted as 'travel agents' by telling tales of riches and adventure beyond the horizon after returning home (Oppenheimer 1932, 2:35). Peasants and workers from all over Europe who had never traveled much beyond their home regions now found themselves mobilized into entirely new environments in World War I. If they were on one of the fronts, they experienced the horrors of modern industrial warfare. But only a minority of soldiers fought on the front lines at any given moment; and many of the military never saw fighting at all. Throughout the conflagration, officers, soldiers, civilian administrators and experts, nurses, and many others affected by the war traveled. For some, the war was the first extended experience with nature, an experience that transformed them into people one often finds in travel advertising, though under quite different conditions. That is, they were fit and athletic-looking, their faces weathered or even suntanned. They experienced the rigors of a life 'out of doors' no less successfully than modern-day campers and backpackers do. They lived a kind of 'classless' reality, radically different than the social hierarchies of normal life, in the same way that tourists experience the unhinged egalitarianism of travel. German soldiers' fond memories of the 'front community,' fraught with a political meaning eventually exploited by the Nazis, were not unlike tourists' memories of the camaraderie of travel. Yet just as tourists compare themselves to each other, soldiers consciously or unconsciously reinforced patterned understandings of privilege and deference, thereby bringing the everyday world back into the trenches. Soldiers were frightened to the point of paralysis by the war, but they also found it fascinating in its bitter spectacle, just as tourists marvel at the promise of danger in sublime natural environments or even in big, overpopulated cities (Eichberg 1992).

Some soldier-travelers were in need of orientation as they were stationed in new surroundings. German physicians traveling to Warsaw after the German occupation of that city in August 1915 could refer to a guidebook published by the German Congress for Internal Medicine, or Deutscher Kongress für Innere Medizin (1916). While this book introduced the physician to medical facilities available to military doctors in the Polish city, it also recommended sightseeing opportunities. Soldiers on leave to Berlin could take advantage of a guidebook published by the city's official travel agency (Centralstelle für den Fremdenverkehr Groß-Berlins 1915). It took account of the brevity of the visit most wartime travelers to Berlin would make, recommending walking, shopping, and coach tours of one, three, and seven days. If they did not travel, soldiers dreamt about travel, often spending long, boring hours in the trenches imagining the places they would visit once the war was over (Keitz 1997, 24).

The war drastically reduced American leisure travel to Europe, stimulating a 'See America First' campaign that put unprecedented numbers of tourists on the roads in the United States (Shaffer 1999; Withey 1997, 337–8). Even so, 250,000 Americans saw Europe's military mobilization in 1914 (Endy 1998, 567). Many Americans were in Europe during the war, and not only as soldiers after US entry into the conflict in March 1917. Touring both the front and occupied areas, journalists and writers moved throughout the continent from the beginning of the shooting. One account by an American, Arthur H. Gleason, a member of the Hector Munro Ambulance Corps, and his wife Helen Hayes Gleason (1916), dealt in part with the former's experience touring occupied Belgium with Baedeker in hand. It was not a positive memory. Aside from the fact there were many German tourists in Belgium's occupied cities—'I saw them everywhere,' wrote Gleason (ibid., 67)—the author castigated the Baedeker guidebook for representing landmarks, city halls, and museums that were now piles of rubble. 'Half down, or a butt-end, or sometimes ashes'—this was the condition of the monuments Baedeker's guide to Belgium depicted (ibid., 66). Gleason's account was at times absurdly naïve—he was sure German tourists would give Baedeker 'a warm time' (ibid., 67) when they realized the disparity between the handbook and the actual condition of the country—but his message came through: the German occupation had brutal consequences for Belgium. He was also correct in pointing out the lag between the Baedeker guide and the condition of Belgium's tourist sites. It would not be until 1930 and 1931 before German and English-speaking tourists respectively would be able to buy updated Baedeker guidebooks to Belgium.

Another genre of war tourism consisted of sightseeing trips to the battlefields. Usually associated with the postwar era, battlefield tourism began soon after the war broke out. Civilians were making trips to the battlefields by the end of 1914 to collect stray bullets as souvenirs. The Cook's agency received enough inquiries by March 1915 that it was compelled to issue a statement saying it would not conduct tours to battle sites until the war was over owing to French opposition. Journalists often made their war reports in anticipation of the tourist value of the scenes they described; travelers would later return to see what became of the smoldering ruins of churches and other landmarks about which they had read. Soldiers talked of the trenches as future tourist destinations. And Germans traveled throughout the occupied regions of both fronts (Lloyd 1998, 23). Even if they carried out-of-date Baedekers with them, German tourists to Belgium had plenty of information from their government agencies, including booklets with descriptions of the land and people along with train schedules and tables showing distances between major towns (Kaiserliches General-Gouvernement, 1915).

After hostilities ended, battlefield tourism became a combination of crass commercialism and sacred pilgrimage. War veterans, widows, and concerned citizens from all the belligerent countries mourned the loss of millions of lives as they viewed memorials, attended ceremonies at ossuaries and military cemeteries, and took part in conducted tours of battlefield sites. The French government promoted battlefield tourism both for its patriotic effects at home and its potential for bringing in currency from foreign tourists, the British and Americans being the most important among them. The US government spent more than 2.5 million dollars sending some 3,600 war widows to France in 1930 alone ('Amerikanische Erholungsreisen' 1931, 3:92). The purveyors of postcards, mugs, and playing cards made money on such traffic, as did the hotel owners and barkeepers who housed and fed the swarms of travelers. So did the guidebook publishers, who hit the market quickly and in great numbers. Between September 1917 and April 1921, Michelin produced 29 different guidebooks, each discussing an important battlefield. Seventeen were translated into English, and one, on Verdun, was issued in a German-language edition. Three volumes on the American experience in the war appeared from Michelin in 1920. The company eventually produced more than 50 guides, including translations and new editions, amounting to 3,500 pages of text (Harp 1999). Germans meanwhile relied on a voluntary organization, the Volksbund Deutsche Kriegsgräberfürsorge, which was in charge of German battlefield graves on foreign soil. It arranged reduced prices for the relatives of the fallen who wanted to visit German military graves and provided information on the accessibility of cemeteries and memorials. The largest of these were on Belgian soil, specifically at Langemark and Menen, each with more than 40,000 fallen German soldiers in individual or collective graves (Mosse 1990, 152-4; Volksbund 1983, 18).

Battlefield tourism treated the leisure traveler as a fragmented personality. On the one hand, travel to the battlefields was clearly an industry regulated by the rules and goals of commercial leisure. It was true mass culture—and not a pretty culture at that. Government ministries warned visitors to the battlefields of France, especially Americans, not to carry away skulls of fallen soldiers as souvenirs ('Schlachtfeld-Piraten' 1929). At the same time, it appealed to a sense of the sacred. The Myth of the War Experience (Mosse 1990) shrouded the bloodletting in a higher politico-religious meaning, providing solace and justification for the loss of so many lives. I have argued elsewhere (Koshar 2000, 98) that the Myth of the War Experience did less to distort the memory of the war than George Mosse maintained. But the idea that the war appealed to travelers as a larger-than-life event, a moment of sublimity in all its enticing terror, remains accurate. Whereas both the commercial and 'specular' aspects of battlefield tourism might plausibly be expected to have created common ground on which travelers could meet, the patriotic or national elements of the phenomenon moved in the opposite direction. The Michelin guidebooks emphasized German destructiveness all along the line and included accounts of German military atrocities in Belgium and France (Lloyd 1998, 116–17). English-language editions of the Paris-based Guide Bleu to Belgium and the Western Front reinforced national stereotypes by contrasting 'British grit' to German 'skill and discipline' (Muirhead 1920, xlvi). Baedeker guidebooks were subtler in tone. Of Compiègne, a popular summer resort occupied briefly by the German army in 1914 and later used as French military headquarters, a Baedeker guide noted only that 'some of its houses are still in ruins, but the public buildings suffered little in comparison' (1924, 401). When deployed in relation to such former sites of war, Baedeker's sobriety amounted to a crass disregard for the origins and effects of destruction. Such 'restraint' notwithstanding, German tourism to the battlefields of the war also stimulated patriotic effects (Mosse 1990, 155). What united tourists on one level separated them on another as memory of the war, facilitated by travel to the battlefields, reinforced national animosities.

Battlefield tourism was just one example of a broader secular trend connected to the impact of the war and to postwar recovery. In Germany, once the material hardships and political strife of the immediate postwar years were overcome, economic indicators moved upward and civic stability of a kind set in as Germany's first democratic republic established itself on the ruins of the Kaiserreich. By 1921, the *Frankfurter Zeitung* could write that 'all of Germany is on the move' (Bausinger 1991, 346). The Comedian Harmonists sang of 'The Weekend and Sunshine' in a popular song of the period as Germans adopted 'the English weekend,' consisting of short excursions to the seashore or a nature area (Nitsch 1926/7). In the second half of the 1920s, the Weimar Republic enjoyed a period of relative stability that brought the possibility of leisure travel to more people than ever before. Continued urbanization and the rationalization of industry stimulated a growth in service employment. The civil servants, retail employees, secretaries, and teachers who peopled the ranks of the new service strata had longer life expectancies than prewar generations did, and they had new ideas about leisure, which now included travel, sports, dancing, radio, and cinema. There were now more than four million owners of radio sets in Germany and more than 5,000 movie theaters. Women played an ever more important role, as the image of the independent and well-dressed 'New Woman' hovered over Weimar leisure culture. The eight-hour day, a triumph of the new Republic, increasingly fell victim to industry's pressure, and the Depression of 1929 put more than six million Germans out of work. Nonetheless, the proportion of German laborers who put in more than 48 hours per week dropped significantly during the Weimar era. The corresponding gains in leisure time along with the expectation that free time was a right even for the manual laborer only increased the prospects of tourism. Even so, only civil servants had the legal right to an annual paid vacation. During the Weimar Republic manual workers and service employees could gain this benefit solely through individual arrangements with their employer or through negotiated labor contracts, of which there were almost 9,000 at the time Anna Siemsen wrote her critique of Baedeker. These contracts gave two-thirds of all workers minimum paid vacations of only three days or less while just 12 percent of workers enjoyed maximum paid vacations of 12 days or more (Dietz 1932, 13; Keitz 1997, 24–33).

The cultural milieu of the Weimar Republic did even more to encourage a new outlook on leisure and travel. Cultural modernism, a product of the prewar era, now burst forth, bringing unprecedented ferment in painting, cinema, architecture, and literature, and stimulating new popular and commercial cultural practices. Travel literature was an important component of the new modernism, and now all but forgotten authors such as Egon Erwin Kisch, Colin Ross, and Armin T. Wegner sold hundreds of thousands of books detailing their travels across the globe. It was fitting that some travel accounts partook of modernist irony, as with the travel writer Arthur Holitscher's *The Fool's Guide through Paris and London* (1925),

71

appearing in four printings as *A Fool's Baedeker* before the Baedeker firm sued the author for misusing its name. Holitscher surveyed the French and London capitals with a pacifist eye and a satirical sense of humor that also poked fun at the practice of travel itself. Plonien (1995) argues that the popularity of travel writing in the Weimar Republic is attributable to 'a loss of world for Germany.' Germany's loss of colonies due to the Versailles Treaty in combination with the economic difficulties of interwar life created a kind of compensatory desire for information about both one's own country and the world through travel literature, in Plonien's view.

Berlin was of course the center of such developments, and Kracauer, writing about the lavish movie theaters in the German capital, saw it as the metropolis of the 'cult of distraction.' In Berlin, the new emphasis on movement and experimentation, on mobility and the active merging of hitherto separate spheres—the increased popularity of photomontage is a fitting example—reached a high point. Berlin took advantage of its centrality to the new age, advertising itself as a cultural metropolis with movies, theaters, museums, restaurants, nightclubs, and much more. Travel to Berlin allowed Germans from all over the country to see the age of cultural ferment first-hand. It allowed them to view the destruction of old prewar forms as the prime travel spectacle of an epoch thirsting for constant displacement. By being on the move, German travelers could participate actively in the creative destruction and recombination of various life practices. So too could the foreign tourist, who sensed he or she was 'dancing on a volcano' in the German capital. 'The foreigner found himself playing the agreeable part of a spectator in a theater,' wrote journalist Heinrich Hauser of pre-Hitler Berlin, 'he could enjoy the drama without being involved in it' (1939, 17).

Berlin attracted as many as two million tourists annually during the best economic times of the Weimar Republic (Spode and Gutbier 1987, 38). It was the most popular urban tourist attraction in Germany and a magnet for foreign travelers as well. Nearly 40,000 American tourists were reported in Berlin hotels and inns in 1930. Other venues in Germany were more attractive to Americans—the Oberammergau Passion Play drew 50,000 US tourists in the same year—but Berlin remained a key tourist site (Grünthal 1931, 2:53; 'Amerikanische Erholungsreisen' 1931, 3:92). From the point of view of the first turbulent years of revolution and hardship after the war, this was a remarkable development. An early postwar poster by the government labor office, reflecting official fears that more and more unemployed would flock to the capital, read 'Don't go to Berlin!' (Franck 1920, 112). Not much later, the municipal tourist agency responded with what became a more popular slogan: 'Everyone at least once in Berlin' (Austellungs-, Messe- und Fremdenverkehrs-Amt 1928). An early postwar English-language Baedeker to Berlin (1923, 50) had an ambivalent view of the effects of the war, suggesting that the German capital was now less attractive as a tourist destination:

The loss of the Great War has effected vast changes in the social composition of Berlin. The brilliance of the imperial court has disappeared. New classes of society with new aspirations have risen to commercial power, while the former calm based on assured prosperity has given way to a restless self-indulgence. The large influx of foreigners, mainly from Eastern Europe, is readily noticed, whereas the activities of the intellectual and professional classes, who now live in comparative retirement, are not immediately apparent to the passing visitor.

The references to self-indulgence and foreign influence (which was often coded as Jewish influence) would find an echo in other tour books. But in the late 1920s Berlin recovered, and for the time being, tourism flourished in the capital of the new republic.

The new travel culture had many permutations. The volume of short-term leisure travel—Sunday afternoon trips or weekend excursions in the countryside—increased tremendously, as German railways recorded a more than sixfold rise in Sunday return tickets from the prewar period to 1929. Wandering became a cross-class phenomenon, made possible by an ever expanding network of youth hostels and a richer variety of inexpensive tour guides, including the series *With Backpack and Hiking Boot*, available for 30 pfennig (Häussler 1932). Overnight stays in German hostels increased from 60,000 to more than four million in the first postwar decade (Keitz 1997, 25, 30). In Berlin, travel associated with the new 'weekend thinking' was very cheap, as roundtrip omnibus and tram tickets to one of the city's outlying parks and nature areas could be gotten for as little as 25 pfennig (Heydenreich 1932, 240). Across the country, there were countless individual variations of the travel experience, not the least interesting being a four-month trip by foot in the summer of 1932 through southern Germany by the 72-year-old Kunrat Döhling. The elderly Döhling went from town to town peddling a book of his own poetry. When he was done, the itinerant bard wrote a travelogue recording the pleasures of talking with local people and traveling salesmen, drinking the local wine and beer, and sightseeing along forest paths and scenic village lanes (Döhling 1933). An idiosyncratic 'business traveler,' Döhling acted like a tourist—and ate and drank as well as he pleased—wherever he could.

Germans traveled abroad as well. Estimates based on overnight stays in hotels indicated that in Austria, Liechtenstein, Czechoslovakia, and the Free City of Danzig, they made up one-half or more of all foreign tourists at the start of the 1930s. They constituted two-fifths of all foreign guests in the Netherlands, one-third in Switzerland and Poland, and one-fourth to one-fifth in Italy. In Hungary, Finland, Yugoslavia, and Great Britain, Germans made up one-tenth or more of foreign tourists. When one measures tourist traffic against the size of the respective populations, however, Germans were not in a leadership role despite their ideal geographical position in the heart of Europe. In none of the 25 countries surveyed by a tourist expert in 1932 did the Germans take first place in terms of 'touristic intensity.' In Switzerland it was the Dutch and the Austrians who visited more intensely than the Germans did, in Italy the Swiss, the Austrians, and Hungarians. In addition, as the Depression wore on, the decline in German travel abroad was steeper than the decline in European foreign travel overall. In 1932, the number of days spent in foreign lands by German tourists shrunk to less than half the total of 1928. Those touristic nationalists who insisted that Germans were unpatriotic because they preferred travel abroad rather than at home were not in a strong position based on the statistical evidence. When they traveled abroad, Germans also spent somewhat less on average than some of their European counterparts did. Parsimonious though they may have been—no doubt because they had taken Baedeker's model of the 'not too demanding' tourist to heart—German travel in foreign lands was indispensable to the European economy even during the Depression years (Bormann 1932, 69–72; Menges 1959, 209).

The role of state agencies and the organs of the travel industry cannot be overlooked in all of this, as Keitz (1997) makes clear. Nor can the role of advertising be ignored. Leisure travelers were now confronted with a flood of brochures, pamphlets, and postcards that drew from the sophisticated design culture of the time. Such developments were monitored by the 'Research Institute for Foreign Travel and Tourism' in Berlin, led by professor Robert Glücksmann, who also edited the institute's quarterly, the *Archiv für den Fremdenverkehr*, until he was forced out by the Nazis because he was Jewish. Its mission was to analyze the evolution of contemporary tourism in its professional, economic, sociological, legal, balneological, meteorological, and geographic dimensions. It also kept abreast of the latest tourist literature, including guidebooks, which were given brief descriptions and reviews.

Once the Great Depression hit, the tourist industry consolidated its resources, which caused a drop in tourist numbers. The low point came in 1933, when domestic tourist travel was down by nearly 40 percent compared to 1928 (Menges 1959, 209). Representatives of the industry were convinced that this did not mean tourist agencies and businesses should cut back on advertising. Rather, they should make better use of all means available to convince Germans that the Depression would not eliminate leisure travel. One way to do this was to encourage those many Germans who traveled abroad—300,000 Germans went to Italy in 1929 alone—to take their vacations in the homeland. Advertising should appeal to Germans' 'social and national' sentiments. Propaganda for the tourist industry should show the potential traveler 'that although many workers were without bread, his fatherland and he himself is made poorer when he continues unthinkingly to travel abroad instead of seeking out the spas and hiking trails of his homeland' (Mariotti 1932, 4:110; Nave 1932, 1:14). It has been noted that the 'See Germany First' argument rested on shaky statistical foundations as Germans in the interwar years were no more prone to travel abroad for their vacations than other national groups were. Still, the inward-looking emphasis resonated at a time when discretionary income for leisure travel was in shorter supply than in the late 1920s.

Travel guidebooks spoke to the new situation, partly by focusing on ever smaller touristic areas that could be visited cheaply and quickly, partly by orienting themselves specifically to less well-to-do travelers. The Meyer's series issued a guide to the Weimar region in 1932 for 2 marks and the Grieben company had inexpensive guides to towns such as Eisenach in the same period (*Weimarer Land* 1932; Grieben 1926). One of the more ambitious undertakings in this Depression-era genre was a series of 300 or so booklets, the Deutschland-Bildhefte, which were published by the national association of German travel agencies and designed to focus on an array of towns and regions. More than 11,000 photographs of architectural landmarks, streetscapes, and natural settings could be found in the series, the motto of which was 'Get to know Germany.' Lavish praise was the modus operandi of each volume, which could be purchased for just 20 pfennig. Heidelberg and its environs were 'altogether a setting of great beauty, an open picture book of the history of German civilization, a field for the tourist offering an abundance of inspiration and recreation,' according to one booklet. The celebration of Frankfurt an der Oder was less breathless, but still altogether positive, as readers were told 'the old and the new, the parks and the favorable site unite to form a charming whole' (Bund Deutscher Verkehrsverbände 1933, 41:4, 75:4).

The Deutschland-Bildhefte included text in German, French, and English, demonstrating the importance attributed to foreign travel in official circles and the travel industry. American travel to Europe and Germany grew after World War I, then receded when the inflation of the early 1920s caused havoc with exchange rates. The mid-1920s saw US travel to Europe increase again, and in 1925 some 300,000 Americans came to Europe, spending 350 million dollars. In that year, among the advertising materials issued by the German Railroads Information Office in New York City was the artist Willy Dzubas' poster proclaiming, in no uncertain terms, 'Germany Wants to See You.' Statistical studies indicated that the typical US university student spent 500 dollars during a stay in Europe, while the 'ordinary traveler' spent 1,800 dollars and the 'luxury traveler' 5,000 ('Office national du tourisme' 1930, 38). It was the last-named group that impressed the public imagination, of course, as luxury ocean liners and fancy automobiles became symbols of the new age for wealthy Americans—and for the not-so-wealthy who followed their more affluent co-nationals' exploits in tabloid newspapers, films, and novels. The well-to-do had their own travel guides as well, including not only the handbooks issued by the ship lines, but also breezily written accounts such as *The Frantic Atlantic* (Woon 1927), which gave tips on how to distinguish social climbers from 'real' society people on ocean voyages.

*Figure 5    A 1925 travel poster (author's collection).*

International travelers from all socio-economic levels were not to be ignored in any event by European businesses trying to reorient themselves after the war. Germany benefited from the secular flow upward. Cook's in England reported that out of 32 European tours it organized for American groups in 1925, 19 included Germany in whole or in part, while in 1926, 30 out of 33 took in Germany. In the first half of 1926, German Consulates throughout the United States reported an average increase of 25 percent in the volume of travel to Germany over the first half of the previous year, with the Boston areas leading the way at about 60 percent.

Boston was considered to be the center of American intellectual life, according to the official journal of the national association of travel agencies, and such data therefore meant that 'it is precisely the educated and well-off circles that demonstrate an ever growing interest in visiting Germany.' In the wake of the anti-German sentiment brought on by the war and furthered by 'Americanization' campaigns in the US in the early 1920s, such perspectives gave hope to German officials in their effort to improve the country's image abroad ('Europas Flugzentrale' 1926, 11; 'Ein Jahr deutsche Verkehrswerbung' 1926, 10). Still, on the basis of ship traffic from US harbors in 1931, France was the preferred European travel destination for Americans, by a ratio of roughly 1.5 to 1 compared to Germany. England ranked a close second to France in the European competition for American tourists ('Fremdenverkehrszahlungsbilanz' 1933, 2:63).

As many as 60 percent of summer tourists from the US in Europe consisted of American women. The New Woman of the Weimar Republic was clearly only the local variation for an international phenomenon. For female travelers from the United States, the tourists' Bible was not the Baedeker but the Chicagoan Clara Laughlin's series of guidebooks (Levenstein 1998, 236, 245–6). *So You're Going to Germany and Austria!* (1930) typified an appeal to college-educated women who had a general understanding of politics and culture but were uninterested in specialized erudition. Although the Baedeker guides were generally 'excellent,' the user of the Laughlin guide read, they were also 'a bit formidable.' It is worth remembering that the emphasis on less comprehensive guides was an international trend and not a reflection of American superficiality or a bias against 'inferior' female travelers. As more middle-class and working-class travelers entered the tourist market, they looked for guides that were not permeated with the classical motifs and high-bourgeois references for which the Baedekers were known. They wanted to have something more than superficial knowledge without having to 'specialize'; they were the products of a 'media cultura,' as an Italian guidebook put it, not the members of an elite armed with deep learning. And yet they still respected old Herr Baedeker: Laughlin's guide to Germany and Austria put Karl Baedeker's first Koblenz office and his gravesite on its Rhenish itinerary (Laughlin 1930, viii; Bertarelli 1924, 9).

Laughlin noted that in the past her travel guides concentrated on France and Italy. But her 'rancor' toward Germany had passed once the passions of war declined, and now that Central Europe was an indispensable part of the American itinerary for US tourists to the Continent, a new guide was needed. The tour book was dedicated to the deceased German liberal politician Gustav Stresemann, and it praised the democratic founders of the new republic, including the assassinated industrialist and democrat Walter Rathenau. Rathenau, wrote Laughlin, 'was so fine a type of the New Germany that it seems to me very important to visit his home.' Rathenau's home was in Berlin, which Laughlin suggested should be given at least three days in the tourist's itinerary. Berlin was 'full of museums,' although many of them were 'for the special student,' not the 'average visitor.' Even those museums for a more general public should not dominate one's visit to the capital, however. 'Pleasure-seekers' were told they should see Berlin 'in preference to almost any other city of Central Europe,' and art lovers, observers of social life, music enthusiasts, and those interested in political history would also find Berlin a necessary part of their tour. Entertainment and comfort were clearly as important as culture and learning. Among the sights 'no one ought to miss' was the giant café Haus Vaterland on the Potsdamer-Platz, with restaurants and exhibits from all over Germany and Europe. Here one could drink beer in Bavaria or sit in the Rhineland watching steamboats go up and down the Rhine River. But even if the entertainments of the capital were as central to Laughlin as museums and monuments were, the tourist should not forget the educative and even civic value of one's labors. 'Every one should wish modern Germany (as distinguished from feudal Germany which lasted until November, 1918) very well, indeed,' wrote the author, 'and be glad to study, or enjoy, its manifestations' (Laughlin 1930, vii–viii, 198–9, 205–6, 216, 218).

### III

Spurred by such developments, a new travel culture emerged in Germany. If leisure travel now took on a theological significance and a more emancipatory ethos, it also focused on sites and subjects previously overlooked or repressed. A telling example of this may be found in a series of guidebooks published by the Munich firm Piper. Entitled *What's not to be Found in the Baedeker* [*Was nicht im Baedeker steht*], this series consisted of guides to London, Paris, Vienna, Berlin, Prague, Leipzig, Hamburg, and Cologne. The idea of offering the traveler something beyond Baedeker tourism spoke to issues of both style and substance. Written by popular authors of the day such as Ludwig Hirschfeld, Eugen Szatmari, and Harro von Wedderkop, the guides were breezy in tone and more 'literary' than the Baedeker. They stressed surprise and humor, and insisted on not taking their subject too seriously. Even so, reviewers noted that each volume also offered 'much of sociological importance' with pithy descriptions of neighborhoods and social life (Review 1931a, 1:31). Hirschfeld produced the first guide in the series, a book on Vienna. He wrote that his original idea was a tour by 'a man and a woman who don't belong together at all, but whom I, the author, have permitted myself to marry a little bit with each other in this book.' The casual intimacy suggested by this fictional relationship was matched by the insistence that a guidebook on Vienna could not survive without 'a little allurement, irony, and skepticism.' Above all, the traveler should avoid the 'catchwords' and 'travel pedanticism' of the Baedeker.

The tourist should see not only the Vienna of relaxed charm and slightly faded baroque but also 'the other Vienna,' a 'real, living, everyday' city that had outgrown the normal tourist slogans (Hirschfeld 1927, 4–6).

It was the 'real, living, everyday' that had been absent, or that was only implied, in Baedeker's Germany before World War I. Roland Barthes wrote in the 1950s as if the leisure traveler's thirst for 'everyday life' was a post-World War II phenomenon (1972, 76). But the desire to get beyond the Baedeker's blindness toward social reality well preceded Barthes' critique. The modernist travel culture of the interwar era now brought earlier intimations to the surface, just as the war itself had broken the crust of prewar social relations. At the center of such transformations was *Neue Sachlichkeit*, or the 'New Sobriety,' which Lamb and Phelan (1995, 71), using Raymond Williams' useful term, have analyzed as a 'structure of feeling' characteristic of the years of economic stability from 1924 to 1929. Lamb and Phelan argue that structures of feeling retain 'an element of emotional response in lived experience' that is distinct from their ideological or economic origins. New Sobriety regarded the world of capitalist modernity with a cool and 'objective' eye, disavowing the idealism and utopian dreams of the past (although not eschewing criticism), and often glorifying the engineer and technician as non-ideological gatekeepers to the future (Lethen 1970). Walter Benjamin's pithy comment—'the construction of life is at present in the power of facts far more than of convictions' (1986 [1928], 61)—fit well with New Sobriety's perspective. So too did sociologist Georg Simmel's prewar musings on the 'blasé metropolitan attitude,' a concept referring to the urban dweller's adoption of an extreme intellectuality in response to the intense stimuli of the modern city (1971 [1903], 325–6, 329).

In travel writing, this perspective appeared in the form of an embrace of the urban experience and an acceptance of reality as an object of consumption. The 'sober' travel account of the Weimar era encouraged a non-ideological (or less ideological) view of the here and now, a love of technology and facts, and a 'distant' openness toward the people and places one observed. It eschewed Baedeker propriety; it gave the cultural monuments of the past an approving though not adoring glance; and it gladly took the traveler through the hectic world of commercial exchange and urban displacement. One of the most successful representatives of this genre, Egon Erwin Kisch, writing in 1925 about the ideal *sachlich* reporter of the age, captured the new trend dramatically: 'The reporter has no tendency to represent, has nothing to legitimize, and has no standpoint' (Plonien 1995, 54–72, 133). Kisch thought the dominant tendency of the age carried society toward oblivion and falsehood, and thus to be 'without tendency' was a critical or even radical position. He would also later express strong sympathies for the Soviet Union and the Communist movement, demonstrating that New Sobriety could issue into more pointed ideological positions.

That the new tendency also had important international political implications could not be denied. Indeed, as Plonien (1995) and others have demonstrated, the new travel culture revealed a desire to 're-map' the world at a time when Germany was without colonies due to the Versailles Treaty. German society thus lived in a postcolonial world well before its Western imperialist rivals did, and the shock of adjustment impelled many to re-visualize not only their homeland but also distant destinations. The metropolis—a new 'living space' characterized by all of the uncertainties of a foreign land—became an important referent for German travel writing in this context (Gleber 1989). Both the United States and the Soviet Union also figured prominently in the re-mapping process since both seemed to mark out compelling paths to the future. The sense of living under postcolonial conditions produced much questionable travel literature, to be sure, such as the racist musings of Colin Ross, one of the most widely read travel writers of the 1920s. But it also gave rise to more tolerant and liberal perspectives on Germany's engagement with a new postwar world.

An example may be taken from the writing of sociologist Franz Oppenheimer. Like so many critics of Baedeker-style travel, Oppenheimer insisted that sightseeing of the past concentrated too much on 'dead monuments' and too little on 'living appearances.' By avoiding the national stereotypes associated with the tourism of 'pyramids and Gothic cathedrals,' and focusing on 'modern things,' argued Oppenheimer, 'the mutual understanding' of peoples could be enhanced, and the 'soul of the people' one was observing as a tourist could be understood. This benefited the tourist as well, since he could thereby also enhance his own 'good national feeling' without feeding that 'evil nationalism' so widespread in Europe between the wars. In Oppenheimer's view, healthy nationalism went hand in hand with cosmopolitanism. If the new and the contemporary were to be the goals of tourism, argued Oppenheimer, then courses on the history, culture, politics, and economy of foreign lands should be organized for tourists by 'experts unswayed by nationalist prejudices.' These would enable tourists to get beyond superficialities once they engaged the host country: 'The situation must stop in which Germans see the French as home-wreckers and absinthe drinkers, and the French see in the Germans only sauerkraut gobblers and beer guzzlers' (Oppenheimer 1932, 2:36). It was not entirely logical that Oppenheimer viewed cultural tourism as something that reinforced ethnic stereotypes. The preservers of monuments and their growing audiences argued exactly the opposite, insisting that the cultural treasures of a nation gave insights into precisely that element of national life that Oppenheimer valued, the 'soul of the people' (Koshar 1998a). Still, Oppenheimer's view represented the voice of enlightenment in an attempt to re-map Germany's postcolonial relationship with a dangerous world.

Soulless or not, Baedeker tourism was due for a facelift, as the publishing firm itself admitted. This no doubt had much to do with economic difficulties. The economic strength of the Baedeker enterprise was weakened by World War I and then severely damaged by the inflation, in which the firm saw much of its capital disappear. Sales dropped precipitously, as only half as many Baedeker guidebooks were bought in 1929 as in 1913. While the regional guides remained successful, sales of foreign-language editions fell drastically, and at the end of 1931 the house of Baedeker stopped publishing guidebooks altogether. Fifty-year old Hans Baedeker, head of the troubled publishing house, saw both danger and promise in the rise of Nazism (Boyle 1986, 4–5; Peters 1987, 8–9). A relationship between the firm and the regime ensued, and Baedeker guidebooks returned to the market. But regardless of political arrangements, secular trends would force a change in address and focus. Karl Friedrich Baedeker, nephew of Hans and chief editor, would note in 1936 that tour guides now had to speak to people's thirst for 'the living and the new.' History and the 'treasures of old Europe' were still important, but they had to be related to 'the here and now' (quoted in Hinrichsen 1988, 38–9).

It was not only in relation to the Baedeker that proponents of contemporaneity made their case. Reviewers of the popular Meyer's handbooks criticized the series for its preoccupation with monuments and its corresponding inattention to 'modern buildings and facilities for cultural, social, political, and . . . economic purposes' (Review 1930b, 3:142). And it was not only the Baedeker that left out the 'here and now.' A contemporary guidebook to England, *England for Everyman* (1933), well regarded for its appeal to tourists across the social spectrum, omitted the major manufacturing cities of Birmingham, Liverpool, Manchester, and Sheffield in favor of the traditional tourist attractions. Another English guidebook, *Walks in Rome*, based on a pre-1914 format but updated for the postwar period, persisted in its high-cultural references to Byron, Hawthorne, Goethe, and many other superstars of the bourgeois world. It even criticized the 'vast modernization' going on in the Eternal City and snubbed its nose at uneducated American tourists, who, when seeing the Colosseum, were said to comment 'it will be a handsome building when it is *finished*' (Hare and Baddeley 1923, 3; italics in original). But it was the Baedeker that stood for the prewar habits and traditions, and therefore it was against that venerable guidebook that the creators and advocates of new guides measured themselves.

A central motif of the 'here and now' was the 'sexual revolution.' As with so many aspects of interwar cultural modernism, the sexual revolution consisted partly of more talk about a previously taboo subject. But there was a programmatic side to it as well. Social Democratic, Communist, and liberal reformers advocated a more open and equitable relationship between the sexes, birth control, the right to abortion, and sex education. Atina Grossmann (1995) has demonstrated there were significant limitations to this discourse. Sex should be more liberated, the reformers said, but it should also be made more *sachlich*, or more 'objective,' and the New

Woman, now both more educated and more attractive to her male partner, should be mobilized to fulfill her reproductive role. Female sexuality was to be directed into the proper heterosexual paths charted by male reformers. Eroticization was to be determined by a fairly narrow canon of male heterosexual behavior. Sexual deviancy was allowed but it was to be controlled if not distrusted. It is often difficult to assess what the relationship was between this discourse and actual sexual practice. What we do know is that the Weimar Republic represented a time of increasing sexual promiscuity, rising divorce and abortion rates, falling birth rates and rising illegitimacy, and higher numbers of women in the work force (Frevert 1989, 186).

It was also a time of increasing cultural representations of sexuality. The lifting of censorship allowed the popular arts to deal more openly with love, romance, courtship, flirtation, and intercourse. While on the one hand this opened the way toward more prurient treatments of female nudity in movies, theater, advertising, cabaret, and other fields, it also encouraged franker portrayals of relationships between the genders. The eroticization of public life was helped by a relaxation of closing hours for bars and nightclubs in Berlin; as of 1926 these establishments were required to close only between 3 and 6 in the morning. Not everyone thought the change was a good thing. Conservative politicians complained that 'in the streets of the big cities it smells of the erotic,' Protestant pastors wrote luridly of 'sexual Bolshevism,' and everyone from anti-alcohol activists to Christian groups called the German capital the 'Babel of sin' (Jelavich 1993, 5; Schlör 1991, 114–15, 225–6). But such protests could do little to stem the tide of sexuality and talk about sexuality that rolled over Berlin, Hamburg, and other cities in the Republic.

Eric Leed (1991, 113–14) detects an ancient 'male reproductive motive' in the history of travel. The male heterosexual 'spermatic journey' takes numerous forms, from classical myths of wandering gods and patriarchs to the life histories of early modern European sailors seeking sexual adventure in the colonies. Feminist literary theory charts an analogous scenario, emphasizing the way in which narrative form traditionally constructs an active male figure penetrating a space or overcoming obstacles that are either literally feminine or coded as female (De Lauretis 1984; Plonien 1995, 9–10). Linking the history of travel and theories of narrativity, one can see that one variation of the spermatic journey in the age of urbanity is a highly commercialized sex tourism, which may be defined as leisure travel regulated by both representations of sexuality and actual sexual encounters. Sex tourism is both a metaphor and something more. Although usually associated with more recent forms of sexual exploitation of minors by foreign male tourists in underdeveloped countries, sex tourism has also played an important role in leisure travel in the Euro-American world (Hall and Page 1999, 130). The Grand Tour was often the scene of heavy drinking and 'loose amours' for the scions of the British upper classes, as one eighteenth-century newspaper complained, and for both British heterosexual and homosexual males, the Mediterranean in particular promised sexual adventure (Löfgren 1999, 200–201; Pemble 1987, 156–64). Sex tourism was a significant element of that 'Platonic libertinism' (Gay 1984, 334) already discussed in relation to pre-1914 Baedeker tourism in the city. And it was seen as a constitutive moment of the interwar travel culture. From the point of view of the German Communist press, ever ready to castigate 'rich do-nothings,' the bourgeoisie's 'dealings with the sexuality of others' was central to the daily life of the better resorts in the Alps, the Riviera, Egypt, and California (Eckert 1932).

As a literary genre, sex tourism had of course already found its place in premodern travel and travel writing. In the more recent and commercialized genre of guidebook literature, sex tourism was the subject of the so-called 'by gaslight' guides to mid-nineteenth-century New York City and turn-of-the-century guides to Chicago 'by day and night,' both catering to male heterosexual business travelers (Foster 1850; Gilbert 1991, 59–60). Other major European cities, but especially London, where a 'secret culture' of sexual license and sado-masochism existed beneath the veil of Victorian respectability, had similar tour books from the 1850s on (Schlör 1991, 187–8). But in the wake of the war, the tumultuous founding of the Weimar Republic, and the extraordinary cultural experimentation of the 1920s, Berlin and other cities saw the evolution of guidebooks that went well beyond what nineteenth-century sex tourism had seen in terms of both openness and quality.

One such example could be found in the *Was nicht im Baedeker steht* series, in which tourists were led to nude 'girl reviews' or urban quarters where prostitutes worked. But these city guides were still quite respectable and they were hardly dominated by the subject of sex tourism. They explored the world of modern urban sexuality only to the degree that it titillated the fictitious, middle-class, heterosexual couple with the time and money to enjoy a week of shopping, museum-going, and dining in one of Europe's major cities. Many 'mainstream' guidebooks now referred to Berlin sexual eccentricities, if only in passing, and even a jauntily written US tour guide to the German metropolis felt compelled to direct attention to the 'serious frivolity of Berlin nightlife' (Milton 1935, 65). The city's tourist agency included a chapter on Berlin nightlife and cabaret in its official tour book, ending with the wish that the pleasure seeker would have fond memories of 'the blond women . . . of the night' (Ausstellungs-, Messe- und Fremdenverkehrs-Amt 1928, 116–25). More specialized publications such as *Berlin Nightlife!* (1920) listed a varied palette of restaurants, cabarets, and nightclubs, and *The International Travel Guide* (1920/1) led travelers to Berlin's and other German cities' gay clubs and hotels. In 1930, Berliners could also buy the report of a 'wander' through the sites of the city's prostitution districts (Schlör 1991, 34; Weka 1930).

No travel guide to sexual pleasure matched the *Guide through Naughty Berlin* [*Führer durch das 'lasterhafte' Berlin*], published in 1931 by Curt Moreck, a pseudonym for the novelist, editor, translator, and cultural critic Kurt Haemmerling. Born in Cologne in 1888, Moreck was a member of several radical artists' groups during the German revolution of 1918. In the 1920s he went on to publish novels, translations, and cultural–historical works, including a study of sexuality in German cinema. The Nazis burned his books in 1933, and after living in personal exile during the Third Reich, he continued to write fiction until his death in 1957 (Geese 1989, 4:458; Raabe 1985, 338–44). Moreck's guide was unusual not only for its comprehensiveness but also its literate style, its high-quality illustrations (by artists Jeanne Mammen, George Grosz, Christian Schad, and Paul Kamm), and its open references to flirting, voyeurism, prostitution, male and female homosexuality, transvestism, and sado-masochism. Moreck's tour book did not deal only with the world of sexual pleasure. It discussed the Berlin criminal underworld and popular entertainments such as wrestling and bicycle races as well. But even in these sections, sexuality and the imagery of sexuality permeated the text.

Annelie Lütgens (1997, 99) argues that in its treatment of Berlin lesbians, Moreck's guide was not only derivative of a more serious guide on this subject by Ruth Margarete Roellig (1928), but it catered 'to the sensationalist cravings of a heterosexual audience.' It is undeniable that there was plenty of sensationalism in Moreck's tour guide, or that the guide was oriented to male heterosexuals. Nor can it be gainsaid that the guide targeted the middle- and upper-class traveler; the appearance of 'slumming' was inevitable. Moreck's work would also have been impossible without the existence of previous works on Berlin sexual practices, including not only the study to which Lütgens refers, but also Hans Ostwald's comprehensive prewar discussion of female and male prostitution in the German capital (1905/07) and his innovative, pamphlet-sized documentary series on Berlin life, the *Grossstadt-Dokumente* (Fritzsche 1994). As for literary treatments, Weimar-era novelists, and most notably Erich Kästner, offered more elegantly written accounts of contemporary sexuality than the guidebook did. In Kästner's *Fabian* (1993 [1931]), the main character visited some of the same nightclubs and walked some of the same streets that Moreck's tourist did. Still, I would argue that Moreck provided a more honest and informative representation of the diversity of sexual preferences in Berlin than was hitherto available for tourist audiences.

Moreck's guide was not only a product of Weimar's sexual revolution, but also of an enlivened literate interest in flanerie, the art of walking, observing, and representing the daily life of the modern city. A product of the nineteenth century, the flaneur was typically a male figure who sought out not the programmed sights of guided tours, but the underbelly of the city, the scenes that revealed everyday social relationships and tensions, or that brought to light the seamy and disreputable. The flaneur often defined himself as the active and critical counterpoint to the allegedly passive tourist, who simply consumed sights for the purpose of personal leisure, not knowledge and perspective. One the most influential flaneurs of the

Berlin avant garde in this period was the editor and writer Franz Hessel, who influenced Walter Benjamin (Gleber 1999, 63). Hessel published a travel account that meandered through the city decrying tourist traps such as the popular café Haus Vaterland—a symbol of 'monster Germany' in the author's jaded perspective (1984 [1929], 57). Hessel lauded many of the city's great landmarks and museums, but it was above all small scenes of daily life, shop windows, and working Berliners that drew his attention. He stressed the aimlessness of the flaneur, who acted as a counter-tourist by resisting the pre-planned agendas of the travel bureaus and omnibus tours. 'To saunter properly,' he wrote, 'one must not plan too definitively' (ibid., 145). His embrace of aimlessness put him at odds with the functionalism and social rationality of the New Sobriety (Gleber 1999, 65). Moreck's guide to underground Berlin, emphasizing dispassionate observation and accepting the modern society of the 1930s, shared much with the New Sobriety persuasion. But it also had an emancipatory and rambling impulse that gave it a point of contact with Hessel's resistant, 'non-functional,' and critical tone.

The big city was a 'conglomerate of unending possibilities,' wrote Moreck in the introduction to the *Führer*. This phrase reflected the new emphasis, not only in leisure travel but also in the wider culture, on unlimited choice and even excess. Like many of the 'sober' travel reporters of Weimar, Moreck viewed the modern metropolis as a vast compendium of possibilities for consumption. But the range of such possibilities was broader than previous travel literature suggested. Moreck stated that each city has both an 'official side and an unofficial, and it goes without saying that the latter is the most interesting and the most illuminating for understanding the urban world.' Using the same metaphors of light and dark that Anna Siemsen deployed, he wrote that 'those who seek experiences, who demand adventure, who want sensations, they must go into the shadows.' Such travelers could not be happy with staying on the surface, but must 'venture into the deep.' In traversing the boundary between the official and the unofficial, between light and shadow, between the surface and the deep, the traveler had to abandon some of the tried and true objects of Baedeker tourism. Monuments and architectural landmarks 'were milestones of boredom.' Instead of fixating on the past, the student of modern Berlin had to experience the 'present in its intensity.' This meant approaching humanity in all its contradictions, seeking out the places where humanity 'mixes like a piquant ragout, where the wide world is at home.' 'Berlin is a city of oppositions,' wrote Moreck, 'and it is a pleasure to discover them' (1931, 7–8). No better motto for the modernist travel culture could have been given. Indeed, Moreck's openness was quite radical when compared to the reaction Walter Benjamin had to German cities. Benjamin, whose work is rightly regarded as a touchstone of Weimar modernism, could be nostalgic, as when he wrote: "Just as all things, in a perpetual process of mingling and contamination, are losing their intrinsic character while ambiguity displaces authenticity, so is the city' (1986

[1928], 75). Benjamin was a lover of great cities, to be sure, but no celebration of the metropolis' 'piquant ragout' could be found in such statements.

The Baedeker would clearly not suffice to understand this 'ragout'; it was the guidebook for those who were happy 'to be driven around in luxury automobiles' in the metropolis. This was an exaggeration since, as has been shown, the Baedeker catered to a broader middle-class clientele than one might have expected, and Baedeker tourism promoted not passivity but self-organized leisure travel. Those who wanted access to 'the other side' needed an alternative travel guide, in any case. Indeed, they needed assistance more than Baedeker tourists did because for them there were as yet no *Führer*, no 'guides,' but only *Verführer*—'tempters' or

*Figure 6   A pleasure salesman in Berlin: 'Just around the corner, sir and madam! There you can have everything you want, everything!' (Drawing by Christophe, in Moreck 1931, 23).*

'seducers.' Moreck used this pun to refer to the many dishonest *Schlepper*, the personal guides and 'pleasure salesmen' who fleeced unsuspecting visitors to the Berlin of the shadows (1931, 9–10). These guides were also known for their ability to circumvent police closing hours: when all the bars shut down, *they* could always lead thirsty carousers to another out-of-the-way place open for business—for a price (Schlör 1991, 112–13). Clearly, the descent into the 'other Berlin,' which was potentially so much more rewarding than the Berlin of conventional tourism, was not without danger. Berlin was a city of unending possibility that nonetheless needed to be categorized and controlled, its darker topographies mapped and measured. Moreck's guide performed the same function for its readers that Baedeker guides did: it reduced the unpredictability of travel and established criteria for the selection of destinations and experiences while freeing the tourist to explore and develop his own individuality. In this case, however, the tourist self was oriented to the liminal aspects of the metropolis and not the canon of travel destinations, the periphery and not the center.

Women played an indispensable role in Moreck's discourse of the city as unending possibility. Under the author's gaze, Berlin was transformed into a topography of opportunities for the male heterosexual viewing of women. In nightclubs such as the Admiralspalast, famous for its chorus lines and nude reviews, he noted—and not without some disdain—that male visitors could see 'cascades of naked female flesh displayed on stage under the spotlights.' Of the bustling, famous Tauentzienstraße, in the shadow of the Kaiser Wilhelm Memorial Church, Moreck wrote that since before World War I it featured 'beautiful women with sweet mysteries.' He praised the voyeuristic possibilities of the Kurfürstendamm, where 'female exhibitionism celebrated...its orgies.' 'What would the woman be if she did not have spectators?' he asked. What Moreck described as competition for male attention had, in his words, a 'eugenic' effect because it drove the city's women to look more beautiful. In the cafes of the Friedrichstraße he invited his readers to look out over the sea of marble tabletops to watch the 'very red lips of the little girls who . . . search for partners' (1931, 16, 24, 38, 70).

In these and many other instances, it is clear that Moreck's guide was an expression of a well-established sexual politics of looking whereby, in the geographer Steve Pile's words (1996, 94), 'the active look is encoded as masculine and the passive object is feminized.' In this case, the feminized passive objects were women themselves. Moreck's gaze drew on an even more specific tradition whereby usually male observers represented and analyzed the urban night as a distinct cultural and social phenomenon. Ever since new technologies of lighting made a modern urban nightlife possible, men represented the night in word and picture. This tradition of visual appropriation found abundant expression in the Weimar-era tourist literature produced for the 'mainstream' traveler. The Hamburg-American Line's guide to Germany identified Berlin's 'Westend,' and specifically the Kurfürstendamm and the Tauentzienstraße, as a district 'where night is turned into day' (1930, 137). In this tradition, men who sought to 'see' in the urban night were confronted with the same uncertainty, chaos, and shadows, the same forbidden pleasures, that they saw in women. Even so, as Joachim Schlör argues (1991, 162–5), the city at night was a 'space of confrontation' between men and women, a realm in which the fantasies, anxieties, and hopes of both male and female were played out in a dramatic manner. Nocturnal Berlin was a place in which the multifaceted 'morality,' or *Sittlichkeit*—a subject on which Moreck had already written—of the era could be observed.

Men who read Moreck's guidebook could do more than observe, of course. They were directed to the districts where hotels and pensions could be rented by minutes, hours, or days. In these establishments, men could have relations with

*Figure 7    Berlin streetwalkers (Drawing by Jeanne Mammen, in Moreck 1931, 31).*

one of the more than 6,000 registered prostitutes of Berlin (Schlör 1991, 208–9), or they could seek out 'unofficial' whores whose existence escaped the city statistical office. Of the prostitutes he wrote: 'The girls, who on the street corners lay out their carpet of smiles before our feet while with a couple of sharp glances they assess our suitability as "cavaliers," embody the eroticism of the city.' Nearby, massage parlors and manicure salons, bathed in gaudy neon lights, were in abundance. On the side streets of the Tauentzienstraße district, one encountered the 'regions of the violent Venus . . . the promenade of the noble ladies of the Order of the Marquis de Sade.' Moreck explicitly linked the emerging world of mass consumption with the development of the sex market. 'In the glow of the picture windows of the "Kadewe,"' he wrote with reference to the giant department store, 'which with its supply of goods satisfies every need of modern humanity, there operate the experts who cultivate the erotic special needs of the world of modern man.' Wearing knee-high boots with stiletto heels, these 'queens with riding whips' could also send a shiver down the spine of unsuspecting tourists like the 'brave provincial, [who was] unfamiliar with the human, all-too-human' (1931, 19, 29, 30).

Moreck's reference to the 'brave provincial' reflected one aspect of the guide's approach to the new age of leisure travel. On the one hand, the idea of the naïve traveler from the provinces who ventured forth into the big city was a well-known trope of travel literature throughout Western and even global culture. It was a widely shared cliché of everyday life in the German capital, where Berliners often referred to all tourists as 'uncles from the province' (Spode and Gutbier 1987, 37). In the Berlin volume to the *Was nicht im Baedeker steht* series, Szatmari picked up on this cultural figure in relation to the city's sexual life. Advising tourists to visit the Eldorado nightclub in the Lutherstraße, he wrote that 'here men dance not only with women, but women with women, men with men, and the good-natured gentleman from Saxony dancing with the blond singer has no idea that this lovely fairy—is a man' (1927, 144–5). But the provincial traveler also had a critical side; he was not only an object of derision but also a source of new knowledge. The writer Hans Heinrich Ehrler used his travelogue of Berlin, subtitled 'experiences of a man from the provinces,' to chart the sexual eccentricities of 'inwardly destroyed' people and to pinpoint the emptiness of the new sexuality (1930, 19). In this equally well-known imagery, the backwater rustic saw more clearly than urban sophisticates did.

Just as the trope of the naïve provincial traveler could always be turned to new critical purposes, Moreck aimed to take sensationalism beyond itself. Uninterested in portraying women as purely passive objects of male heterosexual desire, he traced the historical development of the increasingly independent expression of female sexuality and female tastes on Berlin's streets. While the Tauentzienstraße girls were there to look at, in Moreck's opinion, the author also noted that they

89

*Figure 8    Dancing at the Eldorado nightclub (Drawing by Benari, in Moreck 1931, 173).*

adopted a style—through their clothing, their boyish hair-dos (*Bubiköpfe*), their makeup, and their flirtatiousness—that before the war was considered either extravagant or even disreputable. Now their 'audacious, fresh flirt' had become the norm if it had not already become somewhat trite (Moreck 1931, 25). Still, while the author revealed his nostalgia for the prewar era, he expressed no desire to turn back the clock. Women acted independently, in the author's eyes, with regard to another cultural trend in interwar Berlin. Moreck noted that heterosexual women, in his opinion ever ready to follow the latest fashions of the day, had in some cases corroded the distinctive character of some of Berlin's gay bars by flocking to them when they became famous. Moreck seemed to disapprove of this tendency, but he clearly regarded it as an example of how modern women expressed their tastes in the new Berlin. No one could gainsay the fact that on the streets of the great metropolis, for better or worse, women did much to define the sexual topography.

In his description of the world of the 'five o'clock frau,' Moreck describes a new form of public sociability in which women played a central role. 'Afternoon dance teas' had become a popular attraction for both Berliners and tourists in the 1920s, and for most of the interwar period, the better hotels such as the Adlon and the Esplanade as well as restaurants and dancehalls drew a varied clientele for such events (Grieben 1936, 30–1). The five-o'clock frau went to 'smart' afternoon teas where conversation and dancing were the main attractions. Here men and

*Figure 9    The five o'clock frau at tea, and the male gaze (Moreck 1931, 55).*

women who answered some of the hundreds of 'personals' in the Berlin dailies met their correspondents, and married women occasionally left their wedding rings at home while they met a male partner for an afternoon rendezvous. The ambience surrounding the five o'clock frau was not without sexual overtones, to be sure, but Moreck emphasized that the goal of most such women during this liminal time between day and night was sociability and companionship, whether male or female. Sex might have been the result of an afternoon encounter, but it was by no means the principal goal. Of the married women who traversed Berlin streets during these afternoon hours, Moreck wrote 'they reveal the possibility of a new morality' (1931, 67). The five o'clock frau was for Moreck the symbol of a new and highly modern form of social contact undertaken in a very public venue by women who may or may not have wanted to include men in their activities.

It is possible to regard Moreck's description as yet another male fantasy of Weimar culture's New Woman. Patrice Petro (1997, 41, 42) argues that in the Weimar Republic 'modernity . . . was almost always represented as a woman.' As the capital of modernity, Berlin played a pivotal role in the culture, and contemporaries regularly imagined it in female form. Moreck's guidebook thus shared a metaphorical language with Kracauer, Benjamin, and many others who deployed such tropes. Petro also observes that the tendency to regard Berlin as a woman 'reveals less about women in Weimar than it does about a male desire that simultaneously elevates and represses woman as object of allure and as harbinger of desire.' Historians remind us that World War I was a profound shock to male authority in European societies. Moreck's guide registered part of the shock by pointing out the more frequent appearance of women in public places. It was the prevalence of women on the streets, in the cinema, the sports arena, and bars and restaurants that represented part of women's modernity. From labor and social policy to cultural representation and war monuments, male authority figures tried to re-establish a masculine culture by simultaneously stressing the centrality of women to modernity but also regulating their influence and constructing barriers against them. Petro is interested in teasing out the ways in which women acted as independent agents in this context, particularly in the realm of film spectatorship.

Leisure travel suggests another path along which women broke out of the masculinist imaginary of modernism. I do not refer here to women as travelers, although this is a legitimate topic in need of much development. For instance, Gleber (1999, 171–213) argues that the female flaneur, virtually ignored in literary studies, deserves much more scholarly attention. The same point applies to the female tourist, for whom the official Berlin guidebook included a short chapter on what to do (with or without children) during a short visit to the metropolis (Austellungs- Messe- und Fremdenverkehrs-Amt 1928, 129–34). In both instances, scholarship has fallen behind in recognizing the presence of the woman traveler. But in this case I am referring not to women who traveled, either as flaneur or tourist, but to the way in which women encountered by tourists appear as independent actors in a modernist travel culture still dominated by men.

It is true that the *Führer* is permeated with the spirit of that Neue Sachlichkeit championed by sex reformers. Moreck, like so many other representatives of the new feeling, registered his experiences with a matter-of-factness that rejected extreme expressions of individuality or utopianism. In this sense he did not stray very far at all from Baedeker's bourgeois traveler, who avoided excess in both work and pleasure. But this is also not the whole story. It may be useful to adopt a perspective taken from current postcolonial studies to interpret Moreck's guide to the sexual topography of Berlin. In a most effective analysis of travel writing and imperialism, Mary Louise Pratt (1992, 6–7) argues that the spaces of colonial encounters are 'contact zones,' a term the author takes from the analysis of contact languages. In contact zones, asymmetrical power relationships shape interactions, but at the same time new relationships are improvised that transform the colonizer and the colonized, the powerful and the powerless. Tourists traveling to 'primitive' regions of the world have economic and cultural power, but they as well as the 'natives' they observe are changed by their interactions, if only subtly or in ways that are unclear at first. Something is learned on both sides of the equation. The result is often a subterranean transformation of identities for both visitors and hosts, a transformation that is never captured by a purely diffusionist account of power flowing from imperial centers to colonial peripheries, or from citadels of male power to female spaces.

It is useful in my opinion to read Moreck as an innovative guide to the sexual contact zones of the modern metropolis. In his analysis of the five o'clock frau, Moreck acquires a knowledge of Berlin women that moves beyond the 'gaze' as a static imposition of masculine power and suggests a more interactive set of relationships, indeed, that goes beyond the lack of involvement suggested by New Sobriety. Innovative or thought-provoking knowledge is being generated, in other words, and the women who are being observed by the male traveler are recognized for their attempts to be more than passive objects. Siegfried Kracauer's now famous analysis of the 'little shop girls' at the movies reveals a parallel argument. In this analysis, the author discusses the concentrated gaze of female spectators in the cinema in relation to women's self-actualizing need for heightened sensory experience as they searched for an antidote to the monotonous world of labor within and outside the home (Petro 1997, 52–62). Women's demands to be thought of as more than a prostitute or (what was almost as disreputable) an actress when they appeared alone on the street, and their corresponding demands to have more police protection when they traversed nocturnal urban avenues, also reflected a more active stance (Schlör 1991, 171–5). In Moreck's guide, the women of the afternoon tea and dance establishments along Berlin thoroughfares were no less actively seeking a peculiarly feminine style of sociability. Just six years after Moreck's guide appeared, Nazi writers condemned five o'clock dancing and tea as a 'degenerate social form,' borrowed from the English but also infused with a 'Jewish spirit,' and aimed in particular at young men who were out to conquer the 'fair sex' (Mosse 1966, 47–53). In this context, Moreck's singling out of women as autonomous agents at five o'clock tea appeared all the more groundbreaking.

Some feminist scholars argue that men enforce a discourse of heterosexuality over women by excluding lesbianism as a legitimate form of sexual identification. It is important in this context to point out that Moreck devoted considerable attention to Berlin's lesbian nightclubs and pubs. His work was partly derivative of other, more engaged accounts of Berlin lesbian subculture, particularly the work of Ruth Margarete Roellig (1928). Moreck described many of the same entertainments and itineraries Roellig did. He commented on the seediness of the Café Olala, where women engaged in 'horizontal handiwork' stopped in for a respite from their nocturnal profession. Roellig used the same term to describe the clientele of this questionable establishment. Moreck noted that regulated prostitution was frequent in this district before the war, just as Roellig did, and that the nearby Toppkeller was a favored place not only for lesbians but also tourists and voyeurs. Among the club's frequent visitors were 'lovely women . . . who have made willingness a duty'; Roellig described these same young women as 'lovely and by no means shy.' Of lesbian women in the Domino-Bar, near the Tauentzienstraße, Moreck observed that 'every attempt by men to make an advance was repulsed with a smiling charm.' Roellig wrote: "Every attempt by men to win the favor of these lesbian beauties is turned down with a charming smile' (Moreck 1931, 166, 168, 170; Roellig 1928, 39, 41, 45).

Yet Moreck also went beyond the earlier guide. Roellig's book contained a preface by the distinguished sexologist Magnus Hirschfeld. Hirschfeld made a plea for understanding all forms of homosexual expression, but he nonetheless framed his comments so as to leave the 'normal sexual world,' to use his phrase, very much in charge. He argued that one of the benefits of Roellig's guide was to inform people about alternative sexualities so that problems arising from the union of a 'normal man' and a 'lesbian woman' could be avoided. Roellig herself stereotyped lesbians as 'hotter' and 'less well-tempered' than other women (1928, 20). She was unusually dismissive about some aspects of lesbian subculture, most notably lesbian newspapers, 'none of which,' she claimed, 'in contrast to the newspapers of male homosexuals, are to be taken seriously.' Roellig reacted to these lesbian magazines with the same outrage one found in more conservative circles: 'In the first place, the pictures of naked women on the cover have a crass, showy effect designed above all to entice buyers from every sphere. And then the titles!' (ibid., 7, 20, 23). Roellig was an advocate of the lesbian cause, and her publication had a more sectarian quality even when it argued for the need for more publicity for lesbian culture. Perhaps for these reasons, a degree of critical latitude was possible; hers was the critique of the insider.

Yet Moreck, articulating the broader significance of lesbian life, wrote more understandingly. His accomplishment was all the more remarkable if we remember his audience undoubtedly consisted of mostly heterosexual male tourists. He noted the difficulties lesbians had with police authorities, and he stressed how 'petit-bourgeois morality' stamped lesbians with the 'brand of inferiority' (1931, 164). Above all, he found a thriving and diverse lesbian culture. 'Lesbian love,' as Moreck termed it, found its home in the district surrounding the Bülowstraße, where the Damenklub Violetta, the Hohenzollern Diele, the Mikado, and Café Olala could be visited. While one could find heterosexual couples at such places, for the most part the motto of these establishments was 'men knuckle under here!' (ibid., 158). In the night spots with more appeal to out-of-town tourists such as the Toppkeller, men were encouraged to attend, a fact Roellig pointed out by noting that this club's owners realized male guests drank more than women did (1928, 40). In still other bars, such as the Damenklub Monbijou, men were excluded altogether or allowed only by invitation. But these were not threatening places, and Moreck found that a 'good atmosphere' prevailed in most of them. In the Hohenzollern Diele, Moreck found masculine-looking women with partners who, in the author's eyes, were also attractive to the male heterosexual gaze—'finely-framed, slim, completely girl-like women' who represented the 'female principle' and the 'personification of wifehood' in these same-sex relationships (1931, 160). The distinction between the 'male' and 'female' principle may strike one as 'essentialist,' but it is important to note that Roellig's account dealt in the same currency (1928, 19). Moreck's view cannot be ascribed to some allegedly typical masculinist rendering of female same-sex relationships but rather to the way in which the broader cultural matrix categorized lesbian society.

Moreck argued, perhaps with a little too much wonder, that even alternative sexual relationships ended in the same way 'normal' ones did—in marriage. Indeed, the theme of normality, not of sexual preference but of behavior and atmosphere, permeated Moreck's discussion. In the sites of Berlin's lesbian subculture one found not perversity or orgiastic celebrations but a relatively well-ordered and almost *bürgerlich* routine of social interchange. Baedeker propriety had not been left behind after all, but was re-framed to take in a wider range of sexual relationships and experiences.

Of Berlin's male homosexual subculture, consisting in part of an estimated 80 clubs, bars, and restaurants, Moreck noted a similarly routine quality. Emphasizing this theme was a significant departure from most contemporary approaches to the subject. This was a time when the Cook's travel agency of London led its customers through Berlin's night life and homosexual neighborhoods as if the inhabitants were displays in a curiosity cabinet (Mosse 1985, 132), and when French journalists and travel writers portrayed male homosexuality as *le vice allemande*. In contrast, Moreck argued that Berlin was no 'naughtier' than Paris or London, but that in the German capital male homosexuals were 'partly less ashamed, partly less hypocritical' (1931, 132). Above all, a degree of respectability characterized gay establishments. 'One waits in vain for an orgy in one of these clandestine pubs,' wrote the author. 'Everything transpires in a balanced way, in a well-tempered atmosphere, consisting of a mix of bourgeois propriety and disreputability' (ibid., 133). Sensationalists did not need to apply.

It is possible to read Moreck's guide to Berlin sex as a more commercialized and popular artifact of the sex reform movement of the Weimar Republic. While I find Grossmann's (1995) characterization of the sex reform movement compelling, I do not think Moreck's discourse fits. Without having evidence on the reception of *Führer durch das 'lasterhafte' Berlin*, allow me to make this final point by briefly speculating on who Moreck's imagined tourist was. He was of course a male heterosexual who was drawn to the more salacious side of Berlin culture after World War I. Nonetheless, his views were assimilable neither to the constricted world of Baedeker morality nor to the fascist misogyny of post-World War I Germany analyzed in Klaus Theweleit's work (1977/8). More than the male sex-reformers of Grossmann's research, he was willing to concede the variety of sexual identities one encountered when traveling through a major city. By touring naughty Berlin, he crossed a border, and he helped to build a new travel culture where not only heterosexual women, but also male and female homosexuals operated as more than passive subjects, as more than objects of derision, or as more than players in eroticized *tableaux vivants*. In Moreck's Berlin, the Other looked back, and the possibilities of new representations and new sexual identities were contained in this returned gaze.

In part, the returned gaze was an old problem in the history of tourism that has just now received wider scholarly attention. As tourism has developed, as armies of tourists have occupied countries, landscapes, and urban districts once thought to be 'back regions,' investigators realize that local inhabitants' ability to 'cope with tourists' (Boissevain 1996) is a topic in its own right. Women's ability to establish their own territory, their capacity to reverse the gaze of the male tourist and carve out an independent space within the Weimar imaginary of the city, marks one significant chapter in this history of 'native' coping. And yet, as the history of relationships between colonizers and the colonized increasingly shows, this imaginary was a product of negotiation and compromise, even when power (in this case sexual power) was unevenly distributed. Of the many goals tourism sets itself, the search for meaning is one of the most important. The search for a more diverse range of sexual meanings negotiated between a touristic public and their 'hosts,' both adapting to post-World War I Germany, both benefiting in different though related ways from the business of tourism, was well-served by Moreck's unusual guidebook.

**IV**

'Africa and America are no longer dreams' (Keitz 1989, 3). Such was the slogan issued by a Social Democratic cultural organization in the 1920s. Fired by the enthusiasm of the moment, the socialist workers' movement regarded leisure travel in utopian terms. This put it at odds with the modernist travel culture, whose sobriety suggested anything but passionate expressions and lofty goals. Whereas the socialist travel culture was earnest about the worker's right to leisure, devotees of the New Sobriety wanted distance, irony, and skepticism even when knowledge was to be gained through travel, and even when the 'sober' attitude could be linked to progressive political causes. Whereas the socialist travel culture had its eyes fixed firmly on the future, the modernist traveler enjoyed the displacements of the moment. In these and other ways, the two travel cultures were distinguished from one another even as they shared a common enemy: bourgeois travel in Baedeker's Germany.

Proletarian travelers still needed guidebooks no less than the sex tourist or Baedeker vacationer did. Just as modernist travelers required a guide to the netherworld of the metropolis, the worker needed orientation in a society that did little to educate him as a consumer or direct his still uncertain forays into the leisure regime of a democratic society. He needed advice on economical and efficient ways to use his precious leisure time, on how to get around by foot or using public transportation at a time when only the well-to-do could undertake automobile tours of the Continent. Even then, 'the traveling and wandering worker must have more,' or so read the introduction to the Dietz publishing house's 1932 guide to Germany, advertised as the first travel guidebook primarily for the socialist working class. It was not enough to be the proletarian version of Baedeker's economical tourist. It was not enough to have detailed lists of youth hostels and other cheap accommodations, or to have instructions on setting up tents, building campfires, and cooking out of doors. The socialist worker must also have a guidebook that spoke of 'peoples, of their work, their sufferings and triumphs.' When the 'smoke-screen of bourgeois playing with history' was stripped away, what was left was the flesh-and-blood history of ordinary people, whose artifacts and daily lives must now be the substance of workers' tourism (Dietz 1932, 9–10). This goal matched Anna Siemsen's discourse perfectly; the Dietz publication represented one significant attempt to create the kind of tourist guidebook for which the Social Democratic author called as a necessary entry into the post-Baedeker world.

The seriousness of the socialist travel culture could be seen not only in the introduction's passionate call for ideologically motivated leisure. The second section of the guide featured a short history of the regulation and provision of paid vacations for German workers and employees. It outlined the history of current laws and labor contracts relevant to leisure pursuits, and it compared Germany's progress on giving paid vacations with policies in other countries. The reader was told that only Finland, Latvia, Luxemburg, Austria, Poland, Russia, Czechoslovakia, and Brazil had legislated paid vacations. (Later in the 1930s, the Popular Front government in France would legislate two-week paid vacations for workers, but with mixed results [Cross 1989].) Even in these countries, many exceptions and legal complexities diminished workers' efforts to have the state guarantee paid leisure time. The situation was a complicated one, stated the guide, but the German trade union congress was on record as of 1931 that it was both possible and desirable to legislate a minimum of two-weeks' paid vacation time for all German workers over 18 years of age. 'Secure your vacation, workers! A vacation means reproduction and strengthening of your labor power, a sound national economy cannot do without a negotiated and legally guaranteed vacation!' (ibid., 15)—with these words echoing in his ears, the worker-traveler would set out on his leisure-time pursuits.

That these pursuits were not to be undertaken as a revolutionary assault on Baedeker's Germany was clear from the reference to the role of vacationing in the national economy. Like the Social Democratic movement from which it sprang, the Dietz guidebook situated itself as the artifact of an alternative travel culture *within* the existing society. Like the Social Democratic political goal of using democracy to transform capitalism gradually, the Dietz traveler embarked on a journey that reformed society from within, preserving the gains already made while also distributing resources more equitably. This *démarche* spoke directly to the interests of the mass of socialist laborers, who appeared happy to accept many aspects of German bourgeois heritage, often to the chagrin of revolutionary artists and middle-class educators within the Social Democratic movement (Guttsman 1990, 44–53). It was significant in this context that the Dietz guide allowed advertising; the reader of its itineraries would find information on commercial travel agencies, the Prussian lottery, canned foods, the city zoo, Tempelhof airport, and local swimming pools.

Positioning itself in this manner, the guide could not avoid incorporating many elements not only of Baedeker tourism but also of the new modernist travel culture. The Dietz guide was a walking and tramping guide, which meant that one of its key goals was the enjoyment of nature. The well-established traditions of the Friends of Nature movement were echoed in the guide just as readily as those of bourgeois nature hiking. Introducing the walking tourist to the 'hygiene of travel and tramping,' the guide instructed the reader to pay attention to the 'landscape with its inexhaustible richness of changing images.' This perspective put nature in the same category as the city of modernist sex tourism: as a spectacle representing an unlimited supply of attractions and possibilities for the aware consumer. At the same time—and despite the attention to group travel to be discussed—it put the emphasis on the individual traveler and the quasi-religious elements of his or her perceptions just as firmly as Baedeker discourse did. 'The goal is the enhancement of existential feeling,' read the guide, 'the deepening of inner life, and the conscious appropriation of the world of appearances.' Whoever did not understand this missed the important perception that nature was a 'revelation.' 'For him who has never experienced this, nature appears to be nothing more than decoration, and he himself is nothing more than a snob, a climber, a glutton for kilometers' (Dietz 1932, 16). By deriding the view that nature was 'decoration,' the guide appeared to reject the specular aspects of nature tourism. Yet the hiking Baedekerite would have found little with which to disagree in a statement affirming the revelatory qualities of natural environments. The reverse elitism of this phrase, the sense of superiority elicited with reference to the (no doubt, bourgeois) 'snob,' is also unsurprising, for as we have seen with Baedeker tourism, leisure travel operated between the poles of wide popularity and insistent distinction, for workers as well as for the Bürgertum.

The revelatory quality of nature was nowhere more evident than among German youth, a group that was unusually open to the positive attributes of travel in forest and countryside, according to the Dietz. For schoolchildren and teenagers, 'wandering is a fountain of youth.' This facet was relevant at the historical moment in which the Dietz appeared, a time of economic crisis and deteriorating social conditions. 'The joyful pleasure that touring has inspired among youth from time immemorial finds heightened expression today in contrast to the physical and moral destruction of economic despair caused by unemployment,' read the guide. In this construction, leisure was not merely a practice that reproduced labor power; rather, nature offered an alternative to labor itself, the right to which had been destroyed for so many German laborers in the world economic crisis. The 'educative quality' of tramping could not be denied in this context, as it fostered both the 'steeling of the will' and the 'formation of personality.' Yet the characterological aspects of touring were ultimately connected to 'the social,' as the guide used the term. 'Nowhere can a sense of community, or what we in later life call solidarity and class consciousness, be internalized with less pedanticism than there, where in collective wandering comradeship builds contacts from one to the other.' Comradeship through leisure travel was for youth the best insurance against the 'ego-man in his selfish eccentricity.' A democracy demanded this sense of social involvement, stated the guide, and comradely travel nurtured both the feeling of obligation to the community and the 'love of the homeland,' or *Heimat*. Indeed, workers' wandering was a form of self-taught local history that, when learned in youth, continued to link individuals to their homeland—their nation, region, or hometown—through a storehouse of 'memory images' whose 'deep mystery' could be rediscovered again and again (Dietz 1932, 16–18).

Wandering was not only for youth. The Dietz guide made a point of saying that tramping through forest, countryside, and mountains could be done by all ages.

99

The key was a rationally determined choice of how and when to travel based on an understanding of one's 'physical ability, constitution, and type of employment.' The question of 'mountains or ocean' could be determined finally only by the individual. Those who lacked the necessary physical fortitude were counseled to stay away from vigorous mountain climbing, while those with heart and lung conditions were advised to avoid too much exposure to the sea with its constant wind and the effects of salt-water air. Those who spent much time sitting in office jobs, or whose work consisted of long stretches of repetitive movement were to aim for a balance between vigorous exercise and a more sedentary tourism. For such individuals, tramping in valleys and hills was the right choice to offset 'the harmful effect of bad posture, deficient respiration, and sluggish digestion.' Tourism was therefore both individual and national therapy for the Dietz guidebook, whose approach was summed up in the motto: 'Physical training and touring are the doctor at the sickbed of the German Volk' (ibid., 18–19).

The guidebook's introductory material resonated in a number of directions. While it drew on the conventions of Baedeker and modernist travel cultures, it also marked out an unusually ideological—but hardly revolutionary—position. The Social Democratic party was wedded to democratic reform, and workers' tourism drank from the same well. This by no means ensured the viability of the kind of workers' leisure the Dietz guide represented within the Social Democratic movement, however. Since the late nineteenth century, when an array of cultural and social organizations had grown up as semi-independent entities in the socialist movement (Lidtke 1985), the Social Democratic leadership was anxious about giving leisure-time pursuits too much visibility or power. Seeing movies and going to the museum, taking nature hikes or going on guided tours of historical cities, sharp-shooting and calisthenics—such activities deepened workers' sense of their right to leisure, but, so the fear went, they did little to sharpen the workers' commitment to political struggle. What is more, leisure presented the possibility of greater individuation for the worker. The varied selves of the tourist, presumably brought together in a coherent ideological matrix within the socialist travel culture, were in danger of being split apart once the pleasure of leisure (or the leisure of pleasure) exercised its sway on the worker's mind and body. Youthful wandering in nature under proper ideological guidance might ensure that worker-tourists gained the appropriate political messages. But even here, there were no guarantees. Finally, the socialist travel culture saw tourism as a form of social, or even national, hygiene. Shaped in part by the urgencies of the economic crisis, this viewpoint also connected with the wider language of the sick nation and the need for drastic remedial action then prevalent in German political culture. The urgency of national hygiene could also be expressed in racist terms, and we will see that leisure under the auspices of the National Socialist movement could quickly be linked to a violent, 'biologistic' politics based on eliminating those who were deemed sickly and inferior. The socialist travel culture avoided such rhetoric, but it shared with the Nazis the idea that the national body suffered, that new and more widely distributed leisure practices had something to do with a remedy, and that tourism was an activity with deep ideological and social meaning. But in this latter regard, all German travel cultures of the interwar era, the socialist, the modernist, and the National Socialist, expressed themselves in terms that were structurally related to those of Baedeker tourism. Had not the comfortable bourgeois tourist also believed in the cultural significance and educative value of sightseeing? The post-Baedeker world could not unhinge itself entirely from the nineteenth century in which it originated.

## V

One of the most distinctive themes of the socialist travel culture was group travel, which was not only cheaper but also more ideologically appropriate. Readers of the Dietz guide were presented with detailed information on a number of voluntary groups that organized inexpensive travel for laborers and employees. One such association was the Travel Department of the Reich Committee for Socialist Education, begun in 1924 and headquartered in Berlin, which gave advice on all aspects of 'vacation culture' and promoted group excursions in Germany and abroad, the Paris–Brussels bus tour being one of the most popular. By the time it was listed in the Dietz guide it had transformed its once highly politicized rhetoric, focusing less on a language of social oppression than on the idea that all workers, regardless of their ideological position, deserved leisure travel. Even so, publications by the organization continued to distinguish its worker-tourists from the 'Baedeker-toting spectator' and the 'stuffed philistine' who allegedly ran from site to site seeing everything possible. For the Reich Committee, the key was a kind of 'social wandering' that took in scenes of everyday labor and economic life, peering behind the façades of buildings to understand work relations and class conflicts (Keitz 1997, 131–2, 138). Whether the rhetoric actually contributed to the formation of a distinctly new vacation culture is doubtful, as shall be discussed below.

Other workers' tourist clubs listed in the guide included the Friends of Nature and the Friends of International Cooperation. The Friends of Nature had undergone a turbulent ride since the war, experiencing deep drops in membership in the wake of postwar inflation and then a steady rise in membership in the late 1920s, when more than 800 local clubs existed in Germany. At the time of the Dietz guide's publication, the Friends of Nature had travel agencies in more than 30 German cities. It organized mainly small group tours that were no longer oriented solely toward nature hiking but also included excursions to cities in Germany and abroad.

Here too one found a combination of 'workerist' rhetoric and pragmatic organization of tourism designed to address the individual's desire for relaxation. As with most other workers' touring associations, tour participants were no longer required to belong to the Social Democratic party or a trade union; it was enough to be of a 'like-minded orientation.' There were limits to such tolerance, but they were most visibly and necessarily enforced on the Left as the Social Democrats undertook a purge of Communist members of the Friends of Nature late in the Weimar Republic. The Friends of International Cooperation, nicknamed Fredika and founded in Berlin in 1924, organized workers' and socialist students' exchanges between Germany and 23 European countries. One of its main contacts was the London-based Workers' Travel Association. Fredika also had a working relationship with an organization from New York City, the 'Pocono Study Tours,' which offered three-month excursions by American workers to Europe. Part of the program was a summer adult-education seminar in the Tyrol, where among others, German instructors would give lectures on European labor history and related topics. The Dietz guide noted that the Pocono Study Tours were race-blind, and that any American worker who refused to associate with a black person during the excursion was dropped from the program (1932, 25–32; Keitz 1997, 152–61).

Dietz itineraries tell us even more about the content and history of the socialist travel culture. As with the 1913 Baedeker guide to Germany, the Dietz began with Berlin. It provided general information about the city's visitors' bureaus, but also pointed out that those who wanted 'serious communal–social study' during their tour should turn to the secretariat of the Social Democratic party. Group tours through the city could be arranged through the Republican Student League, the student arm of the Social Democrats, as well. The language was combative: a 'modern Berlin' had grown up only with the accession to power of the Social Democrats, who overcame the 'failure' of the previous city administration, run by liberals and the Prussian-dynastic regime. Socialist administration consolidated the sprawling urban center into 8 urban districts, 59 villages, and 27 estates. Few people knew that at the center of the old Berlin was a 'landed estate,' the huge Imperial Palace of the Kaiser and his family. The legal status of the palace enabled the dynasty to 'escape regulation and supervision by the city administration.' 'Also this old, graying pig-tail was finally cut off in 1920,' read the Dietz, and the new 'red Berlin' would see to it that such historical landmarks and traditions would find a safe home in the new regime. Red Berlin was a giant; only New York City and London had bigger populations, and only three other cities had a larger area. Dietz stood the conventional guidebook description of Berlin's confessional makeup on its head, omitting mention of the city's large Protestant majority and instead writing that out of more than four million people, about one-tenth were Catholic. Even more revealingly, it emphasized that more than 300,000 Berliners mentioned no confessional affiliation at all, and that 170,000 were Jews. An evocative characterization followed: 'Comparatively, this would mean that Nuremberg would be entirely Catholic, that all of Magdeburg would be free-thinking, and that all Augsburg would be Jewish' (Dietz 1932, 62–4).

Berlin was above all a city of production and consumption in the Dietz perspective. Detailed statistics were given for occupational makeup, housing, meat and agricultural production, transportation, city finances, utilities, libraries, hospitals, and sports facilities. Later in the guide, the reader would find tours of important industrial and commercial sites—the Borsig machine company, the giant Siemensstadt complex, and the Berlin electrical works, the 'most modern of Europe' (ibid., 1932, 94–5). Although a degree of pride was evident in such material, it was clear also that the guide found the overall effect to be questionable. Like the Baedeker and many other tour books, the Dietz stressed that many fine old buildings existed in Berlin, but that a coherent historical core of the kind Nuremberg or Frankfurt had was nowhere to be found. But while the Baedeker offered just one regretful line about the absence of an 'organically developed artistic image of the city' (1927, 30), the Dietz accused the previous city administration of having no 'love for the homeland' and of fomenting a 'ruthless Americanization' of the metropolis. The Dietz guide's anxieties about the modern city were evident as it developed its overview of Berlin. It worried that in the oldest part of Berlin one could detect the prior existence of a fishing village only from the morphology of the streets around Fischerstraße and the Petrikirche; it advised a 'melancholy stroll through Old Berlin' in the subsequent itinerary. The Baedeker treated matter-of-factly this absence of what once had been. In the nearby Mühlendamm, the Dietz found 'castle-like, less tasteful buildings of the Municipal Savings Bank' where the Baedeker, in less emotional tones, found only 'fortress-like' buildings (Baedeker 1927, 150; Dietz 1932, 67, 87). Despite differences in tone, the similarity in word choice indicates that the Dietz borrowed heavily from the Baedeker in these and other descriptions.

The Dietz's city overview soon became a history lesson about the exploitation of the local population by the Hohenzollern dynasty. What had once been a 'real city-republic' in the fourteenth century was soon lorded over by a Hohenzollern monarch who, after a brief period of cooperation with the city, put down an uprising and began a centuries-long period of dominance. The city's degradation found fitting expression in the tearing down of the Roland statue on the Moltenmarkt, a symbol of municipal autonomy in the medieval age. The next 400 years of history was a blank spot in the Dietz's introduction as it picked up the narrative only in 1848, when a 'second uprising' against the 'cowardly Hohenzoller Friedrich Wilhelm IV' took place. Only on 9 November 1918 did the half-millennium of monarchical rule end for Berlin, which still suffered from its long history of submissiveness. The population's passivity was well-symbolized by the fact that the Hohenzollern palace could still be observed without obstruction in the center of the city while the Rathaus was imprisoned between 'unimportant, ugly commercial buildings.' Even more galling was the fact that Kaiser Wilhelm II had given the city a new Roland fountain in the Avenue of Victory. This structure, read the Dietz, 'was the ugliest fountain to be found in recent times in German cities.' These and other symbols of past monarchical crimes were evident for all to see in the modern Berlin of the Weimar era and the Dietz applauded the fact that the Revolution had not done away with them. They were a sign of the 'patience with which a liberated people tolerates the memory of its harsh suppressors and persecutors.' Even so, it was indefensible that Hohenzollern symbols remained while there was 'neither a monument of liberation, nor a street of 9 November, nor a monument for the first truly democratic and social Reich President Friedrich Ebert' (Dietz 1932, 68–70). This observation was accurate. Not only had the revolutionary struggles of the first German republic damaged relatively few monuments and historical structures of Hohenzollern vintage; the Republic itself did relatively little to symbolize its triumphs, leaders, or roots in German history (Koshar 2000, 90–1; Speitkamp 1997, 15).

The Berlin itinerary proper began with a Baedeker-like orientation to personal taste: the guide would offer only summary information, enough to allow one 'to see with one's own open eyes and senses.' Yet the strongest impression to emerge from the itinerary is the consistently politicized, manipulative view. The point was clearly not to let the tourist decide for himself, but rather to create a systematically critical impression of the city. The boulevard Unter den Linden was to be appreciated less for its pulsating crowds than for the fact that its eastern closure was dominated by the structure that one critic called the 'beginning of the present age's wretchedness in monuments,' the equestrian statue of Frederick the Great. Of the palace of Kaiser Wilhelm I, an elegant structure more pleasing to the eye than the mammoth Imperial Palace, the Dietz could only mention that it was not equipped with a bathtub. The old Kaiser had to have a tub brought to him from a nearby hotel when he wanted to bathe. The famous Zeughaus had architectural importance, but above all it was 'the site of pilgrimage for all war-loving German national philistines, including their wives, offspring, and pedagogues.' Its museum had interesting material on military history, but it was also filled with 'lots of other stuff.' Berlin was a city of movie houses, as we have noted, and this fact did not go unnoticed. But moviegoers from out of town should also beware: the great film production company Ufa was owned by 'the German national devourer of socialists Hugenberg.' Once outside the capital, Potsdam came in for especially heated criticism: it was the 'mecca of all reactionaries.' The critical perspective also demanded that much would be omitted or repressed. Berlin's nightspots were no secret to most tourists, but the good socialist worker would have to seek them out on his own. Around the Friedrichstraße, the reader was told only that there were many 'bars and clubs oriented to out of towners,' and those seeking more information about such entertainment were referred to the newspapers and boulevard press (Dietz 1932, 70, 71, 72, 76, 97, 108).

Embedded in this perspective was a narrative that gained specificity as the reader moved from the general introduction to the detailed itineraries. Not only could one read the broad history of Hohenzollern oppression in the city's monuments; there was also a story to be told of the Bürgertum's cowardice. 'We will see,' read the guide as it summed up the complex of buildings around the Opernplatz (today: Bebelplatz) and Zeughaus, 'that the Berlin Bürgertum never made a serious attempt to confront this dynastic Berlin with a modern-bourgeois one.' This was to be seen most clearly in the account of the Reichstag and the nearby Avenue of Victory. The Reichstag was not a symbol of democracy at all, but of the monarchy. 'Every hall, every room, every corner usable in any way' did not praise the people, but rather added up to a 'more or less clumsily implemented glorification of the ruling house.' The ugly Avenue of Victory, Wilhelm II's pompous, monumental street commemorating Hohenzollern dynasts, was even more scandalous after 1918 than before. 'It appears that the Republic will be forever burdened with these and many hundreds of other Hohenzollern mementos,' read the guide, which attributed the commemorative hangover 'singly and solely [to] the guilt of the Bürgertum, which selfishly watched over the preservation of Hohenzollern kitsch and trash' (ibid., 1932, 75, 78–9). The fact that the Revolution had not done away with the monuments of the past—in clear contrast to both the French and Russian revolutions—was a source of regret rather than civic pride.

The Dietz guide did not paint an unrelentingly negative picture of bourgeois political history. When it stepped outside the capital and considered places such as Freiburg in Baden, it did not miss the chance to point out that the lovely Gothic cathedral there was both a symbol of 'mystical spirit of medieval religiosity' and of the 'self-assured consciousness of the urban Bürger' (ibid., 258). But in Berlin, the bourgeoisie was accused of both sins of omission and commission, of not fighting hard enough to secure democratic rights and cultural autonomy, but also of jealously defending the symbols of kingly power it should have opposed. Such statements gained meaning and impetus from the trope of the failed bourgeois revolution, a constitutive element of socialist discourse in Germany since the nineteenth century. Whereas they were accurate as far as they went, these criticisms ignored the constant struggle, the daily give-and-take that took place in Berlin city politics between middle-class liberalism and the monarchy during the Kaiserreich (Mommsen 1993). This struggle was reflected in the Baedeker's characterization of the German capital as a hybrid of Prussian-dynastic will, administrative and commercial success, and liberal bourgeois cultural accomplishment.

The other key part of the Dietz narrative was based on the triumph of progressive political and cultural forces. This had a strong future-oriented slant. The guidebook treated the 'fearful appearance of the rental barracks,' the crowded and unsanitary residential quarters of the proletarian East, as a historical occurrence already being overcome by clear-headed Social Democratic policies providing health clinics, swimming pools, and other important urban amenities. Its reticence to go into much detail about the daily life of the *Mietskasernen*—strangely comparable to the Baedeker's one-sentence treatment (1927, 31)—can be attributed in part to the fact that the Communist party had much support among their inhabitants. In general, though, the guidebook's modus operandi was to turn Baedeker imagery of Berlin inside out, giving places neglected in the mainstream literature much more attention and de-emphasizing other attractions. Berlin museum life was handled peremptorily, for example. The Wertheim department store was a standard attraction in tour book literature, but the Dietz singled out the building not only as the 'most beautiful and elegant of Berlin's department stores' but also as 'a revolutionary act in its time.' Not much was said about why the building should be regarded in this way, and readers would have to glean from the text that Wertheim's was revolutionary because the socialist Paul Göhre, writing before World War I, had done an important sociological study of it employees. The famous city library earned attention because of its impressive holdings of more than 300,000 volumes. Particularly noteworthy was the fact that more than 8,000 of these dealt with social and economic history, some 1,100 with social policy, and another 400 with socialist theory. The educative strain in the socialist travel culture gravitated to such details. Modernist architecture also came in for special consideration. Max Taut's Hufeisensiedlung, a modernist housing development that stood in stark contrast to the proletarian rental barracks, was 'unconditionally worth seeing,' and Ludwig Mies van der Rohe's exciting residential buildings in North Berlin were treated as models of 'new building' (Dietz 1932, 74–5, 80, 86, 88, 91).

Even more important were the traces of working-class struggle. This perspective meant, first of all, that buildings associated with the Social Democratic and trade union movement were pushed center stage, even if they were architecturally unremarkable. More dramatically, Berlin was transformed into a site of popular martyrdom, a move the Dietz guide shared with other political guidebooks of the 1930s including those of the Nazi party, and which anticipated the post-World War II German Democratic Republic's 'antifascist' commemorative strategies as well. Dietz editors approved of the restored and 'highly restrained' Neue Wache, a memorial to the war dead designed by Heinrich Tessenow. This was one of the few monuments referring to World War I mentioned by the guidebook. That it received any attention at all indicated that the compilers did not regard it solely as part of the nationalist culture from which most other war monuments sprang. Such places as the cemetery of the martyrs of 1848 in the Friedrichshain, the city's oldest park, and Treptower Park, which had been a place of 'unforgettable Social

Democratic prewar demonstrations,' were approvingly discussed. The architecture and art of the Imperial Palace received short shrift, but its notorious political history, including the incident in which the Prussian monarch and his wife were forced by their enemies to review the badly disfigured corpses of 1848 demonstrators killed by the military, got much attention. The Friedrichshain cemetery was a 'site of pilgrimage of all Republicans' and it contained a 'mass grave' of those killed in the street battles of 1919 as well. Since the disturbances of 1919 were caused mainly by the revolutionary actions of the Communists, the Dietz guide did little to develop the information on this site. Indeed, throughout the guide, the memories of 1848 or of prewar Social Democratic political mobilization were more central than were memories of the founding of the Republic. When the guide mentioned the Friedrichsfelde grave of Rosa Luxemburg, the socialist theoretician murdered by Prussian paramilitary police in January 1919 in Berlin, it referred to her only as a Social Democrat, not a radical Left critic of socialism and an early Communist, which she became during and after the war. The Baedeker guide did more to point out the traces left over from the Berlin battles of 1919—such as bullet holes on monuments and other public buildings—than did the Dietz publication (Baedeker 1927, 144; Dietz 1932, 72, 73, 82, 88, 89). The deep split on the Left that did so much to weaken the Weimar Republic had clear effects on the socialist travel culture's vision of the topography of the German capital. This topography necessitated a twofold move: liberal democratic accomplishments were downplayed in favor of a narrative emphasizing Hohenzollern brutality while Communist activity was banished to the margins of post-World War I history.

When it moved to areas other than Berlin, the Dietz guide also reflected the perspective of the travel culture from which it originated. The title of one chapter was 'The Ruhr Region as Tourist Destination,' a wording that signaled how unusual it was to consider this, one of the greatest mining and steel centers of Europe, as a site of leisure travel. The gateway to the region was Dortmund, the 'blacksmith of profit on the Ruhr,' and the second largest city of the country in terms of area. The factories of the Ruhr valley were places of science-fiction-like furor where men worked before the flames and poisonous gases of the blast furnaces as they turned ore into iron, and iron into steel. Here one could see the miners, the *Kumpel*, who swung their pickaxes against the 'dusty coal' 700 meters below ground. And here one could see row upon row of dirtied housing tracts, the laboring men of which (women were not mentioned) were fired by the conviction 'that the important things of the world were divided inequitably, that a more just and more social order must make its way.' This conviction buttressed the 'creative energy of a great movement, the socialist,' which overcame the war and the postwar problems of unemployment to give Dortmund new housing, parks, swimming pools, and clinics. 'Difficult struggle and much sacrifice' of the kind postwar socialism stood for in the Ruhr would, the guide confidently stated, lead to the 'progress of mankind and the victory of humanity' (Dietz 1932, 185–7).

But if the Ruhr symbolized a socialist future in which human wants would be more justly addressed, was it really a tourist destination? 'Is it not foolish,' asked the Dietz, 'to spend one's short vacation time in this coal-pot, the parade ground of heavy industry?' The response stressed that the 'proletarian traveler' could learn much from a visit to the Ruhr, thereby continuing the tradition of educative, socially conscious tramping. But the broader emphasis was on enjoyment. Despite the industry, smoke, and poverty, the 'general aspect' of the land was 'so different, so much pleasanter than is usually assumed.' The 'iron tanks of industry' did not yet extinguish the 'original, idyllically lovely character of the landscape.' The hiker could see forest paths, still river valleys, and flowing cornfields. Scenic artificial lakes represented 'a harmonic triad of nature, technology, and architecture.' All the major cities had sports fields and parks, and Essen's Gruga athletic complex was 'almost American in pomp and grandiosity.' Industrialists may have made themselves at home here as aggressively as the crassest 'golddiggers in unpopulated California,' but they were unable to wipe out the area's many historical churches, half-timbered houses, and romantic castles. The Folkwang Museum of Essen, with its fine collection of modern art; the schools and workers' organizations; modernist architecture in Dortmund, Essen, and Gelsenkirchen—all were grist for the tourist mill (ibid., 187–90).

If such sites could appeal to everyone, the 'class conscious traveler' or the ordinary worker, no one was to overlook the Krupp works in Essen, creation of the 'cannon king of Wilhelmine Germany.' The Krupp complex, 'this factory in the city, this city in the factory,' occupied an entire urban district and made products that were known to every household in the country (ibid., 191). The Baedeker was fascinated with Krupp as well, but the postwar versions of the guide praised the 'unsurpassed' measures for employees' welfare taken by the firm and advised travelers to see the workers' colony Altenhof, in Essen-Rüttenscheid (1925, 5). The Dietz was less sanguine about the state of workers' housing, noting, though not with specific reference to Krupp, that 'the slum conditions attributable to the architectural principles of turn-of-the-century capitalism are still a long way from being eliminated' in all Ruhr cities. Yet on the whole its treatment of Krupp and other industrial sites hinged on a twofold schema made up of the working man's commitment to a better future and the wonders of modern industrial technology. The guidebook's statement on the Duisburg harbor, the world's biggest inland harbor, was typical: 'The unforgettable activity in this industrial harbor gives one an inkling of what industry can and must do in this highly technological age' (Dietz 1932, 193). More than Berlin, still weighed down with the stone reminders of Hohenzollern oppression, the Ruhr gave hope for a socialist future of productivity and welfare for ordinary laborers despite the injustices of the industrial system still working there.

For all its ideological zeal, the Dietz guide was not above treating various sites in purely touristic terms, and to the considerable degree it did, it lost its distinctiveness in relation to bourgeois guides. This tendency was more apparent once one moved to destinations outside Berlin or the Ruhr, that is, to places where the penumbra of political conflict was less visible. On the scenic Rügen island, 'Germany's biggest and most beautiful island,' travelers were invited to consider local legends of the pagan goddess Hertha, whose rites were linked to the 50-foot-high semi-circular mound found at this spot. The Baedeker, too, mentioned this aspect of the scenic area (1925, 150). The nearby island Hiddensee invited the nature hiker to consider the great variety of birds to be found there. The Black Forest and Alps with their numerous scenic views, hiking paths, and villages were given sufficient attention in the guidebook, as they were in most mainstream tourist literature. In the case of the Alps and many other areas, though, even seemingly clichéd treatments of popular tourist destinations reminded the reader that an important social process, indeed an act of emancipation, was underway. The section on Munich and its environs began with the following: 'The Alpine regions have more and more become the favored vacation and hiking destinations for the working class' (Dietz 1932, 114, 120–1, 321).

## VI

A strange combination shaped the Dietz handbook: an inside-out view of tourist attractions foregrounding that which the Baedeker and other guides glossed over; heavy-handed ideological criticism paired with a celebratory narrative of working-class sacrifice and triumph; and numerous itineraries that differed little from those of less politically engaged guides. It is difficult to say how flesh-and-blood worker travelers responded to such material. There was much agreement on a general point: workers deserved and needed leisure travel for their physical and psychological health. A female employee writing about her vacation in 1925 put it clearly: 'A deep bitterness would take hold of all people compelled to work for wages or salary if their vacation, for which they have so strenuously struggled, would be taken away from them' (cited in Keitz 1997, 192).

Leisure travel was not only a physical necessity but also a symbolic value. And virtually without exception, literature on workers' travel, like the Dietz handbook, stressed the limitations on workers' leisure time and financial resources, and the corresponding idea that as much as possible was to be made from one's vacation. Workers needed advice on getting 'the maximum recovery and strengthening of their health' during their vacations, wrote a correspondent for the General German Trade Union Association newspaper ('Reisen und Wandern' 1929). 'The worker should not leave his wanderings to chance,' wrote a correspondent to the Communist press, 'but should be expedient, since he can make only a few trips.' In the case of this anonymous contributor, expediency meant drawing out the appropriate, that is, Communist, political meanings, of one's travels. Leaving the Duisburg train station for Amsterdam late in May 1928, the writer was moved by the early-morning sight of street sweepers, whose labors led him to exclaim that 'in the not too distant future workers themselves will build their state on the ruins of the capitalist state apparatus.' The same writer made a point of questioning the 'illusions' held by two Social Democrats he encountered in Amsterdam. These comrades, according to the writer, mistakenly believed that Social Democratic successes in Reichstag elections held earlier in the month would lead to a new coalition between Communists and socialists ('Auch der Arbeiter,' 1928). The question of what expediency meant for non-Communist worker travelers, however, was an open one in this writer's perspective.

When the Kassel chapter of the Friends of Nature discovered in 1980 the photo collection of one of its most active members, the lathe operator Paul Schminke, they found little in the way of a utopian or didactic spirit. Taken mainly by Schminke for his family and Friends of Nature comrades, the photographs covered more than a half-century of tourism starting in 1914. A Social Democratic supporter of 'social tramping,' Schminke nonetheless took few photographs of ordinary workers in everyday life and even fewer recording the political struggles of the working-class movement. His hobby had little to do with the workers' 'photo sport' movement of the Weimar period, for which the Dietz offered a section of information and guidance. Schminke's photographs were highly subjective views of scenic castle ruins, pleasant natural settings, and family and friends (Erdmann and Lorenz, 1985). A talented amateur picture taker, Schminke was no politically engaged intellectual, and his touristic sensibilities strike one as having been thoroughly in line with those of Baedeker's universe even if he might have disdained using the Baedeker guidebook. Was he typical of his time?

We have seen that the Reich Committee for Socialist Education's travel department promoted the idea of ideologically motivated 'social wandering.' But the Reich Committee's itineraries were barely distinguishable from those of commercial travel agencies. Participants who signed up to go on so-called 'study excursions' did not expect to get rigorous instruction of the kind one might expect in an adult education class. Rather they preferred a more general approach to sightseeing that hardly differed from what one would find in a less ideologically situated commercial tour. This caused not a little consternation on the part of tour organizers and ideologues within the organization, such as Herbert Kriedemann, who continued to insist 'we don't travel for pleasure!' Yet such individual dissatisfaction with the lack of political rigor could not carry the day. By the early 1930s comments from tour participants showed that it was not the 'educational content' of the excursions that drew praise but rather decent organization and accommodations in the best hotels for the money (Keitz 1997, 138–142, 144–5).

The Reich Committee struck a note of harmony and avoidance of controversy in its publications: its guidelines for group excursions in 1930 explicitly mentioned that 'combative persons are advised to stay away.' Its programmatic statement regarded leisure time as a product both of workers' emancipatory struggle and the effort to bring all nations together. But it was also much less ideological than the Dietz guidebook was. For the group's Rhineland tours, the program emphasized 'fabled castles and splendid landscapes,' for the East 'rural beauties,' and for Frankfurt the pleasures of the 'old historical Reich and commercial city.' Normandy in France featured numerous 'historical sites' but also 'great rural charm.' Excursions to Switzerland, the Riviera, Dalmatia, and many other foreign destinations received similar treatment. Travelers had the chance to meet their worker brethren in foreign countries, as in the 12-day tour from Brussels to Paris, in which an evening was set aside to meet 'Paris socialists' (Reichsausschuss 1930, ii, 1–3, 16). But such encounters were not the centerpieces of these tours, which were hardly the stuff of engaged politics as advocated by the Dietz handbook. Travel accounts indicate that socialist workers noted if a region or city flew Republican, conservative, or trade union flags, but such observations were usually offered only in passing (Keitz 1997, 200; Warum 1927).

As for the idea of group travel, there was much commentary extolling the necessity of collectivized tourism so as to achieve a truly socialist perspective. A German Communist's account of his visit to the Russian 'Riviera of workers and peasants' on the Black Sea could give no higher compliment than to say that 'everything was [done] together' (Eckert 1932). Nonetheless, everyday practices put a premium on individual decision-making and individual activity, even when people took part in group excursions or social tramping. Choosing a travel destination was an individual decision, and not an insignificant one from the point of view of women workers who regarded such choice as an act of independence. This was doubly so for women who espoused alternative sexual identities, as with lesbian workers and employees, who could get advice on choosing vacations from publications such as the journal *Garçonne* (Altenberg 1932). Workers who saved enough money to take a one- or two-week vacation regularly saw this in terms of their own economic acumen. During the vacation, moreover, 'continued vigilance and diligent saving' on the part of the individual were necessary lest the trip be discontinued prematurely. Family travel was a key part of working-class leisure, also in group tours, but here too an individualized mode of perception prevailed. The travel account of a male printer from Berlin touring northeastern Germany with his family in 1928 all but eliminated his wife and children from the scene (Keitz 1997, 193, 201, 202–8). Excursion tours offered by socialist travel agencies allowed for much individual variation both in the mode and timing of travel to particular destinations and in the itineraries adopted once workers arrived. Recalling a practice first established with the Cook's agency, the Reich Committee for Socialist Education explicitly welcomed single women travelers for excursions (Reichsausschuss 1930, ii).

The national–liberal travel culture had been characterized by a clear, though understated, national pride. In contrast, modernist travel appeared to be unconcerned with questions of nationality and nationhood. The emphasis was on the emotions of the moment, and their ironic representation, rather than on tradition or the projection of the national community into the future. Between these poles, the socialist travel culture tended more toward the former than the latter. The Dietz handbook was unfailingly critical of German nationalism and everything associated with it. Yet it was aware of the historical and cultural treasures Germany possessed, its natural grandeur and rural beauty; and it was proud to direct the traveler's gaze to the impressive industrial and technological might of the nation. More than a commitment to social wandering or some version of collectivized leisure, it was this national pride that showed through in travel accounts and other kinds of travel literature penned by workers. Reacting to the exhibits of various German regions in the Dresden travel show, a correspondent for a trade union newspaper exclaimed: "One is amazed to see how much beauty there is in Germany' ('Reisen und Wandern' 1929). The travel section of the socialist journal *Kulturwille* regularly featured excerpts from classical bourgeois travel writing of the nineteenth century by novelist Theodor Fontane or the cultural historian Wilhelm Heinrich Riehl. These excerpts reflected a sense of national identity that socialist editors felt little need to qualify (Fontane 1929; Riehl 1929). Even when the national unit to which one belonged appeared in a questionable light, as when German workers toured the World War I battlefields of France, and even when 'war romanticism' was to be avoided, there was patriotic pride that German soldiers fought bravely alongside their national comrades (Hartmann 1929).

What the socialist travel culture clearly shared with both of the other travel cultures was a sense of the international dimensions of contemporary tourism. From the outset, Baedeker's Germany situated itself in an international tourist market, and the national–liberal travel culture depended on the consumption of tourist sites both at home and abroad. The new modernist travel culture gained its character from an appreciation of avant-garde art from throughout Europe, of the international style in architecture, of jazz from America, and of the nightlife of Paris, London, New York, and Berlin. The socialist travel culture's internationalism was more ideological—it stemmed from Marx's original idea that the proletariat had no country—but also in many ways more accomplished because of the limited resources of those who participated. All of the organizations touted by the Dietz handbook worked very hard to establish international exchanges and group tours throughout the industrial world. Workers' travel accounts are full of impressions of German workers going to conferences in Paris, London, Amsterdam, and Moscow. The socialist travel culture extended from the small-scale weekend tour or Sunday outing close to home to well-organized and collectively conceived group excursions abroad. It is difficult to say what the precise effect of international tourism was for workers lucky enough to take advantage of it, but the intention, the idea that 'Africa and America are no longer dreams,' was clear. The worker's self was no more 'collective' than was its counterpart in the modernist and national–liberal travel cultures. But it was just as international and, given the obstacles it faced, all the more impressive for that fact.

## VII

Modernist sexual identity and class consciousness offered two alternative referents of leisure travel to Baedeker's vision of Germany. They were not the only alternatives, to be sure. A more ideologically pointed form of class struggle regulated Communist travel culture, which derived the necessity of revolution, not gradual reform, from inequities in the distribution of capital. Traces of this more radical travel culture have appeared throughout the preceding pages. A grassroots nationalism based on love of one's immediate homeland, one's *Heimat*, also posed an alternative not only to Baedeker liberalism but to the excesses of eroticized travel and the ideological impulse of class identity. The *Heimat* revival of the Weimar Republic had many dimensions as it spanned the political spectrum, from the moderate Social Democratic Left to the conservative and nationalist Right where it found its most willing political representation. It gave tourism a central place not only because leisure travel generated income for hard-pressed municipalities but also because travel gave Germans a chance to immerse themselves in the landscapes, architecture, cuisine, literature, and art of the many homelands of the nation. To mention these other alternatives is to point to the central and debilitating fact of Weimar leisure culture, namely its fragmentation due to both political contention and severe economic crisis.

This is not the way the proponents of alternative travel cultures saw the matter, however. They regarded their efforts as both novel and comprehensive, not fragmentary or partitive. The advocates of a modernist sexuality saw eroticized travel, irony, and skepticism as elements of a healthier worldview, a new theology, in which leisure fed off the dynamism and incessant movement of techno-urban environments. Leave the monuments behind, they said, and in doing so free your self from bourgeois values that repressed true emotions and deferred the pleasures of the moment. Socialist travelers turned Baedeker topographies upside-down, seeing German cities as records of class oppression rather than national accomplishment. Yet they retained enough of the bourgeois outlook to moderate their claims and balance their insistence on reform. Both attempts at synthesis rested on the idea of distance between leisure pursuits and political identities. Moreck's sexual topographies achieved coherence precisely because they operated at a distance from the political conflicts of the time even when they derived dynamism from them. The Dietz guidebook's socialist tourism preached working-class solidarity, but it also carved out a niche for simple pleasure and individuality, if not always willingly. In relation to Baedeker travel, the Dietz publication narrowed considerably the space between leisure and society. But in relation to another alternative travel culture of the era, that of National Socialism, it operated more closely to the Baedeker model, which originated in the idea of leisure culture as a sphere distinct (though never disengaged) from the world of work and politics.

The foregoing leads one to an unhappy hypothesis, namely that it was the National Socialist travel culture that was the only 'successful' travel culture of the time. More than other alternatives, it seemed to combine the appearance of cross-class popularity, focused ideological appeal, and social relevance. It seemed to unite various tourist selves in a coherent whole. It did so by *claiming* to collapse distinctions between leisure and society, and by insisting that 'race' represented a more dynamic and galvanizing concept with which to bring German leisure travel into line with the political demands of the age. It is therefore necessary to spend somewhat more time, in the next chapter, on this radical challenge to Baedeker's Germany.

# Chapter Three

# Savage Tourism

## I

One of the oddest products of interwar travel literature was a satirical travelogue of Nazi Germany written by a fictitious 'Zulu reporter,' Usikota, whose dispatches to his homeland were published in the *Zulu Post*. Appearing in 1938 with the English left-wing publisher Victor Gollancz, *Zulu in Germany* was an absurdist tour through Hamburg, Nuremberg, Münster, Berlin, Munich, and the provinces, in which the protagonist conducted interviews with Nazi leaders, including Hitler himself. Along the way, Usikota learned that regulated prostitution in Hamburg stemmed from the regime's attempt to 'satisfy a fundamental human appetite' within the unruly SA, the Nazi paramilitary group. He likened the Germans to two cannibals once civilized in Zululand, who, when returned to their native village, were again roused by the 'sickly smell of roasted human flesh.' After only 14 years of freedom, the Germans, like the cannibals, reverted to their accustomed authoritarianism when the 'old smell of Tyrant's meat' wafted their way. In Hitler's Germany, the pen had been replaced by the 'dung fork,' cows marched to the Horst Wessel Song, and Usikota himself was suspected of having 'Jewish blood.' Seeing thousands of 'Hitler's children' at a youth group meeting, the reporter naïvely asked Nazi leaders how many wives the White Father had, and after making his pilgrimage to Berchtesgaden, he asked the Reich Chancellor why he begot no offspring. In Nuremberg, he learned the legend of the feared monk of the thirteenth century, Rind Fleisch Streicher, who incited anti-Semitic violence and killed 100,000 Jews. Finally, the Zulu traveler himself, concluding that 'educate the people' must be the saving slogan of the day, ran afoul of the SA. In an epilogue to the book, Usikota's editor wrote of how the unfortunate reporter's flesh was 'eaten by savages' the day before he was to depart Germany (1938, 25, 42–3, 54, 85, 100, 115, 144–5, 183, 188, 191).

Walter Benjamin wrote that 'what completes the isolation of Germany in the eyes of other Europeans . . . is the violence . . . with which circumstances, squalor, and stupidity here subjugate people entirely to collective forces, as the lives of savages alone are subjected to tribal laws' (1986 [1928], 73). This (racist?) equation of Germans and 'savages' now found expression in Usikota's picturesque travel narrative, in which Nazi rogues and villains turn out to be more savage than the supposed savage himself. The Nazi idea of 'blood and soil' as the wellspring of a purified and tribal Volk put the emphasis on sessility, territory, and place. In Usikota's narrative, the solid 'huts' of Germany, its forests, rivers, and mountains, created a cumulative picture of a people nested, fortress-like, in their primeval homeland. Yet it is worth pointing out that for foreigners as well as for Germans themselves, the impression of 'rootedness' and national stability was gained to a significant degree through movement and travel. This was obvious in the case of the Zulu reporter, but it applied as well to the people he encountered, who were constantly on the move in demonstrations, marches, nature hikes, tours by auto, train, and ship, festivals, torchlight processions, village celebrations, and hunting expeditions. Germans acquired the reputation of being a peripatetic people, so much so that an American travelogue joked that 'every German infant' was born with a hikers' knapsack on its back (Van Til 1938, 18). In Germany in the 1920s and 1930s, leisure travel in fact lost its elite and middle-class character and began to assume the form of an emergent mass tourism. Nazism played a role in this transformation, although it was more qualitative than quantitative. Tourism increased by only between 10 and 15 percent from the Weimar Republic to the Nazi regime. Rather than bringing about a sharp break with the past, Nazism furthered a gradual secular rise in tourism that, despite two world wars and the depression, characterized the whole period from 1913 to the mid-1950s (Keitz 1997, 214–15).

What was significant about the Third Reich was that this secular development was given new political meaning, as the culture of travel was reformulated to meet Nazi ideological goals. Every member of the 'people's community,' the *Volksgemeinschaft*, was to have the right to travel for leisure purposes. But neither liberal values nor modernist sexuality, neither gender nor class, were to be the defining moments of the National Socialist travel culture. Instead, race determined the boundaries and the possibilities of the nation, and hence the experiences and expectations of revolutionized leisure. The impetus of the new synthesis was deeply democratic, but paradoxically so because its many enemies were to be deprived not only of free movement but of their personalities and (if need be) their lives as well. It was claimed to be 'totalistic' because it presupposed that the distance between leisure and politics was to be demolished. Indeed, from the point of view of the regime's ideological goals, leisure was more important to politics than ever before. The 'construction of the Reich' could not take place successfully only in the sphere of labor, argued the Nazi editor to a glossily done collection of essays and photographs entitled *The Volk after Work*. Much more crucial was that part of life in which the Volk comrade understood the duty to be fulfilled 'toward himself, his family as a core cell of the new state, toward his Volk, and toward voluntarily and freely chosen authority.' Since one's national duty could be realized 'only outside the occupational labor of the individual Volk comrade,' the sphere of leisure, 'free time,' consumption, and travel assumed an unprecedented importance in the new order of things (Müller-Gaisberg 1936, 10).

As for foreign visitors, they were encouraged, like Usikota, to get a firsthand perspective on the positive conditions brought about by the new regime. They were invited, as the state tourist agency's 1938 motto put it, to 'travel in happy Germany,' where 'joy' was the 'guide and teacher in tourist questions' (Esser 1938, 4). They were encouraged to look closely at the happiness with which Germans went about their daily chores. A Deutsche Lufthansa advertisement from 1938 also peddled 'joy,' as it appealed to foreign guests with the slogan 'Visit Happy Germany.' It presented its case with a large map of the country in which a photomontage of Germans from a variety of social backgrounds could be seen. From sailors in the north to Bavarian peasants dressed in traditional garb in the south, from Hitler receiving a joyous crowd of young women in central Germany to a crowd shot of swastika-bedecked faithful around Munich, the map presented a gleaming picture of a satisfied nation ('Besucht' 1938). But joy was a Janus-faced phenomenon in the Nazi travel culture. Its one side referred to the tendency of expanding the leisure capital of larger and larger groups of people, a goal toward which all industrial nations also worked. No less than in the democracies, leisure was on its way to being an *individual* right, even a kind of entitlement, in Nazi Germany. But the other side spoke to the collective barbarity, indeed the political cannibalism that finally did in the unlucky Zulu traveler. Scholars emphasize this duality of National Socialist culture, but their studies focus on everyday leisure only to a limited extent. In this chapter, the reciprocal identification of normality and abnormality, of pleasure and savagery, of movement and 'roots,' will be examined through the lens of tourist literature.

## II

The automobile was the primary symbol of that mobile sessility that framed the new travel culture. From the beginning of his Chancellorship, Hitler announced his vision of a nation on wheels in which a vast network of modern highways enabled Germans to drive affordable vehicles not for commuting to work but for vacations and weekend outings. 'So long as the automobile remains only a means of transportation for . . . privileged circles,' he said in 1934, 'it is with bitter feelings that we see millions of honest, hardworking, and capable fellowmen . . . cut off from the use of a vehicle which would be a special source of yet-unknown happiness to them, particularly on Sundays and holidays.' The Chancellor insisted on finding a solution, saying that 'one must have the courage to grasp this problem in a decided and comprehensive manner. What will not be possible in one year will, perhaps, prove to be a commonplace fact ten years hence' (Nelson 1965, 35–6).

The military motivations underlying Hitler's vision cannot be discounted, of course. The technical possibilities of the compact car, or *Kleinauto*, became apparent behind the lines in World War I, and the military was already looking ahead to the next war in the 1920s. In 1930 the Reichswehr devised a mobilization plan that called for the seizure of 100,000 private automobiles to transport 300,000 troops (Möser 1998, 209, 221). Small, nimble, and fuel-efficient cars were precisely the kind of transport needed by a mobile army. Numerous designers and engineers, not the least Ferdinand Porsche, later the creator of the Volkswagen, called for an affordable, efficient small car as well. Opel, the market leader in small- and medium-sized cars in Germany, had both the technical and financial means to produce a 'people's car,' and in fact its Opel Kadett possessed many of the features (compactness, affordability, versatility) that the Volkswagen would later incorporate and perfect. But Opel was a 'foreign' firm, bought by General Motors in 1929, and political obstacles lay in the way of its manufacturing a car for the German masses (Ortlinghaus 1996, 55–8). Against this backdrop of possibilities, Hitler's vision resonated more widely than that of his contemporaries, partly because he was in a position to put the state's power behind it.

The *Autobahn* program was central to Hitler's fantasy of German automobility (Sachs 1984, 48–55). Here too the Reich Chancellor stepped into a context full of opportunities. The country's first superhighway, the Avus in Berlin, was planned in 1909 and opened to traffic in 1921. It became an important tourist sensation and a signature of the fast-moving, gleaming modernity of the German capital. Mussolini opened up the first major stretch of his nation's *autostrada* in 1924, and Italian travel guidebooks, brimming with patriotic pride, encouraged their readers to drive the roads issuing from the 'grand work realized by the Fascist regime' (Touring Club Italiano 1939, 12). German travel agencies, city administrations, and automobile clubs agitated for more and faster roads well before Hitler trod the political stage. Building on such precedents, the Autobahn project made great progress under Hitler, creating some 3,800 kilometers of roads and constructing 9,000 bridges. Impressive though this was, it fell far short of the planned 7,000 kilometers. Autobahn construction put many unemployed to work, but here too the target numbers were never approached, and the pay and housing conditions of the laborers were abysmal.

Even so, not only did the new network of roads enable millions of tourists to get around inside Germany more easily than ever before, but it also helped to represent the new travel culture to itself and the outside world. The Autobahn's promoters argued that the aesthetics of the 'liberal age' no longer applied in the building of the new superhighways. The liberal age cared only for technological solutions and profits. The age of the Autobahn, by contrast, integrated beauty into all design decisions, making the engineer as much of an artist as the architect was. Autobahn bridges were designed with such distinctions in mind; they forsook the tall steel or wooden arches of the railways, the symbol of the liberal culture of the nineteenth century, in favor of low-slung side rails that created an almost seamless image between the bridge and the road for passengers. Commentators remarked, and not without a hint of criticism, that the motorist barely perceived he was traveling over a river or a valley when driving on the new Autobahn bridges (Schütz and Gruber 1996, 7–13, 100–101). Nonetheless, the Autobahn was quickly turning Germany into 'the motorists' paradise,' according to the state agency promoting tourist travel. 'A new traffic era is beginning,' read an agency publication, 'and a new culture arises.' This culture depended on a blending of 'technology, art, and nature' that gave tourism 'a new romance of fantastic beauty' (Reismann 1939, 5). Concrete romanticism did not preclude practicality and comfort, however. 'Comfortable motoring' was the goal of the German government, another state publication told American travelers, who were assured they could buy American gasoline at most German filling stations (Reichsbahnzentrale für den Deutschen Reiseverkehr 1934, 18–19). The new travel culture, nationalistic to the core, did not preclude the use of 'foreign' blandishments to attract capital from free-spending American tourists.

As for the German automobile industry, the progress made from 1933 to 1939 seemed impressive, with automobile production increasing more than sixfold. Looking back at the five years that had passed since Hitler's first major speech on the motorized nation, delivered at the annual Berlin Auto Show in February 1933, a publication of the Reich Committee for Tourist Travel saw the matter in glowing terms. It stated that 'the German motor industry has experienced an expansion which at that time was generally thought impossible' (Küke 1938, 4). This triumphalism was for the consumption of foreign guests. But readers of the trilingual (English, French, and Spanish) publications of the Reich Committee who looked more closely would have found that the US still contained 24 times as many cars as Germany did even though its population was only twice as large. In addition, most cars in Germany were expensive, their upkeep was financially prohibitive, and only the middle and upper strata could afford them. This was neither changeable nor regrettable from the point of view of some. Representing the 'elitist' strand of German car cultures, the head of BMW felt that not every German needed an automobile; mass transit would work for most people, or motorcycles, per capita ownership of which was as high in Germany as in Britain in 1932 (Möser 1998, 210; Ortlinghaus 1996, 9).

Even so, the culture of automobility was at home in Germany. It was not quite the way Nazi propaganda put it, namely that 'the enthusiasm for motoring has indeed taken hold of all classes of the German people' ('A Summary' 1939, 1). But there was a general public interest radiating well beyond those who owned automobiles. Among the consumers were children, who 'drove' around Germany's expanding Autobahn system in a popular board game with colorful landscapes

*Figure 10   Advertisement for the 1938 German automobile show (author's collection).*

(Falkenberg 1991, 289–90). Automobile magazines such as the *Allgemeine Automobil Zeitung* featured regular articles on the newest designs, automobile maintenance and travel routes, and surveys of readers' opinions and letters to the editor. Readers opined that Germany had failed to produce a sports car matching the power and maneuverability of Italian designs, and that German drivers needed lighter, more powerful, and streamlined cars that took advantage of the burgeoning road system ('Der Sportwagen' 1936, 11–14; 'Der Wagen für die Autobahn' 1936, 8–13). Articles on 'The Automobile from Front to Back' educated readers about the workings and care of each part of the car ('Das Auto von vorn bis hinten' 1936, 13). Women readers received advice on what cosmetics to wear while on motoring tours (von Stein 1936, 26–7). The camping movement, normally regarded as a product of the 1950s in Germany, was the subject of one feature (Thero 1937, 1026–8). And the Berlin automobile show gained thorough and at times critical attention from contributors, who bemoaned the conservatism of German auto design (Kapitän Nemo 1936, 12–15). The 1936 Berlin auto show attracted more than 800,000 visitors, and the 1937 guide to the exhibit noted that the affair had become a popular tourist attraction. More than 30 countries were represented among the visitors to the 1939 show, including every European country. For Germans, too, the auto show was part tourist outing and, for those who dreamed of buying a car, part shopping expedition (Reichsverband der Automobilindustrie 1937; 'A Summary' 1939, 2; Müller-Gaisberg 1936, 284–5).

Hitler's idea of German automobility looked beyond all this, nonetheless. What would later be known as the 'people's car,' the Volkswagen, was to operate on a vast network of inter-local auto routes through which Germans from all social levels would get to know their country. The Volkswagen had a military rationale, but it was also the product of 'perhaps the largest single state-planned project promoting consumerism in Germany' (Möser 1998, 219). Supplied with capital by the German Labor Front, the Strength through Joy organization (*Kraft durch Freude*, or KdF) took command of the project. The VW would be known as the 'Strength through Joy Car,' or KdF-Wagen, even though its registered name was *Deutscher Volkswagen*. Using a sophisticated advertising campaign, Strength through Joy mobilized about 300,000 Germans to enlist in a lay-away savings program. Contributing a minimum of 5 marks a month entitled certificate holders only to be eligible for a car; it did not guarantee them an automobile at the end of the process. No interest was given on the savings program, and there was no guarantee of a full refund if the car was not delivered. The Volkswagen was indeed *not* delivered during the Third Reich, although a giant plant near Fallersleben (now Wolfsburg), envisioned as the biggest automobile plant in the world, was begun with great fanfare in 1938. It eventually used thousands of slave laborers to produce military vehicles during World War II.

The social utopia of automobility envisioned by KdF planners had significant limits. The automobile savings program was entirely voluntary, and in fact German consumers demonstrated much reticence about it in the face of regime propaganda and daily pressure from party officials and employers. Only one-quarter of the Volkswagen plant administrative staff contributed to the lay-away scheme. Nazi officials initially hoped they could link the savings program to a broad campaign of obligatory driver education, but this proved unworkable given the need to mobilize as many savers as possible. It was not the German worker who put his hard-earned marks into the savings plan, moreover, but rather members of the middle strata. Workers made up at best just 5 percent of the total number. The people's car campaigners stated publicly that they wanted to harness first-time car owners, but this goal was achieved only to a limited degree, as about two-thirds of VW customers planned to buy their first automobiles (Mommsen and Grieger 1996, 179–202).

Nonetheless, the German travel culture was as much about what could be as about 'real existing leisure.' This was clear from the way in which travel guidebooks resonated with the imagery of a motorized nation. They were never as effusive as the Nazi tourist publication that, after describing a motoring tour in a wintry landscape, exclaimed 'we are once again at peace with God and the world' (Müller-Gaisberg 1936, 286). But they embraced the culture of automobility fully. Although tour books included brief tips for motorists before World War I, such information now became a central element in itineraries as automobility was connected with access, authenticity, and even anti-tourism. Arguing that the tourist was now compelled to use the automobile, the Satchel guide to Europe (Crockett and Crockett 1933, xxxiv) stated that 'In no other way, can the *real* Europe—the Europe that is seldom apparent in tourist centers—be seen to the best advantage.' Given that annually more than 130,000 tourists' automobiles entered Germany, this statement no doubt found willing listeners—all the more so because they found parking: Berlin was known as one of the few big cities in which parking places were readily available (Hauser 1939, 8; Küke 1934, 1:24). The Baedeker guidebooks registered the advance of the new highways in the German landscape. The 1938 guide to the Tyrol, after recognizing Hitler's 'world-historical act' bringing Austria into a Greater Germany, also gave readers detailed information on plans for the extension of the Autobahn from Munich to Rosenheim, Reichenhall, Salzburg, Linz, and eventually Vienna (Baedeker 1938, v, xxiii). In the same year, travelers could purchase a Baedeker to the nation oriented specifically to automobile tourism and co-sponsored by the German Automobile Club. It too took full account of the burgeoning superhighway network, maintaining that 'the automobile traveler can get to know Germany today in a way that was inconceivable two decades ago' (Steinheil 1938, 5). The Grieben guide to the 'Eastern March' spoke of Hitler's 'world-historical act' just as proudly as the Baedeker did, and in a detailed appendix on automobile touring in Austria it noted that the Alpine terrain made it 'of particular interest for the motorist' (1939, 267). Guidebooks failing to measure up to the new culture of automobility—such as the Meyer series and even Baedekers of the earlier 1930s—could count on criticism from tourist industry publications (Review 1930a, 3:142; Review 1931b, 2:64).

The new road system was a subsidiary corporation of the German State Railways, and the Hitler regime tried to balance road, rail, air, and water transport. Even so, the German railways appeared to be on the defensive. A cartoon from *Simplicissimus* in 1930 likened the railways to a destitute war veteran in the Depression. Standing next to a superhighway with automobiles rushing by, the beggar, with a train locomotive for a head, supported himself on a crutch while holding out a hat and saying 'I too have seen better times' (Schütz and Gruber 1996, 15). It was not only automobiles but also omnibus companies and light motorcycles that competed for the leisure traveler's allegiances. Part of the problem, too, was outmoded infrastructure. 'It is still true that in some parts of Germany travelers are as a rule glad to be seated at last in the train which is to take them out of a dismal, dark, smoky railway station into the pleasant countryside,' read a Reichsbahn publication. This situation was to be improved with brighter, more architecturally up-to-date train stations in Düsseldorf, Duisburg, Oberhausen, Nuremberg, and Stuttgart (Happ 1938, 20).

New train stations could not address the overall impression that auto and bus travel was cleaner, more efficient, and more adaptable to individual tourist needs. Nor could they relieve the pressure on the Reichsbahn's profit margins, eaten away further by discounted rail prices given to the Nazi party's leisure organization. Nonetheless, the railway remained an important mode of travel. After the Depression, the number of railway passengers declined to a level below that of the pre-World War I era, but rail traffic slowly picked up, and in 1937 volume exceeded that of 1913 once again. Travelers were offered vacation packages at discounts of up to 60 percent, and big families received reduced prices for tourist outings. Foreign guests were made similarly attractive offers including reduced ticket fares, good exchange rates, and lowered visa fees. The upward trend continued in the next two years, but it is difficult to separate tourist from military travel for 1938/9, when the annexation of Austria and mobilization for World War II increased train use (Petzina et al. 1978, 68; Keitz 1997, 224–6; Schwarz 1993b, 91). Only better-off European and American travelers would realize the vision of a motorized world in the 1930s, in any case, and the airplane was limited to an even smaller group of travelers. The majority of those who traveled any distance from home still used the trains and would continue to until well after World War II. The railway, stated one Nazi publication, still provided 'the cheapest accommodations' and 'the most reliable means of long-distance transportation' (Müller-Gaisberg 1936, 274).

If the KdF promoted the idea of individual automobility, the bulk of its energies in the realm of tourism were devoted to mass action. Modeled on the Italian Fascist leisure agency, *Dopolavoro*, and designed to raise the productivity and political loyalty of workers, Strength through Joy undertook campaigns to create healthier, more beautiful factories and offices, and it provided cheap, organized weekend tours to the countryside, the mountains, or historic cities. It organized two-week package ship cruises to Italy, Portugal, the Portuguese island of Madeira, Yugoslavia, and Norway, and in 1936 it began to build giant vacation complexes such as the never-completed Prora resort on Rügen island on the Baltic Sea, designed to accommodate 20,000 individuals. Soon the largest travel agency in Germany, the organization managed it all with great flair, advertising its successes and using testimonials from individual workers to make a claim for the egalitarian character of the enterprise. 'It was really all splendid and made no end of impressions on me, beginning with the voyage with my fellow-workers,' one KdF tourist to Madeira was quoted as saying. 'It was the first long voyage any of us had ever made in our lives. And to think that there were thousands of us on three huge ocean liners—it just shows what can be done when everybody lends a hand' (Moes 1935, 26).

At its height in 1936, the KdF accounted for nearly 10 million overnight stays in German hotels, more than 11 percent of all overnight stays that year (Spode 1982, 299). So enormous were its demands on the German rail system that the Reichsbahn was forced to deploy outmoded, fourth-class rail cars to handle the overload. Still, the actual practices of the organization worked against the rhetoric of equality and 'massification.' Not only did more white-collar workers than manual laborers take advantage of KdF tours, which remained beyond the financial means of many workers, but the regime, often in conjunction with participating businesses, also used Kraft durch Freude tourism to reward 'selected' workers and employees with special discounts, free vacations, and extended leisure time. This reintroduced hierarchies of privileged access to leisure rather than lessening differences between workers. As before 1933, and despite regime rhetoric of the 'touristic emancipation of the worker,' no general legislation existed to regulate paid vacations for all laborers (Keitz 1997, 215–23, 226).

The KdF theoretically offered workers and employees a chance to visit parts of the homeland to which they never had access. This meant that regions still not exploited fully by the private travel industry could be brought into the tourism market, including East Prussia, Masuria, and the economically depressed Eifel region in western Germany (Pasewaldt 1938, 508–9). These were also border regions that had special political significance for the regime as national hostilities heightened before World War II. The KdF was in a position to mobilize parts of the population, workers in particular, that never before traveled for leisure, or that traveled only infrequently. Incorporating the worker in the racial community depended on circulation and interaction between workers and between workers and other members of the Volksgemeinschaft. A 1937 KdF guidebook explicitly noted that KdF tourists were strangers: 'Whoever travels with Kraft durch Freude doesn't know his travel companions so well. One may come from a factory in the north, another from a bakery in the south. The third comes from a workshop, and the fourth was unemployed a few years ago' (Schulz-Luckau 1937, 10). On KdF boat tours, long amounts of time were spent on ship with individuals one had just met in group singing, calisthenics, and propaganda sessions. The journey itself was a contact zone just as much as or even more than the destination was.

The journey did not always run smoothly, as the Swiss writer Jakob Schaffner, a sympathetic participant in two KdF tours, reported in 1936. KdF touring was not yet perfected, argued Schaffner, and it was not always 'comfortable' to experience the sometimes rough and ready accommodations one found on KdF ships (1936, 12–13, 21). Critics argued that KdF tourists were forced to take part in ideologically correct calisthenics and social events. It was said that workers, who always constituted a tiny percentage of Strength through Joy tour participants, were envious of the middle-class KdF travelers with whom they came into contact. Some observers noted that the Kraft durch Freude vacations took little account of the actual physical capacities of participants, who were at risk because of poor health or special medical needs. Families with small children got short shrift as well, and the KdF plan to build massive resort spas like the Prora development was a tacit admission that the charge was true. The Prora complex was designed to have large apartments, bathing facilities, and dining halls appropriate to the needs of families as well as singles. Supporters called it the 'Eldorado of the vacationing family.' Finally, friction between hotel or restaurant owners and KdF tourists was a frequent occurrence (Kahl 1940, 22–36, 63; Spode 1980, 304).

If the people's car represented individuality, the KdF tours were based on a collective concept of travel in which the Nazi ideological message theoretically carried the day. This gave it a point of commonality with the socialist and Communist travel cultures of the Weimar era. Even so, KdF propagandists made a point of saying, partly in answer to critics who complained of overcrowding and mass organization, that 'every individual, regardless of where he travels, can always do and act as he pleases at his destination' (Kahl 1940, 24). This opened the door to a degree of individual flexibility. The point is reinforced if it is remembered that many KdF tourists traveled individually or with families in the 1920s and most likely chose group tours with the Nazi agency for economic rather than ideological reasons. They were accustomed to a degree of personal latitude during their vacations, as all good Baedekerites were. Baranowski's evidence (2000) suggests 'an individualist search for pleasure and self-fulfillment' in which KdF tourists 'drank to excess, danced, played games, flirted, and made love in the lifeboats after the sun went down.' In short, they acted much like the 'unorganized' German tourists American kayakers encountered on the Moselle, Elbe, and Danube: 'With the young folk on the rivers the sex bars are down and the gentlest passion is definitely a catch-as-catch-can pastime' (Van Til 1938, 83).

Considered against the broader development of tourism from 1933 to 1939, individual or familial travel was the norm. From short Sunday outings *ins Grüne* to the ever increasing number of package excursions by private travel agencies (Hauser 1939, 15; Keitz 1997, 223–33), the individual remained at the center of the Nazi travel culture. The individualizing coordinates of tourism were deftly caricatured in a *Simplicissimus* cartoon layout by Karl Arnold entitled 'Preparations for Vacation and Travel' (1938, 294–5). In one of the cartoons, a young woman leans over the counter of a travel bureau. 'And do you know,' she asks, 'what the temperature of the water is in Wolfgangsee from the third to the eighteenth of August?' Another question about picnic spots on the Autobahn makes the same point: that individual tourists had become quite precise in their planning and

*Figure 11   Miniature golf on the Hapag steamer 'Resolute' (Reich Committee for Tourist*
*Travel, Germany [July 1934]: 3).*

unusually demanding about getting the right information. The author of a guidebook to less publicized tourist regions of Germany approached the issue in a related
way, writing that whoever travels 'with heart and feeling' will reach the same
conclusion he did: that the discovery of 'unknown Germany' is a highly individual
matter (Zeddies 1937).

The main effect the Nazi regime had on such 'normal' tourism was to redirect
more travel inward toward the homeland, including those 'unknown' parts off the
beaten track. Currency restrictions did much to strengthen this tendency, as
Germans were able to take very small amounts of German marks out of the country;
before Germany's takeover of Austria every German visiting that country except

business and commercial travelers paid a Reich tax of 1,000 marks. But the inward-looking movement was also a continuation of earlier trends. The national rail agency had begun issuing 'German travel booklets,' or *Deutsche Verkehrsbücher*, after World War I in cooperation with the provincial travel bureaus. These handy booklets included high-quality photography and a map for selected tourist regions. Their covers carried color drawings by established German artists. By 1934, the series was producing over a million books a year (Winter 1935, 1072). In addition to these booklets, the Reich rail agency distributed posters, illustrations for magazines and newspapers, and films. And despite economic difficulties, the Baedeker remained an indispensable element of the travel culture. Even a heavily ideological Nazi publication on tourism noted that preparations for a vacation always included close reading of the Baedeker guide (Müller-Gaisberg 1936, 262). The image of the diligent tourist silently reading his or her guidebook reinforces the idea of the essentially private and personal nature of preparation for the well-organized leisure outing.

The secular development of tourism suggested continuity with the past, which in turn found expression in tourist guidebooks. Guidebook itineraries still focused on the standard fare of monuments, museums, natural environments, and scenic towns. Addresses of Nazi party offices, Nazi-inspired architectural landmarks such as the redesigned Königsplatz in Munich, and the Autobahn became 'naturalized' elements of the tourist experience. Scenes of Nazi party history also found their place in the mainstream guides. The Baedeker led visitors to the Hofbräuhaus in Munich, described—in small print—as the place where Hitler first announced the Nazi party program in 1920. At the Feldherrnhalle, they were instructed to see a monument to the martyrs of the 1923 Nazi putsch, and advised parenthetically that passersby were obligated to give the 'Hitler greeting.' (They were not told that many local people, avoiding the annoyance of saluting as they walked or rode by, found alternative routes around the Feldherrnhalle [Koshar 2000, 117].) Tourists in Obersalzberg were directed to see the 'stately mountain retreat' of Adolf Hitler (Baedeker 1938, 6, 35). But all such information was nested in a broader stream of information, in typically encyclopedic form, that did more to reduce the impact the new regime had on the tourist landscape than to place it in the foreground. The stunning normality of it all came through most strongly.

For those Germans still lucky enough to travel abroad individually, meanwhile, countries such as Italy remained important as tourist destinations. At the end of the 1920s, 300,000 German tourists went to Italy annually, making up one quarter of all foreign tourists in that country. Germans were the single largest group of tourists from abroad in Italy, followed at a considerable distance by North Americans, who accounted for almost 17 percent of the total (Mariotti 1932, 4:110). For the KdF, Italy was a favored destination as well; in 1939 before the start of World War II, 145,000 Strength through Joy tourists visited the southern peninsula,

*Figure 12 A honeymoon in the south (Drawing by Erich Schilling, Simplicissimus 43, 16 [24 April 1938]: 187).*

as Mandel (1996, 149) points out. But Mandel (149–50) also notes that the Italian state travel agency ENITEA (Ente Nazionale Industrie Turistische e Alberghiere) advertised heavily in Germany, appealing above all not to groups but to individuals traveling by rail.

ENITEA was only the most visible element of a much broader push on the part of the Italian state, provinces, and cities to improve tourist accommodations in Italy and also to make propaganda for the regime among foreign tourists (Cavazza 1993; Trova 1993). The program bore fruit, especially among the more educated or well-to-do strata. Air travel between Berlin and Rome more than doubled between 1933 and 1937 in terms of the number of passengers booked by Deutsche

Lufthansa. No other Lufthansa route out of Berlin to a foreign city save for one was more popular in 1938 (Statistisches Reichsamt 1934, 171; 1938, 244). Since air travel was still a luxury for most Germans, this increase must be attributed to the upper classes, not the middle and lower strata of KdF tourism. Intellectuals also strengthened the trend, aided in part by a 1938 cultural agreement exchanging teachers and students between Italy and Germany (Petersen 1988). Among German writers and novelists, there was a 'rediscovery of the Mediterranean,' a tendency that had little to do with interest in Mussolini. For some younger German literati, Italy (as well as Greece) represented not the bright future of fascism but German engagement with classical Western culture, an engagement strong since the eighteenth century. The two perspectives were by no means mutually exclusive, but a continued adherence to the classical world could be expressed outside the political context of the time (Graf 1995, 324–35).

Travel to Germany from abroad flourished in the prewar years of the Nazi regime, to G due partly to the efforts of the Reich Committee for Foreign Travel, founded in June 1933. 'Foreign tourists have once again flocked to Germany in increasing thousands,' stated the Satchel Guide in the first year of Hitler's rule; by 1938 the number of foreign tourists in Germany was more than double what it had been in 1931 (Crockett and Crockett 1933, 197; Schwarz 1993b, 101). The proportion of American visitors to Germany hovered around one-tenth of all foreign visitors from 1934 to 1937, although in absolute terms American stays in Germany doubled in this time span (Statistisches Reichsamt 1934, 53; 1938, 74). The proportion of English citizens among foreign tourists to Germany also rose dramatically, increasing to nearly 19 percent in 1936/7 compared to less than 7 percent five years before. Some British travelers responded to impressive advertising from the German railways, including a spread in *The Times* that read: 'See Germany for yourself. You will find truth in personal contacts. A hearty welcome awaits you' (Schwarz 1993b, 93). The well-organized youth hostel system in Germany continued not only to draw travelers from abroad but also inspired emulation, as similarly structured youth hostel associations were formed in England, Switzerland, and Scandinavia (Kiesel 1933, 15–23). The German travel culture continued to participate in and shape international developments in leisure despite the regime's insistence on national singularity.

Foreign travel in Germany increased partly because of Hitler's interest in appealing to foreign opinion. He was concerned that the foreign reactions to his violent consolidation of power and the boycott of Jewish businesses would ruin Germany's international status and deprive the country of important income. 'It is certainly not exceptional,' wrote Reich travel bureau director Hans-Gert Winter of his correspondence with potential tourists, 'that men and women inquire if they need to bring a revolver on their vacation to Germany!' (1935, 1083). Tourism policy makers referred again and again to the Nazi regime's peaceful aims and represented leisure travel as a primary means of achieving stability between nations. Tourism 'is valuable from the view of foreign policy in that it furthers understanding in the world and thus prepares the path leading to the attainment of the noblest aim of humanity: peace amongst nations,' wrote Hitler's state secretary for tourism, Hermann Esser (Reichsfremdenverkehrsverband 1938, n.p.).

England was a linchpin of Germany's attempt to normalize its image in the light of Hitler's desire to forge Anglo-German cooperation. It was important to demonstrate that the economic crises of the Weimar era were overcome, that the civil strife of the last days of the Republic was ended, and that the Nazi regime wanted peace and prosperity for the Continent. Hitler sent his chief party ideologue Alfred Rosenberg to London in May 1933 'to clear up certain misconceptions which existed abroad in regard to recent events in Germany.' Acting as a political tourist, Rosenberg botched the job, inciting public criticism when he placed a swastika-bedecked wreath at the main British World War I memorial. Such gaffes did little to dampen the Nazis' desire to enhance the regime's image abroad, however, and soon there were plans afoot to bring not only British opinion makers but also ordinary tourists into Germany (Schwarz 1993b, 76–9, 93, 101). Even then, many had the impression that Americans were welcomed more openly than the English. After telling a mildly suspicious boathouse operator from Ingolstadt they were from the United States, a couple kayaking on the German Danube noted that now 'we were American, not English, and there was no accretion of hates to block his liking us' (Van Til 1938, 54).

Since its extraordinary growth in the second half of the nineteenth century, Berlin was an important symbol of German national connectivity. It had also been a leisure mecca for foreign guests, and the Nazis quickly grasped that Berlin would be an important window on the new Reich. At first severely prohibiting Berlin's ribald nightlife, the Nazi regime soon eased restrictions. By the summer of 1939, Heinrich Hauser could write that 'a craving for pleasure and a night life no less febrile than that of the past' greeted the foreigner as well as the German visitor to Berlin. Americans, Englishmen, and Frenchmen were seen less frequently in the capital, but Romanians, Hungarians, and Greeks were now more plentiful. Alcoholism and fast money characterized late 1930s Berlin, argued Hauser, who also wrote that Berlin nightclub shows were 'now nuder and more daring than those almost anywhere in the world.' A more prurient approach still obtained in provincial cities, but Berlin was different, and the new emphasis on nudity could be interpreted in terms of Nazi race policy: public displays of sexuality promoted a healthy desire to produce more babies for the fatherland (Hauser 1939, 18–19).

Berlin was also a showcase for the regime during the Olympic Games of 1936. As the Games approached, the Nazi propaganda office, headed by Josef Goebbels, regarded the event as a crucial opportunity in which the city's museums, landmarks, streets, hotel lobbies, and taxis would represent the regime to foreign travelers.

Like Hitler, Goebbels was convinced that foreign travel to Germany was essential to the legitimacy of the state, and he and other officials believed that propaganda was most effective when it was hidden or muted. In the official state guide to the 1936 exhibition 'Germany,' held in the Funkturm assembly hall in Berlin for domestic and foreign guests at the Olympic Games, visitors read that 'Germany itself is the best propaganda. It is enough to show Germany to our guests in order to free them from all prejudices' (Gemeinnützige Berliner Ausstellungs-, Messe- und Fremdenverkehrs-GmbH 1936, 11). The exhibition was designed to show visitors the essentials of the new Germany, meaning both the usual images and photographs of scenic historic towns and monuments, but also contemporary painting, architecture, photography, music, technology, science, and manufacturing. The history of the Nazi movement as well as its efforts in the fields of youth welfare, racial science, and education were also on display, but photographs of party meetings and of Hitler and other party leaders were kept to a minimum. In keeping with the overall strategy of the regime, the guide also avoided all hints of direct or violent anti-Semitism. The 'Germany' exhibit and, one year later, the 'Give Me Four Years' Time' exhibit celebrating Hitler's 1933 promise to transform the German nation, were major tourist successes, high points of a National Socialist exhibitionary strategy that has gained only sporadic attention in historical scholarship (Thamer 1998, 366).

A milestone in international sports history and a key building block of Nazi cultural politics, the 1936 Olympics in Berlin also shaped the history of leisure travel, furthering a tendency toward spectacularization that began before Hitler was born. *Olympische Spiele 1936*, a slick magazine full of sophisticated photography and advertisements for automobiles, luxury goods, and banks, whipped up enthusiasm for the games months in advance. Berlin was a 'sea of flags' during the Olympics, thanks in part to the support of German business. Even Jews were to participate in this festive cloaking of the capital, although since they were disallowed to fly party or national flags, they were supplied with Olympic flags instead. Parties and banquets took place throughout the city, as dignitaries in both the Nazi party and state agencies tried to outdo each other. The head of the International Organizing Committee, Baillet-Latour, complained that the festivals overwhelmed the main event. 'An end must be put to the endless receptions and festivals outside the Games,' he stated. But the gigantism of the entire enterprise was not to be stopped as the 'Olympic spirit' demanded more and better cultural productions. The Games were an unprecedented audio phenomenon as well, as a sophisticated radio network transmitted some 2,500 reports to Germany and abroad. Even the road construction program provided a tie-in, as 1,000 German youth group members along with 500 foreign journalists and 300 Olympic athletes were transported to the festive opening of an 85-kilometer stretch of the Berlin–Magdeburg Autobahn. All this necessitated an openness and hospitality toward foreign guests that many Berliners may have found difficult to keep up given their reputation for rough humor and sarcasm. Racial prejudice was also to be temporarily retired in this context, as businesses were instructed to show 'Jewish-looking' travelers from abroad the same courtesy they showed other guests. The regime also removed the many signs reading 'Jews not wanted' and prohibited street sales of the racist *Der Stürmer* tabloid (Schwarz 1993b, 99–100; Teichler 1976, 292–4).

The Olympic Games did not amount to an unmitigated propaganda success for the regime. The American journalist William Shirer, no admirer of German culture, wrote that 'the Nazis have put up a very good front for the general visitors, especially the big businessmen.' Well-off Americans were impressed with the Nazi 'set-up,' reported Shirer, and those granted an audience with Göring believed him when he said there was no religious persecution in the Third Reich. But US ambassador to Germany William E. Dodd, a distinguished historian and Jeffersonian democrat, thought differently, remarking that incessant propaganda had 'a bad influence on foreigners' (Shirer 1941, 65–6; Schwarz 1993b, 99). Domestically, it appears that the Games offered distraction for Germans upset by Hitler's political brinkmanship. In March 1936, Hitler had violated international treaties to remilitarize the Rhineland. The Games settled the jangled collective nerves of the nation, or so thought the French diplomat to Germany, François-Poncet. He wrote that 'fatigue from the excitement that the occupation of the Rhineland brought with it' made people willing to 'yield gladly to the anticipated release of tension' promised by the Games (quoted in Teichler 1976, 293). It is crucial to note how opposite was the reaction by German Jews. Victor Klemperer, disgusted with the propaganda messages fed to thousands of foreign tourists during the Olympics, thought the decline in open anti-Semitism could only lead to something worse. 'The Olympics will end next Sunday,' he wrote on 13 August, 'the . . . Party Rally is being heralded, an explosion is imminent, and naturally, they will first of all take things out on the Jews' (Klemperer 1998, 181). But for the majority of the 'Aryan' population, the Olympic Games worked in the same way less spectacular tourist experiences did: they normalized relations, offered a welcome alternative to political tensions, and cloaked the core violence of the regime in a highly modern and aesthetically compelling ambience.

Much the same could be said for those millions of foreign travelers in Germany throughout the prewar years. Evidence from various guidebooks suggests how their expectations were framed to situate the new regime within pre-existing tourist culture. For English and American tourists in Germany, the Baedeker guides remained essential, and the Satchel Guide did not hesitate to recommend the venerable guidebook for travelers wanting in-depth knowledge of the country (Crockett and Crockett 1933, 197, 223). There was much continuity in this regard. Other guidebooks suggest something of the way in which the new Germany's political life was addressed. The English-language Grieben guide to Berlin handled German politics of the Weimar era in one sentence: 'After the disaster of 1918 attempts were made to gather up the broken threads,—a difficult task.' At least this was not the radical condemnation of the Weimar 'system' that the Nazis regularly used. As for what came afterwards, the Grieben stated disingenuously that Hitler's first years in office 'were marked by characteristic changes in the outward aspect of the city' (1936a, 12). A humorous American guide to Berlin was uninterested in politics, but it found it difficult to take seriously the nationalist pathos of the Wilhelmine Avenue of Victory, an attitude that carried over implicitly to the scenes of Nazi power. It passed over the Moltenmarkt's famous 'house of Ephraim the Jew,' an architectural gem from the eighteenth century, without comment on the anti-Semitic persecution going on in the German capital. It got the details of the Reichstag fire wrong, attributing damage to the building to 'the conflagration which occurred in the spring of 1933, just before Hitler came to full power.' The fire occurred in February, and it is debatable as to when or whether Hitler achieved 'full power.' More telling perhaps, was the absence of any detailed discussion of the new regime or its effects in this tour book (Milton 1935, 39, 79, 81).

Such 'normality' was partly a function of the depoliticizing effects of the tourist experience. Tourists traveling in Germany were not looking for the signs of racial persecution or class warfare. Leisure demanded 'getting away from it all.' The secular transformation of tourism, now motivated more strongly than before by the desire for recreation, worked to soften the hard edges of the dictatorship. But so did conjunctural trends. Growing economic prosperity, the improvement of transportation, and the renewal of German cities made it possible to forget the political turmoil through which Germans had gone just years before—and to ignore the violent means taken to re-stabilize the country. But the image of normality was also the result of the regime's political program. To a degree impossible to measure precisely, the normality of tourism in Nazi Germany was a managed normality, an effect of totalitarian cultural politics. There were exceptions to this picture, to be sure. William and Bee Van Til, American travelers in Nazi Germany whose main interests were not political but rather boating and backpacking, were not unaware of the regime's persecution of Jews or of much surreptitious criticism of Nazism within the country. While they enjoyed idyllic days traveling by 'folding boat' (*faltboot*) on the Danube River, they did not fail to notice the 'slimy printed lies' of the German newspapers (Van Til 1938, 15–17, 28, 78–94, 105–14). Yet this travelogue, entitled *The Danube Flows through Fascism*, left the larger impression of a modern, friendly, and clean tourist country with resources that appealed to many tastes and inclinations.

The concept of managed normality overlooks the fact that tourism was 'over-determined,' a product of many different social tendencies and institutions. Many non-party organizations participated in the fashioning of a touristic imaginary that hid or counterbalanced the regime's deeper political reality. Shortly before World War II, the State Railways produced a slick color brochure entitled 'On the German People and their Culture.' A celebration of the regional diversity of the country, the brochure featured German peasants dancing, 'traditional' peasant costumes (*Trachten*), scenic thatched-roof homes, and idyllic small towns nestled in green valleys or at the foot of snow-capped mountains. The scenes enticed the German traveler to see his or her homeland, rich in folklore, traditional cuisine, and solid peasant values. Were it not for the small swastika on the cover and the Nazi flag on the last page, both skillfully integrated so as not to alter the ambience of rural authenticity, it would have been difficult to tell that the brochure was produced in the Third Reich. The approach was sophisticated, the presentation highly modern. The concluding paragraph put Germany in the middle of Europe: 'The German looks around in the world and recognizes without envy the accomplishments of other peoples. Just toward other nations, proud of his fatherland in the heart of Europe, he has earned the right to be called a carrier of progressive civilization and a representative of European culture. Whoever gets to know the land of the Germans, will respect it, whoever lives in it, will love it even more' (Reichsbahn-zentrale, 'Vom Deutschen Menschen,' n.d.). Here Nazism appeared to follow the culture rather than manage it, to emerge from a centuries-long tradition rather than to revolutionize society. Yet the regime wanted to use tourism to promote an image of peace-loving Germany, at ease with itself and respectful toward others. The folkloristic scenes, the brightly colored pictures of peasant costumes, folk dances, and frothy beer mugs linked up with a totalitarian cultural politics whose strength was the normality with which it could be represented in the 'land of the Germans.'

## III

What was at was at the core of the Nazi travel culture, the other side of the 'joy' evoked in Autobahn travel, Kdf tours, the Olympic Games, and everyday tourism? To gain a deeper appreciation of this dimension, it is useful to turn to a 1937 guide to Berlin written by Julius Karl von Engelbrechten and Hans Volz, two members of the paramilitary SA, or *Sturmabteilung*. Entitled *We Ramble through National Socialist Berlin*, the book transformed the metropolis into a Nazi psychotopography in which the history of the Nazi movement, its street battles and key meeting places, its memorials and sites of martyrdom, were laid out in 275 pages of detailed itineraries.

The guidebook was part of a broader development whereby the Nazi movement created a memory of itself and memorialized its martyrs in a ritualized and quasi-religious 'cult of death' (Baird 1990; Koshar 2000, 127–8). It is important to note

*Figure 13    Peasant dancing in folkloristic Germany (cover to Reich Committee for
         Tourist Traffic, Germany [June 1938]).*

that this macabre memory-work had important commercial dimensions as Nazi
history reached a wider public in postcards, souvenirs, memoirs, film, radio, and
numerous illustrated books. SA postcards depicting the humiliation of former
Social Democratic politicians appeared soon after the Nazi seizure of power. One
postcard from Chemnitz depicted two SA men cutting a swastika into the hair of a
Jewish man. Its caption read: 'Clean-up action in Chemnitz' (*Braunbuch* 1978
[1933], 249, 298). The party's propaganda minister and Berlin district chief
(*Gauleiter*) Josef Goebbels had published a history of Nazism in the capital, and
Engelbrechten himself published a chronicle of the Berlin–Brandenburg SA the
same year that the guide appeared. After 1934, when the Nazis purged the SA and
executed its leader Ernst Röhm, the SA rewrote its own history to emphasize

*Figure 14    The cover to* We Ramble through National Socialist Berlin *(Engelbrechten and Volz 1937).*

respectability, both political and moral (Mosse 1985, 159). The SA guidebook to Berlin was thus one aspect of a process of commercialization and marketing of Nazi history and terror. Not to be overlooked is that such memorabilia was bought and presumably 'enjoyed' individually.

The book used the more populist term 'ramble' (*wandern*), which befit the plebeian character of the SA and linked it to a tradition of working-class, youth group, and artisan travel. Carrying the subtitle *A Guide through the Landmarks of the Struggle over the Reich Capital*, it portrayed Berlin as the front line in the battle between Communism and Nazism. It quoted Hitler's description of the last weeks of 1932 in which Germany stood 'a hair's breadth from the brink of Bolshevik chaos.' And it noted that the Berlin party took the full force of the struggle, losing 'almost fifty' comrades to street violence. This number was rather low, of course, and it reflects the fact that despite Nazism's revolutionary rhetoric, its rise to power was a relatively contained affair, just as its assault on the state was modulated if not controlled. But the guide's creators did not want to go into this aspect of the movement's history; instead, they argued that Berlin deserved special attention in party memory because it was the site of the 'bitterest struggle over power' in the Weimar era (Engelbrechten and Volz 1937, 7). It achieved this status because National Socialism had made it a central goal to penetrate the Berlin districts in which the Communist party was strong. The audacity of this effort should not be overlooked: in early 1928 the Berlin SA numbered only about 800 compared to 11,000 in the Communist paramilitary group, the Red Front-fighters' League (Rosenhaft 1983, 19).

Despite the existence of other Nazi literature on Berlin, no synthetic guidebook to the sites of SA and party history existed for the city in 1937. The special problems of assembling such a publication were noted. 'A big part of the information comes from oral reports and representations, which are based solely on memory,' read the preface. This meant that errors or oversights were likely to have crept into the text, and the authors invited readers to contact the SA if they had corrections. We have noted that since the nineteenth century commercial guidebooks also rested on this interaction with readers. But this suggested a larger issue as well. The guide was to have not only 'practical worth,' argued the authors, but also 'historical importance.' Given the many 'changes to which the landmarks were exposed' since 1933, many of the *Sturmlokale*, the pubs and taverns favored by the SA, could no longer be found, or their names were changed due to new ownership. The topography of Nazi conquest was also being transformed by ambitious regime plans for the urban renewal of Berlin, which in Hitler's vision would be renamed Germania, the center of a global racial empire. This urban renewal project included getting rid of many sites of the former Communist party's activity. 'Thus it was important,' wrote the authors, 'to capture these things in word and image, since after the passage of a few years, it might not be possible at all, or it might be possible only with the greatest effort, to verify the precise location of the relevant sites.' One cannot disregard the fact that the SA itself was a victim of changes within the Nazi movement. It had been the target of a bloody coup on 30 June 1934, as Hitler paid tribute to a conservative military that feared the SA as a radical people's army. As many as 200 SA leaders and members were killed in the purge— far more than were killed in the struggle against red Berlin. The purge reduced the organization to a second-line propaganda group within the movement. This event found no mention at all in the chronology of Nazi party history included as introductory material in the guidebook. The sense of having little time to establish its place in National Socialist memory may therefore have been an additional spur to assembling the disparate pieces of the story of the SA's struggle. The sense of urgency was palpable as readers were alerted that the guide was there 'to memorialize the dead, to admonish the living, and to keep vigilant the memory of a difficult time, that of the struggle over red Berlin' (Engelbrechten and Volz 1937, 8–9).

In formal terms, the guidebook was a true hybrid. On one level, it followed well-established conventions of the genre. The authors divided up the city according to accepted guidebook models, leading the individual tourist from the western and eastern section of the historic inner city to surrounding suburbs and peripheries, and then finally beyond the city borders. They interspersed 60 photographs and 30 maps with practical information on opening times for museums and galleries, and they alternated font sizes to indicate essential and more specialized information, just as the Baedeker and other guides had since the nineteenth century. Just as Karl Baedeker and his sons claimed they visited most of the sites included in their travel guides, moreover, the SA authors listed only places they had seen. Such veracity was designed to avoid semiotic static, and to create precisely the kind of transparency and orderliness that travel guides always tried to establish. This was to be entirely 'truthful' discourse.

Yet on another level the guidebook reflected the 'primacy of the political' (Mason 1972) within the Nazi movement. It included a fairly lengthy (22-page) introduction to the history of the Nazi party in Berlin, contradicting the general tendency of tourist guidebooks to pare down elaborate historical background, or to move such background to the back of the book. In addition to the historical introduction, it provided a list of Berlin SA units and statistical tables on Reichstag and Presidential elections during the Weimar period. It gave no practical information about hotels, restaurants, and travel arrangements. Its main introductory map was a skeletal sketch of the city's principal traffic arteries whose main purpose was to highlight the 'sites of murder' (*Mordstellen*) of Nazi party members. These were marked with small black crosses as well as the last names and year of death of each individual. The guide's sense of place was that of the necropolis, the city of the dead. 'The German cult of heroism was tied more to death than to life, more to destruction than to victory,' argues historian Jay Baird (1990, xi). Again and again, the guide reenacted its ode to death as it wandered through the great city.

Fascist movements throughout Europe were preoccupied with death, and it was Mussolini's dramatic commemoration of his movement's martyrs that set the standard in this area. But one should not be too quick to attribute the cult of the martyr only to fascist groups as the theme of heroic death for a cause had been the stock-in-trade not only of World War I commemoration but also of Communist writing. Documenting the first five months of Nazi terror against political enemies, the famous Brown Book, published by Communists in Basel in August 1933, included a long list of workers and intellectuals killed at the hands of Hitler's followers (*Braunbuch* 1978 [1933], 332–54). One of the districts treated by the

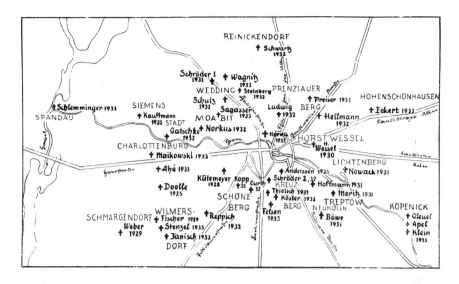

*Figure 15    Berlin as a necropolis for the SA tourist (Engelbrechten and Volz 1937, 44).*

Nazi party guide, Berlin–Charlottenburg, was the subject of a leftist novel on working-class life under National Socialism. *Our Street*, written by Jan Petersen and published by the Gollancz house in England, began with a list of 18 workers from Charlottenburg killed by the SA before 1933 or by the Nazi state after Hitler came to power (1938, 7). Antifascist resistance movements throughout Europe would assemble their own pantheons of victims in the war and in the postwar period. Tourism would draw on this tradition after 1945 no less enthusiastically than Nazi-era SA tourism did. And of course the East German state would build its official ideology on remembrance of the Communist dead, most often to the exclusion of the memory of other, less politically 'correct' victims such as Jews or Catholic priests. Former Nazi concentration camps such as Buchenwald, Sachsenhausen, and Ravensbrück—foci of a Communist cult of martyrology— would make up an important part of East German tourist itineraries (Reiseführer 1981, 118, 140, 214).

The SA guide's historical introduction charted the 'gradual rise of the party' in the 'city of millions,' presenting the story as a kind of brown Bildungsreise. It told a tale of heroic struggle from 1925, when the NSDAP could garner just 137 votes in municipal parliament elections, to the moment in March 1933 when it gained the absolute majority, though only after preventing 44 Communist parliament delegates from taking their seats. It highlighted Goebbels' formative effect on party fortunes, portraying the Berlin chieftain as a mighty struggler against 'the Marxist parties,' an epithet lumping together the Social Democrats and Communists, and against figures such as the 'Berlin Jewish vice-president of police Dr. Bernhard Weiß,' whom Goebbels nicknamed 'Isidor.' It stressed that the party victory depended on the deft organization of propaganda, and that the huge Nazi demonstrations in the 'Sportpalast,' in the Potsdamer Straße in the west, were central events giving the party visibility and a sense of dynamism. Much of the guidebook's historical account was a lifeless march through electoral results, the creation of numerous National Socialist subgroups, Hitler's public appearances, SA forays into Communist strongholds in working-class Berlin, and the SA's central role in establishing the terror regime in 1933. But the general point came through clearly enough: that the Nazi party had been victimized by a 'Marxist terror' against which only the bravest could struggle, and against which fierce reprisals were not only defensible but also necessary. The party's enemies made it a regular practice 'not only of carrying out countless nocturnal attacks on individual Nazis'; in some areas of the city 'it was even impossible to walk the streets in daylight if one was wearing a party, SA, SS, or Hitler Youth pin,' claimed the handbook. The true extent of the terror was reflected, so the authors argued, in the 47 dead party, SA, and SS members killed at the hands of the Communists and their allies (Engelbrechten and Volz 1937, 11–15, 18–19).

It was only when the narrative turned to the formation of so-called Sturmlokale that a semblance of the daily life and individual identity of SA men emerged. The pub or restaurant so designated was a central institution in Berlin political life of the period, and many street battles and political confrontations crystallized around Sturmlokale. They were combination bars and soup kitchens, and sometimes they were outfitted with beds so that SA men could use them as their home away from home. The Communist party knew where most of the major Sturmlokale were located, and Communist neighborhood newspapers often published the addresses and proprietors of these SA hangouts (Rosenhaft 1983, 19–20; Swett 1998, 127–8). The Sturmlokal was used both as a 'fortified place in the battle zone' and as a place affording 'rest and security against the enemy [and] refreshment and strengthening.' Also used for regular stormtrooper meetings and social gatherings, it was at the center of the 'SA spirit.' This meant that the Sturmlokal was also a locus and symbol of manly comradeship. Despite the viciousness of the political struggle going on in red Berlin, the SA man needed nothing more essentially than solace and warmth. 'In the Sturmlokalen, men who were often repudiated by their families due to their political belief experienced that which was almost always lacking at home,' read the guide. At the SA pub, men could find 'the warm heart, the helping hand, the interest in them as persons, the harmony of feeling, thinking, and will in a circle of their community'—all woefully absent elsewhere. The Sturmlokal was thus a place where 'a feeling of being at home and a joy in life' could be gotten, and where an 'iron moral and material wall against the Commune and reaction' could be built (Engelbrechten and Volz 1937, 19–20).

In one respect, this portrayal represented the Sturmlokal as the space of a reconstructed and nurturing nuclear family where SA members achieved an individual sense of self-worth unrecognized in the wider society. World War I had done much to subvert families, as husbands and fathers were removed for long stretches of time from home, killed at the front, or returned to their loved ones as injured or psychologically scarred shadows of their former selves. They would often find that their wives had gained a new feeling of independence, and that sons and daughters regarded their fathers with distrust if not outright hostility. The SA members who were 20 years old or older around 1930 undoubtedly remembered such difficulties, and may have acted the part of the resentful son who rued the return of fatherly authority after the war. These same SA men were most likely unemployed or underemployed during the Weimar Republic—as their fathers might have been after the war or in the Depression—and they were struggling with the typical problems of youthful restlessness and confusion. The handbook recalled fondly that often the proprietor of the Sturmlokal took great chances opening up his establishment to the 'raw lads' of the SA, who were shunned by more respectable restaurants and inns. The kindly Gastwirt would often also lose money, since many SA men could not pay for food and drink, and he risked material damage as well, since the 'battle over the Sturmlokale' regularly featured broken windows, bullets, and hand grenades—to say nothing of heavy drinking. The innkeeper played the role of the understanding patriarch, while his wife, regularly called 'Muttchen,' or 'little mother,' throughout Berlin, upheld the familial atmosphere. The oldest SA Sturmlokal was located in the Köpenick district; its nickname was 'Aunt Anna.' The theme was taken up again a few pages later when the efforts of the National Socialist Women's League (*Frauenschaft*) in Berlin was discussed. Women belonging to this organization undertook traditionally female tasks, preparing meals and ensuring that hot coffee was available for SA men during electoral battles and demonstrations. These women were true 'mothers in the Fatherland' (Koonz 1987) to the young SA men seeking etched-in familial relations. And the SA men could play the roles of dutiful sons or even knights in shining armor, as when they protected the Nazi League of German Maidens, the junior analogue to the Frauenschaft, from 'a threatening Communist attack in 1932' (Engelbrechten and Volz 1937, 20, 22, 29, 193–4).

In another respect, the Sturmlokal may have been a site of homoerotic identity. There is a tendency in scholarship and popular culture to conflate male homosexuality and fascism, as Andrew Hewitt (1996) points out. Yet it is reasonable to argue that homosexuality was an element, if by no means a dominant one, in the life of the SA. The memory of World War I was crucial to this story. The wartime 'front community' depended on male bonding and willingness to sacrifice for a fellow warrior. Veterans would later say that the comradeship of the trenches was the most valuable experience of the war. Some of the SA fighters had lived this experience, but others had not, and for them, the comradeship of anti-Communist struggle in the Nazi party substituted for the missed solidarity of the Great War. Ostensibly based on securely heterosexual role models, the comradeship of the trenches also had homoerotic overtones that reappeared in postwar culture (Mosse 1985, 114–32). Without recognizing that it was doing so, the SA guide drew a hidden connection between itself and the sections of the guidebook to 'naughty Berlin' treating Berlin's male homosexual subculture. But it did so by a process of inversion whereby a repressed homosexuality was put in the service of a reactionary political cause upholding conventional gender roles and attacking homosexuality itself as a perverse departure from the image of the soldierly male (Peukert 1982, 119–20). For their part, Communist party street cell newspapers and leaflets drew attention to Sturmlokal sleeping arrangements, furthering the image of SA homosexuality (Swett 1998, 127). The Nazis themselves unwittingly upheld such ideas. Beside the charge of treason, the homosexuality of the SA leader Ernst Röhm was given as justification for his summary execution in the putsch of 1934, even though Röhm's sexual preferences were known for years (Bracher 1970, 239).

Finally, the life of the Sturmlokal reflected analogies between SA practice and tourism. Just as war and leisure travel possessed many similarities, SA marauding and fighting were like tourist outings for the young men who participated. Like contemporary adventure tourists who seek just enough danger to challenge them (but not enough to kill them), SA men embarked on anti-Communist raids and paramilitary sorties that were potentially deadly, but which, given the frequency of violent interactions that took place, rarely resulted in fatalities. The Sturmlokal meanwhile provided some of the same features that the holiday resort or youth hostel did: a home away from home, where parental authority could be kept at arm's length, and where a classless camaraderie of travel (and perhaps also homosexual adventure) could be experienced. SA violence became the stuff of SA memory, a kind of second-hand leisure travel, as Nazi-era tourists wandered through the sites of former paramilitary tourist struggles. We have already noted the commercial dimensions of this process.

Most tourist guides to Berlin began with the great boulevard Unter den Linden and the Brandenburg Gate. The SA guide's itinerary began with the Reichstag. This choice reflected the overall strategy of the guide, which inverted the history of the Reich capital to fit the heroic narrative of Nazi party struggle. The process of inversion demanded that the Reichstag would be an empty center, an absence. This inversion swam against centuries of Western urban history, for, as Roland Barthes argued, city centers have always been thought to be 'full'—of buildings, power, and 'truth' (1982, 30). Although electoral statistics reflecting the rapid rise of the Nazi party were given, it was stressed that the party systematically violated everything for which the national parliament stood. After the first significant Nazi electoral victory in September 1930, the 107 party delegates appeared wearing their brown shirts despite a police ban on political uniforms. In February 1931, the delegates withdrew in protest from the parliamentary chamber singing the Horst Wessel Song, the main Nazi anthem. Adolf Hitler became a Reichstag deputy only in the March 1933 elections, and, the guide was anxious to point out, the Führer never set foot in the Reichstag building during the 'time of struggle.' On 27 February 1933, a fire that the Nazis claimed was set by 'Communists' caused significant damage to the Reichstag. The party used the incident to unleash a massive wave of terror that was crucial in demolishing the already weakened democratic institutions in Germany and paving the way for the more fully established dictatorship to come. The Reichstag itself housed part of the infamous trial of the hapless drifter accused of arson and taking part in a Communist conspiracy, and the building remained open as a ruin for guided tours (ten till five daily, with abbreviated hours on Sunday). Reichstag sessions, which under the Nazi regime became pointless exercises of acclamation for Hitler's policies, were now held in the nearby Kroll Opera House (Engelbrechten and Volz 1937, 49–51).

If the Reichstag was the eviscerated heart of the narrative, other sites were replete with historical content. The National Club, opened in 1919 in the elegant Hotel Prinz Albrecht in the Hermann-Goering-Straße, formerly the Sommerstraße, was one such place. It was here, we are told, that 'Hitler's first contact with the nationalist circles of northern Germany took place' in 1921. In a secret meeting, Hitler answered numerous queries from nationalist leaders regarding his plans for solving the 'Marxist and Jewish question.' It was here, the guide said, where Hitler explained that 'concentration camps' would be necessary in order to carry out the Nazi takeover 'with the minimum of bloodshed.' It was here too where Hitler gave a speech in 1922 in which he laid out in more detail his plan for building, with the help of nationalist groups, a broad front against 'the Bolshevist danger.' He emphasized that a 'national dictatorship' would also work to repress the 'fateful influence of Jews, Freemasons, and political Catholicism,' and that other nationalist groups could play only a temporary role in the formation of the offensive against Marxism. Only the Nazi party, Hitler said, had the will to bring together all 'sound national forces,' including youth, in the struggle (ibid., 52–3).

The Kaiserhof hotel, one of Berlin's oldest and largest, was also regarded in the light of its connection to Hitler, who used it as his headquarters from 1931 until the seizure of power. (For most of the Weimar period, he stayed in the Hotel Sanssouci.) The guide gave a detailed accounting of Hitler's stays in the elegant hotel, offering a day-by-day breakdown for 1932 and early 1933, and chronicling Hitler's arrivals and departures during his negotiations to become Chancellor. In smaller print, it excerpted a previously published party account explaining why the 'leader of the workers' made the much-criticized choice of a luxury hotel— the tourist guides called it 'palatial' (Grieben 1936a, 15)—from which to assault red Berlin. The issue was clear: 'Why did the Führer pick out this as his workplace, the "comfort" and modern amenities of which were undoubtedly of little use to us?' The guide assured its readers that the 'atmosphere' of this well-appointed hotel was of little consequence to the hard-working Führer; 'purely pragmatic reasons determined the choice of precisely these headquarters.' In the first place, Hitler had to take account of the 'mentality of his counterparts in negotiations,' and it was important to choose a place that fit their 'psychological perspective.' More significant was that the Kaiserhof 'symbolized . . . clearly the struggle of world views between the two antipodes, the final battle between the new Germany and the ruined system.' Hitler's staying in the Kaiserhof caused the same 'fear and terror' in Berlin that the cry 'Hannibal ante Portas' once did for ancient Rome. And finally because the Kaiserhof lay in the protective zone, the *Bannmeile*, designed to protect the Reichstag and Prussian state house from violent political demonstrations, Hitler's residence there reminded people yet again of the 'complete failure of the state.' The Führer was portrayed as a general in his 'field headquarters,' and his minions received praise for their help in organizing his frequent trips, his press conferences, his meals, and the negotiations that accompanied his dealing for the Chancellorship. No 'turbulent scenes' or 'nervousness' characterized Hitler's entourage, claimed the guide in opposition to press reports. Instead the Führer managed his Kaiserhof entourage with 'self-confident deliberation' (Engelbrechten and Volz 1937, 63–67).

Hitler was not the only Nazi party luminary whose history the guide read in Berlin's physical environment. Goebbels too had been central to the Nazi cause in the Reich capital, more central in fact than the Führer. One of the buildings most closely associated with his part in the Nazi victory was the Sportpalast on the Potsdamer Straße, which he called the 'tribune from which we speak to the metropolis.' The guidebook included copious information on this memory site, recalling the assemblies in which Goebbels could *not* speak, thanks to Prussian state prohibitions, as well as those in which he delivered his rousing tirades. Here the first party assembly that appealed directly to Berlin workers was held under Goebbels' slogan 'Into the factories!' Here was held, on 8 January 1932, the shortest Sportpalast assembly on record, a ten-minute affair at which Goebbels spoke quickly because of time constraints imposed on him by the police. Two days after the Reich Chancellor Heinrich Brüning prohibited the SA, on 15 April 1932, Goebbels played a sound recording of one of the Catholic Center politician's recent speeches before 18,000 Sportpalast faithful. He followed up with sarcastic commentary (ibid., 201–10). The Sportpalast would of course continue to be integral to Goebbels' efforts, most notoriously in World War II, when the propaganda minister would get Berlin throngs to bellow for 'total war.'

The guidebook's inversion of the meaning of Berlin topography also explains its inattention to architectural history, so central to both the Baedeker and socialist travel cultures. Paul Wallot's design and construction of the Reichstag received one line, the architectural and political history of the Brandenburg Gate 13 words. For the Brandenburg Gate, the significant thing was that the SA and SS were banned from marching through it due to legislation protecting the Reichstag and other key public buildings from political violence. Only on the evening of 30 January 1933, the day Hitler was handed the Chancellorship, did Nazi columns march through the Gate in a giant torchlight procession. For the Berlin Cathedral, often criticized by tourist guidebooks for its overbearing ornamentation but appreciated nonetheless for its massiveness and regal siting, the guide noted only that it was the scene of an important memorial service for two SA men killed in street-fighting in February 1933. The architectural history of the Reich Chancellery received somewhat more attention, but the detail was geared almost exclusively to the history of the party and the renovation of the Chancellery once Hitler gained power. The detailed index of names at the back of the guide listed no modernist architects at all, of which Berlin had a great many. This is unsurprising, given that the Nazi party attacked the functionalist 'new building' of the Weimar era as 'cultural Bolshevism.' Yet given that the guide's mission was not only to praise Nazism but vilify the enemy, the absence of any mention at all of a modernist architect is significant. Even more striking was the way in which politically acceptable architects from German history such as Karl Friedrich Schinkel, master of that stark neo-classicism that characterized so many Berlin buildings, was reduced to insignificance. He was mentioned just twice, while Georg von Knobelsdorff, architect of the Opera House and many other great buildings, received no mention at all (ibid., 51, 55, 58, 59-61).

It would be one-sided to lay such inattention to cultural or architectural history only at the door of the guide's politics. Many other guides of the period, such as the Grieben company's abridged version of its Berlin handbook (1936b), carried little architectural or art history. It should not be forgotten that Moreck's Berlin book castigated tourists' interest in the musty monuments of history. When the Baedeker firm itself conceded that its guides were in need of revision so as to account more for contemporary concerns, the death-knell for the textured cultural tourism of the nineteenth century was definitively sounded (Hinrichsen 1988, 38–9). The SA guide's emphasis on recent history and the corresponding indifference to Berlin's rich art-historical heritage were part of a general trend whereby society and the travel cultures it spawned lost an important web of connections with the more distant past. With the contemporary past, by contrast, with that part of experience still being formed in the events of the day, the guide retained an intimate relationship, more intimate than that held by commercial guidebooks.

The broader memory of the SA emerged in the walking itineraries, borne partly by repetitive references to SA bureaus and offices in every district, but also by information on institutions that gave the SA a more obvious public presence. In the Taubenstraße (formerly Friedrichstraße), readers were invited to visit the 'Revolution Museum of SA Regiment 6,' open 12 hours daily to the public. This museum contained 'an unusually rich and well-ordered collection of booty taken by the Berlin SA in the struggle against the Red Front.' The collection included everything from Communist pamphlets and newspapers to uniforms, flags, pistols, bombs, knives, and many other accoutrements of the street battle that raged in Berlin in the last years of the Republic. A particularly valued artifact was the Soviet star taken from the monument to the murdered Communist leaders Rosa Luxemburg and Karl Liebknecht in the Friedrichsfelde cemetery. This monument, a modernist triumph by the famous architect Ludwig Mies van der Rohe, was demolished soon after the Nazis took power. Another sensation was the so-called 'Communist hit list,' found in the Karl-Liebknecht-Haus, the Berlin Communist headquarters, during Nazi party raids in February 1933. On this list one found the names and addresses of important Nazi party leaders who were to be eliminated. Here too, it was said one found the automobile license numbers of National Socialist and SA members as well as the addresses of businesses that had dealings with the party (Engelbrechten and Volz 1937, 59). Not just Germans but also foreign tourists visited the museum, as reflected in the Irish evangelist J. Edwin Orr's travel account of the mid-1930s. Orr noted that the Nazis were not alone in their belief in left-wing hit lists; Protestant church leaders were also convinced that Communists had a roster of pastors and other religious figures who would be assassinated when the party came to power (Orr 1937, 100–102).

A consistent theme of such material was the victimization of SA men at the hands not only of the Red Terror but the authorities, the two merging into the same thing at many points in the guide. The attentive traveler was led to the Police Presidium, nicknamed 'the Alex' in Berlin slang, located in the Alexanderstraße. Headquarters of the revolutionary Spartacists in 1918–19, the Alex was a symbol of the entire Weimar system for the Nazis. Here many SA men were incarcerated, and from here many more were sent to the 'horse stalls in the Magazinstraße,' which became an 'SA mass prison.' The walls of the prison had to be repainted constantly because inmates filled them with graffiti and political slogans. SA members nicknamed the presidium the 'weekend house of the SA' or 'Hotel I A,' in reference to Department I A, the political police. They transformed a popular tourist slogan of the day for their own uses: 'Every German once in Berlin—every Berlin SA man once in the I A!' Other prisons were included in the tour, including the Plötzensee in the Charlottenburg district, where both SA and SS men served time. Hitler would use the Plötzensee to execute his would-be assassins in 1944, and after World War II it became one of the most important sites of West German memory of victims of the Third Reich (ibid., 83–6, 126).

Another leitmotif of SA memory was the commemoration of martyrs to the Nazi cause. At each location where an SA man fell, the guide referred the reader to the circumstances of his death, which usually consisted of a short description of how 'the Marxists' had done him in. At the corner of Hollmannstraße in the Kreuzberg district we find the site where the SA member Friedrich Schröder was 'shot down by Communists' on 17 July 1932. Schröder was a 23-year-old employee in an insurance company. We learn he was taken to a nearby hospital, the Krankenhaus am Urban, where he died. At this hospital, a handful of other SA men died, including Harry Anderssen, whom, according to the guide, 'Jewish doctors and the overwhelmingly Marxist medical staff purposely did not help because he was a National Socialist.' As for Schröder, the plaque dedicated in 1934 to his memory read in part: 'Let the heroes not die in your soul.' Anderssen was 'slain by Red death' in 1926 in the nearby Stallschreiberstraße, and he received not one but two plaques, one at the site of death and another in the foyer to the Prussian State Bank, where he was an employee (ibid., 72–3, 171). The level of detail and attention to life history are quite striking in such sections, leading one to conclude that Nazi martyrology, despite its totalitarian claims, depended very much on bourgeois biographical traditions that put the individual at the center of things.

No SA martyrdom was more intricately recounted than that of Horst Wessel, who with 32 separate references in the guidebook's index was in third place in the Nazi pantheon, behind only Goebbels with 53 and Hitler himself with 46. The son of a Lutheran minister and a former university student, Wessel was a notoriously brutal SA-Sturmführer hated by local Communists. Wessel was an effective SA leader, rapidly rising in the ranks and commanding a group made up mainly of former Communist party members. He believed sincerely that the Nazi movement would better the lot of ordinary Germans, and he reveled in the idea of agitating for National Socialism in the heavily proletarian district of Friedrichshain, a Communist stronghold. At the time of his shooting, he lived with a prostitute he had saved from a beating by local pimps. A local tough with ties to the Communist movement murdered Wessel on 14 January 1930, although the severely wounded SA man held onto life in a local hospital for more than a month. Prior to his shooting, Wessel had become less enthused about the SA, partly due to his association with the prostitute, but this did not prevent Goebbels and the party from using the murder to transform the young Wessel into an anti-Communist icon (Baird 1990, 75–83; Rosenhaft 1983, 22–3).

The traces of Wessel's life appeared throughout the guide. The high schools he attended, his parents' home, the neighborhoods in which he agitated, the numerous memorial plaques, the Horst Wessel Platz (formerly Bülowplatz)—all received due attention. On the Horst Wessel Platz, the former Karl-Liebknecht-Haus, the Communist party headquarters and editorial office of the newspaper *The Red Flag*, was renamed after the martyred SA man. It was an SA march on the Bülowplatz, the guide explained, that inspired Wessel to set his poem 'Die Fahne hoch' to music, giving the Nazi movement its anthem. In the nearby Großen Frankfurter Straße, the apartment where Wessel was murdered was now a historical site, preserved in roughly the same state it had been when Wessel died, but presumably without the blood stains, of which there were many as he was shot in the face. The SA guide excerpted the report of the SA doctor Conti on the day of the shooting, which among other statements noted that the bullet lodged in the cervical vertebra after tearing away three-quarters of the victim's tongue and the entire uvula. Nothing was mentioned, of course, about the fact that SA cronies did not get care for Wessel immediately, refusing to call on a nearby Jewish doctor and rifling through their comrade's personal papers to remove compromising material. The reader was given additional detailed information about the course of Wessel's agony in the hospital, where the room in which he died was now a shrine open to visitors at any time. Included in the information was the complete excerpt of Goebbels' feverish article in the Nazi newspaper *The Attack* on the occasion of Wessel's death. As with much of the memorialization of Wessel, Goebbels' writing sensationalized the event: 'How the bullet devastated the fine head of this heroic young man. His face was deformed. I could hardly recognize him anymore.' Travelers who wanted to pursue the legend further were directed to the St. Nicholas Cemetery, where Wessel and his brother, also an SA man but the victim of a much less exploitable death, a ski accident, were buried. The guide recalled how Communist groups tried to overturn the vehicles carrying Wessel to his final resting place, and how during the memorial service they whistled loudly outside the cemetery grounds (Engelbrechten and Volz 1937, 88–103).

One of Wessel's haunts was the Fischerkietz, in the western part of the center, a heavily working-class district whose population was dominated by the Communists. It is significant that the guide gave much attention to such areas of the city, which were ignored in Baedeker tourism and whose social conditions were usually passed over. But the SA guide did no better than the standard guides when it came to describing the everyday life of the workers who lived there. It is true that the 'bleak conditions' of housing in the Fischerstraße and Petristraße were mentioned, as were the densely packed houses and inner courtyards lacking light and ventilation (ibid., 74). Yet beyond such trite remarks, there was little to give the traveler an idea of real circumstances, and even less to tell him how to go about wandering the district 'socially,' as the Weimar Social Democratic tourist might have. Compared to the guide's detailed life histories of martyred SA fighters, the evocations of collective experience in the slums of Berlin were superficial indeed.

What one was given instead was the location of Communist and SA bars alongside an account of how Horst Wessel's Sturm 5 became the first SA group to penetrate the Fischerkietz. Similarly, the guide called attention to the so-called Wanzenburg, a slum apartment building in the nearby Molkenmarkt. Here again the 'unbearable hygienic and sanitary conditions' of the building were noted with little attention to detail. Instead, it was emphasized that the slum once belonged to 'a rich Jew' who exploited the mostly unemployed working-class families living there. When some of these hapless families were evicted, the SA undertook to return them to their dwellings, in some cases hauling furniture piled in the courtyard back into the building. This, the guide claimed, was done 'without consideration of the political preference of those affected,' which brought the SA 'much sympathy among the inhabitants.' This narrative mirrored the stories Communist propagandists told about slumlords in the Nazi movement during the Republic. These 'Nazi House Pashas' were accused of sexually harassing female tenants, whose poverty forced them to trade sexual favors for economic survival (Swett 1998, 127). Like so many parts of this old area of Berlin, the Wanzenburg was torn down in the urban renewal program ordered by the regime; the fate of the Jewish landlord went unmentioned (Engelbrechten and Volz 1937, 74–5, 78). In all such cases, although there were passing references to social life, the primacy of the political was unchallenged. The SA lived and died by the sword; its violent history now became the stuff of political tourism anchored by the martyrology of heroic individuals.

## IV

The duality of the Nazi travel culture was revealed in all its horror during World War II. But even here there were gradations in the extent to which leisure travel brushed the genocidal core of the Volksgemeinschaft. For many of the Alpine resorts of southern Germany and Austria, little had changed, except that the former French, English, and American visitors were replaced by German tourists. These tourists appeared to be unaware a war was going on. 'Fur-bedecked women bathed in the most expensive perfume' were common sights at the resorts in 1942, prompting complaints not only from some locals but from SS informants, who pointed out the questionable morality and prodigious alcohol consumption of such guests. 'It is simply impossible to understand,' wrote one SS official, 'that certain people on the home front can amuse themselves in such a manner while on the other side, soldiers, men of the same blood, daily put their lives on the line at the front' (Boberach 1984, 10:3586–7). Lack of awareness that war meant austerity was not only a characteristic of well-to-do travelers, according to the SS. Cognizant of the need to ration transport facilities, government and the press had tried to get Germans to observe the slogan 'Whoever travels for pleasure will be penalized.' But many ignored the slogan, or even laughed at it, and the SS maintained that single women were often the worst offenders. They took short vacations by train or visited friends in far-off cities, and on crowded trains they refused to give up their seats to badly injured Wehrmacht soldiers. Such recalcitrance forced the regime to ease travel restrictions. In general, pleasure travel during the war was causing massive transport problems throughout the Reich and the East, where trains were needed not only for moving troops but also for the deathly business of moving Jews to ghettos and killing centers. Pleasure travel remained strong well into the war, as traffic for the Pentecost holiday of 1943 was heavier than in any year since 1939 (ibid., 11:4399–400; 14:5421–2). In these instances, the desire to travel for leisure competed with the military and racist goals of the regimes, creating friction between 'fun' and politics, and between individual desire and state goals.

Just as in past wars, World War II was an opportunity for German soldier travelers to see parts of Europe they had never seen before. In some cases, it was a matter of getting to know an area that 'returned' to the Reich, as with Alsace, for which there was an updated Baedeker guidebook. 'After a twenty-two-year break,' read the introduction, 'the blessed and fateful land on the Upper Rhine is today once again a living member of the German Reich and belongs among the most beautiful and valuable travel destinations available to Germans' (1942, v). Soldiers and civilians could use the guide to travel to historic cities and ski resorts, or they could follow the progress of the 'Greater German War of Liberation' of 1939–40, which the guide treated as a completed historical epoch. The area of the Maginot Line, built by the French as an 'impenetrable' defense against German attack, consisting of bunkers, anti-tank installations, and minefields, could be viewed from the region's highways or visited for more in-depth inspections. Points at which the Wehrmacht broke through the fortified line in 1940 were of particular interest. German rebuilding projects in various cities could be observed as part of the Third Reich's program of reintegrating and modernizing the province. Visitors to the capital city Straßburg could see the great 'towering cathedral, which once again as in days of old has become a symbol of the Reich' (xxvii, 6, 11, 18, 36, 38).

Other locales had a more exotic cast. Paris was a central attraction, and Hitler's infamous visit to the conquered city followed a path many other German tourists emulated during the occupation. The German army encouraged leisure travel in the French metropolis, and Wehrmacht soldiers responded, taking advantage of their status as conquerors and receiving much positive reinforcement from local inhabitants. Observing the German occupation of Paris, William Shirer wrote that 'most of the German troops act like naïve tourists.' They were not just impressed by Parisian landmarks but humbled: 'they bare their blond heads and stand there gazing,' wrote the bemused correspondent (1941, 413). Soldiers were aided by guidebooks to Paris, such as the one approved in August 1940 by the Kommandant of the city. This pocket guide featured brief descriptions of the main sightseeing destinations, including the Place de la Concorde, the Avenue des Champs-Elysées, La Place de l'Étoile, and the Eiffel Tower. Its tone was not as plebeian as the US military guide to Rome, which led fresh-faced GIs to areas 'chock full of interest' in the historic heart of the city (United States Army 1945, 21). But it could be as uncritical as any commercially produced guide of the period was. It enthused over the Eiffel Tower, stating that it was 'the greatest wonder of technology' when it was built and still the 'highest monument of the entire world' today. It referred to Notre Dame as 'a wonderful Gothic work of architecture,' and did not refrain from drawing attention to the theological significance of the building, noting that it housed 'true relics of the Holy Cross' and 'several parts of Christ's crown of thorns.' Not forgetting the interests of its target audience, it pointed out that the Montmartre district was widely known for its 'pleasures and night life.' Anti-Semitism was entirely absent: the only reference to Jews occurred in the description of the St. Paul Church in the rue Saint-Antoine, situated 'in the middle of the Jewish district' (*Erinnerung an Paris 1940*, 7, 10, 12, 13–14).

Whereas it represented Paris's main sites in an overwhelmingly positive and essentially unpolitical light—in great contrast to the SA guide—it also took the opportunity to praise Germany. The huge Trocadéro was built for the world exhibition of 1878 but substantially expanded for the International Exhibition of Art and Technology in 1937. The 'most imposing building' in the exhibition was the Deutsches Haus, where, according to the guide, 'German art and science and the colossal progress in various areas of human activity' amazed all visitors. Behind the Louvre, soldiers were encouraged to see the Saint-Germain-l'Auxerrois, site of the sixteenth-century St. Bartholomew Day's massacre in which 'the high point of persecution of the Protestant Huegenots' was reached. 'Many of the persecuted French Protestants fled to Germany,' recounted the guide, 'where they found protection and aid.' If such sites were opportunities for representing Germany as a land of tolerance, then others enabled the guidebook to criticize French politics and history even more than Saint-Germain-l'Auxerrois. The Place de la Concorde was 'grand and beautiful,' but it also reminded the visitor of the 2,800 people executed there in the French Revolution. 'Bloody revolts' took place on the Place Bastille in 1848 and 1871. The historic Hôtel-de-Ville was a new building, erected after the Commune destroyed the original structure. In such descriptions, France emerged as a land of bloody revolution and violence—precisely the opposite of the homeland from which order-loving, productive Germans came (ibid., 2, 6, 12, 17).

The mass slaughter of World War II was literally and figuratively many miles away from the point of view of the 1940 soldiers' guide to Paris. It was much closer in the East, the site of the first great wave of National Socialist 'ethnic cleansing' and ultimately of the destruction of European Jewry, the Final Solution. Here an independent Poland stood in the way not only of Nazi plans to reunify East Prussia with Germany, but also of the larger initiative to 'return' parts of Poland and Eastern Europe to the German sphere of influence. The so-called 'General Plan East' was designed to reduce Poles to secondary citizens, minimally educated and deprived of the most basic rights, and to remake Eastern economic and social life to benefit the German state. Those parts of Poland that were to be directly integrated into the expanded German Reich were now ripe for touristic exploitation. Travel was a way of getting to know the domain of Nazi conquest and re-educating travelers to see the German qualities of the architecture, the urban layouts, and the landscape. In one respect, such travel was hardly unusual, for in the modern era, 'travel in another country . . . represented an assertion of national strength' (Endy 1998, 573). This was true for Germans on the Eastern front just as it was for American travelers to Europe before World War I, when travel abroad extended US power internationally. Yet German travel in the East was not quite this innocent, as it depended not only on such assertion but also on a violent demolition of Polish society.

One such place where travelers learned to see the Germanness of the East was the city of Posen, a Prussian provincial capital before coming under Polish rule after 1918, and now the capital of the Wartheland district, or *Gau*. Tourism in this area was booming, as rail lines between Berlin and Posen were so overcrowded with leisure travelers that government and military personnel, including soldiers on leave, were unable to find places on many trains. Overcrowding was so bad on some lines that passengers stood in the lavatory for the whole trip, and some disembarked through the windows when they reached their destination (Boberach 1984, 7:2466-67; 11:4399–401). A Woerl guidebook for Posen was available in 1940. The guidebook's preface left little doubt as to the historical context: 'on the occasion of the liberation of the German East from Polish domination, the city of Posen also returns to the Reich.' The guide was designed for those 'folk comrades' involved in the 'new order' of the East, particularly the 'great work of settlement' being undertaken in Poland. These included administrators, soldiers, journalists, and many party officials, but also those who were ready to make Poland 'into a new Heimat.' Writing a guide for 'a region which finds itself in a process of transformation—during a time of war no less' made it difficult to guarantee the accuracy of all information. But the need for such a guide was clear (*Illustrierte Führer durch die Gauhauptstadt* 1940, 4).

Political themes and cultural prejudice worked throughout the introductory material and the descriptions that formed the centerpiece of the guidebook. Poles who came to the region in the remote past never developed a 'notable culture . . . but rather lived apathetically and without spiritual striving.' Posen was lost to Germany due to the 'document of shame of Versailles,' and although its historical and cultural roots were thoroughly German, its Germanic character and population were drastically reduced in the period of Polish governance. 'For their part,' stated the guide, 'the Poles went about making Posen into a university and convention city, naturally in their own style.' Several important architectural projects ensued, producing 'huge buildings . . . [that] have the effect of alien bodies, which the German cultural sense definitively rejects.' More seriously, 'Germandom in the old German city of Posen was almost completely eradicated, driven out, and suppressed.' Now, thanks to 'the Führer's act and the bravery of our army,' stated the guide, the city 'will continue the old tradition of its German past.' The main theatre would be renewed, the traces of 'Polonized' German settlers' culture from the Bamberg region in the seventeenth century would be preserved, and Paul von Hindenburg's birthplace, identified with 'a commemorative plaque over the house entrance,' would be the scene of yet more German pilgrimages. The only reference to anti-Jewish persecution in the 69-page guide came in the description of the Old Market Square near the Rathaus, where one found the Fremdengasse, once the Judenstraße, which with several side streets formed the 'separated and barricaded ghetto of Posen' (ibid., 6, 9, 13, 28, 39, 40, 46).

Such references to Poles and Jews had more to do with the kind of prejudice exhibited in the military guide to Paris than with Nazi goals of racial extermination, which in any case were not yet fully worked out in 1940. The difference was that the Poles had no positive characteristics in the Woerl guide, whereas French accomplishments in technology, architecture, and culture were appreciated in spite of the bloody political history of the contentious nation. In both guides, Jews hardly appeared. For the Woerl publishers, Posen was a site of cultural and political transformation, a link in the chain of the 'new order.' The Poles had repressed 'Germandon' and done miserably with the city's architecture. German influence had to be re-established with force. But the fate of other, 'inferior' peoples remained unclear, and the interrelation between leisure and political conquest operated at the level of older patterns of cultural stereotyping. One could say the same about the military guides to the Eastern Front, such as the German army's tour book for Warsaw (Feldeinheit 22 444, 1942). In 28 pages of brief descriptions of that city's ruins and other tourist sites, the guide took considerable notice of Polish deficiencies in military strategy and architecture. But not once did it mention Jews.

Leisure travel's relationship to Nazi violence may be seen at a somewhat more advanced stage in one of the most disturbing travel guides of World War II, the Baedeker guide to the General Government, a part of Poland occupied by the German military but not integrated into the Reich. In 1942 the Baedeker publishing house was commissioned to produce a travel guide for the region that enabled officers, businessmen, administrators, and tourists to get around in the new territory. The guidebook married the traditional Baedeker form—from the red cover to the densely packed itineraries, copiously detailed maps, and informative index—with the Nazi war of conquest in much the same way the earlier Woerl guide did. But this linkage was more disturbing given the Baedeker's long association with a travel culture built on respect for the individual and liberal values.

Once again, Polish shortcomings were plain for all to see. 'The street conditions were for the most part very bad during the Polish time,' one read in the introductory material. In another section, Ernst R. Fugmann, of the Institute for German Eastern

Planning in Krakau, attributed the 'very great backwardness of all branches of the culture' to 'the essence and the race of the local inhabitants and an attitude toward life that is completely alien to German culture.' A shortage of hotels, unreliable non-German restaurants (except those with signs reading 'for the Wehrmacht' or 'Germans allowed'), damaged rail lines and public buildings (attributed largely to the unreasonableness of Polish resistance to the German army in 1939) all reflected the abysmal state of the new territory (Baedeker 1943, xv–xx).

The anti-Semitic element was now more apparent than in the other guides even if it was still not very frequently expressed. Introductory essays on geography, art, and economic history either treated the Jews as a metaphor of everything that was wrong with Polish culture or blamed the Jews directly for a host of problems. Of the Polish nation, Fugmann wrote, 'its people is a mixed outcome of [the meeting] of East and West, indistinct, reserved, and unchecked at the same time, and its bridge-keeper was for centuries the Jewish trader.' A few pages later, the same writer noted that the 'failures of centuries-old Polish economic mismanagement' and 'proletarianization' of a great many Poles occurred in part because 'the Jewish commercial stratum' reaped the lion's share of economic profit (ibid., xxiv, xxix). For the most part, however, silence was the rule with regard to 'the Jewish problem.'

Silence was most deafening when it came to the guidebook's treatment of the sites of the Judeocide. Belzec, a major extermination center, was identified as an outpost on the border between the districts of Lublin and Galicia (ibid., 137), while Treblinka and Sobibor received not a line. Lublin was a major center of Jewish life in Poland and the capital of the district named after it in the General Government. The Baedeker devoted seven pages to the city, and in its short historical background section (in small print) it described how the town declined due to centuries of war, plague, and fire. But it was 'above all through the spreading of the Jews' that the city lost its former stature from the eighteenth century (ibid., 129). Jews had made of Lublin a 'citadel,' the Baedeker continued, with a Talmudic school and the largest Talmudic publishing house in Europe. A parenthetical sentence followed: '(In 1862 the city had 57 percent Jews, now it is Jew-free [*judenfrei*])' (ibid., 129). This chilling reference, which parroted National Socialist language, ignored what in grim actuality was a bloody onslaught on Lublin's Jews in the previous year. From mid-March to mid-April 1942, about 90 percent of the 40,000 Jews of the city were killed through deportation to an extermination camp or execution on the spot (Browning 1992, 52). As for Auschwitz, it lay outside the General Government, but it was a hub of the killing operations against Jews and others, and it was never more deadly than at the time the Baedeker was being used as a guide to the new Poland. But Auschwitz was mentioned only in passing, as a small industrial city en route from Vienna to either Kracow or Warsaw (Baedeker 1943, 10).

One would not have expected a travel guidebook to go into detail about the location and character of mass killing. The nature of leisure travel prevented delving into such matters; the tourist wanted 'to get away from it all,' especially during wartime. That Germany was still at war in 1943 suggests another reason for the silence. Leisure travelers to the new Poland could be expected to tour the major cities and view the key landmarks, but military installations, labor camps, and of course the death camps were off limits. Also, the extermination camps were meant to be cloaked in secrecy, except for a select few, even though information about what went on there reached not only the Polish and German people but the rest of the world as well. The Nazi leadership did not trust the German Volk with detailed knowledge that the logic of racial war demanded total extermination of innocent people. Nonetheless, the juxtaposition of silence and genocide, of leisure travel and mass murder, makes the Baedeker's lack of concern all the more frightening. The Holocaust was quite literally a parenthetical event in Baedeker's Nazi-dominated world—and an obliquely mentioned parenthesis at that.

German renewal constituted the other side of the coin to the narrative of Polish and Jewish failure. In economic and cultural life, in the building of new schools and roads, and in the Germanization of place names, German policy throughout the General Government appeared in the guidebook as a giant project of improvement and modernization. A 'Jew-free' Krakow or Lublin appeared as a necessary component in a larger project of transforming the urban, economic, sanitary, and cultural coordinates of the Polish lands. And yet the guidebook was unable to grasp the General Government as a place of unchallenged or definitive German racial domination. The Baedeker preface made its usual disclaimer about not being able to guarantee the accuracy of all information, but it added that in wartime, and in an area so recently occupied and transformed, 'much is still in a state of transition' (ibid., vi). Background essays characterized the area as a transitional zone of 'eastern Middle Europe,' in which the Vistula region, like another famous riparian contact zone, the Rhineland, brought together different geographies, and in which history revealed a palimpsest of German, Polish, and Russian influences. The guidebook noted openly that the Polish language and culture would appear strange and inferior to Germans, but that daily interaction between Germans and Poles was nonetheless taken for granted. Itineraries led the reader to monuments and urban physiognomies whose histories reflected not principally the violence of the German occupation but the historical and cultural ambience of long-term German activity. The Baedeker's view arguably had more to do with pre-World War I images of Mitteleuropa, or Central Europe, which saw this region not as a field of total German domination but of 'natural' cultural and economic expansion by Germans, the common denominator of an area with many different nationalities. Oriented to a process of 'amalgamation and adjustment' (Meyer 1955, 189) rather than unlimited and genocidal expansion, this view corresponded more readily to the national–liberal travel culture than to that of National Socialism. It rested on a discourse of 'anti-conquest' whereby the 'guilty act of conquest' enables, often without acknowledgment, the 'innocent act' of seeing, a mode of representation common to European imperialist ideologies (Pratt 1992, 66).

No matter what the outcome of Nazi expansion was to be, the traveler was invited to enjoy the present state of disequilibrium in all its sublimity. 'Today,' read the Baedeker, ' the obvious discrepancy that exists between the large-scale aspect of the landscape between the Elbe and Vistula and the cultural gradient east of the old political borders makes a powerful impression on the traveler' (1943, xxi–xxii). We know that this view was ruthlessly exploited in the Nazi program of racial conquest—the guide to the General Government affirms this. The discrepancy between Poland's identification with a Central European landscape and geology on the one side and the 'Eastern' quality of its political culture on the other would finally be eradicated with the most brutal means possible. The sublimity of the moment of violent transformation, so exciting for the touristic gaze, would eventually give way to the routinized authority of total German control in the East. But for how many users of the trusted Baedeker guidebook did the older vision of gradual 'amalgamation and adjustment' still operate, however naïvely?

For one group of travelers in the East, Wehrmacht soldiers, the touristic view had a most intimate relationship with the racial war of annihilation. Here the dual nature of the Nazi travel culture was starkly evident. Recent scholarship on the Germany army in World War II reveals a level of involvement in the Nazi war of extermination far beyond what earlier generations of researchers assumed or admitted (Heer and Naumann 1995). Analysis of soldiers' letters home indicates a continued degree of fascination with the 'touristic' elements of war for the ordinary soldier. In both world wars, German soldiers, like soldiers everywhere, reacted to foreign cultures with cultural prejudice, especially with reference to Eastern Europe and the Balkans. Yet in World War I, this prejudice was expressed as a reaction to social and physical conditions, whereas in World War II, it was expressed more often as an antipathy to people or to 'races.' Criticism of a country tended to become hostility toward an entire people (Latzel 1995, 453). Soldiers in the field saw different conditions than tourists did, of course. Moreover, soldiers had direct access to the means of destruction whereby racial prejudice could be translated directly into death-bringing action. They were also more directly exposed to the propaganda of racial struggle than tourists were. It may be that the cultural prejudices of the Woerl guide, or the references to racially 'cleansed' parts of the General Government in the wartime Baedeker, also lent themselves to the murderous actions undertaken by the German army and SS in the East. There was quite possibly a slippage between older forms of cultural reaction and 'biologized' ways of seeing that may have been 'normalized,' and thereby enabled, by the guidebook's gaze. But the question is ultimately undecidable.

## V

Of all the alternatives to the Baedeker vision discussed here, the National Socialist travel culture was the most formidable—and certainly the most dangerous. It rested on sounder infrastructural foundations than did Weimar leisure travel because it developed as part of a broader social and economic recovery from the Depression. It claimed to represent all 'Aryan' Germans, a claim against which the proponents of ideologies of class or sexual revolution appeared sectarian or hedonistic. It collapsed distinctions between leisure and politics, arguing that everything, and especially one's 'free time,' was now subject to the racially motivated projects of the new regime. It claimed to do away with the antinomies of egalitarianism and social distinction with which previous travel cultures worked, creating the basis for a new collective mode of leisure travel that allegedly gave millions of German workers 'strength through joy.' It connected leisure travel with the most modern means of transportation, including above all the automobile, as important for the fantasies it generated as it was for use in daily life, which was still limited. It turned tourist topographies inside out, replacing older histories and narratives with new ones based on the memory and intentions of a winner-take-all struggle against Communists, Jews, Social Democrats, liberals, and many others. Its central political impulse, the political and cultural domination of Europe by a 'superior' race, became nested in the normal workings of leisure practices that absorbed the swastika as an everyday indicator of the new order. Its racial ideology shaped the perspectives—and the bloody actions—of paramilitary and military 'travelers' in German cities and on the Eastern front. In its representations, policies, and practices were co-mingled the stunningly normal workings of a modern leisure infrastructure and the politics of what Bartov (1996) refers to as 'industrial killing.'

Can one conclude from all this that the National Socialist travel culture was the most 'successful' of the three alternatives to Baedeker tourism discussed in the preceding pages? It pays to recall once again the key goal of the National Socialist approach to travel. Nazi propagandists insisted they were revolutionizing leisure culture, bringing 'work and free time . . . into harmony' in a 'socialist structure' (Müller-Gaisberg 1936, 9). Travel guidebooks of the era, whether those of the Berlin SA or the venerable Baedeker publishing firm, were influenced by such intentions, to be sure. The SA guidebook embodied this impulse in pure form. The young men who fought for the Nazi paramilitary formation in Berlin were violent travelers who mixed street-wise savagery and fun, youthful destructiveness and leisure, fierce anti-Communism and male companionship. The primacy of the Nazi political message shaped their views and determined their actions. The SA guidebook to Berlin allowed them to be time travelers in the heart of the formerly red metropolis, where they could visit the sites where their comrades had fallen and remember the pubs and streets in which they undertook their struggles. All distinctions between private life, work, public culture, and political engagement seemed to be obliterated in the guide's psycho-topography.

Even so, against this 'triumph' of the Nazi travel culture, one can suggest many qualifiers. The SA guidebook was in part a compensatory act by an organization whose political star had fallen in the National Socialist polycracy. A central motivation of the guidebook's creators was to remember what was soon to be forgotten in the transformation of the German capital into Hitler's megalopolis. In formal terms, the SA guide to Berlin departed little from tried-and-true travel guidebook conventions. Given that a central motivation of tourism had become recreation and release, it would not be too speculative to suggest that the repetition of 'sites of murder' in the SA guidebook would wear heavily on even the most dedicated Nazi follower. And what of the strong individuating tendency of this, the guidebook inspired by a brutal collectivism more than any of the other guidebooks discussed here? From the life histories of Nazi martyrs to the narratives of comradeship in the Sturmlokale of Berlin's violent streets, the guidebook appealed strongly to the individual SA man's memory of his contributions to the party's rise to power. A transpersonal narrative of martyrdom to a cause became a deeply personal recollection of savage tourism.

As for the broader guidebook literature available to the German and foreign tourist public, the Baedeker model remained dominant, even if the firm slipped economically and fell behind other publishers in terms of its ability to recognize the tourist value of the 'new' and the modern. Guidebook itineraries of the time incorporated the buildings and symbols of the new order, but they did not necessarily give them center stage. Travel guidebooks to the Eastern front, the cutting edge of Nazi racial extermination policies, did much the same. Frighteningly, a 'Jew-free' urban district in a Polish city could be encountered with as little commentary as a historic fountain or a scenic country lane. In part, this reflected the regime's propaganda strategy, which, many exceptions notwithstanding, favored understatement as much as hyperventilation. The state travel agency's skillful integration of swastikas into otherwise thoroughly entertainment-oriented travel brochures and guidebooks captured perfectly this subterfuge. Even so, Nazism's totalitarian impulse may have come up against a certain immutability not only in guidebook itineraries but in the many tourist practices that were being learned and re-learned by more and more Germans on a daily basis.

By immutability I do not mean to imply that something was unchanging. What I do mean is that tourist culture was wedded to a set of conventions and practices, always traceable in the guidebook literature, that preceded the Nazi regime's leisure politics and persisted even as they were mobilized for ideological purposes. These conventions arguably had ancient roots, but they achieved particularly effective expression in the Baedeker's evolving vision of bourgeois travel. This accumulating tourist 'script' always presupposed an individual traveler capable of making his (or, to an increasing degree, her) own decisions. It combined attention to practical preparation but also to the joy of anticipating travel and fantasizing about what would be seen and done on a trip. Not even Nazi travel literature, rigorous to a fault, denied the individual tourist this right (Müller-Gaisberg 1936, 261-2). It maximized freedom while also modulating the chaos that could ensue from having too many options, too many travel routes, and too many sites to take in. Itineraries, asterisks, and variations in print size combined to give the reader a tolerably concise set of markers and cues with which to navigate the tourist landscape. Above all, Baedeker's vision suggested that the ability to travel was within reach of everyone— in theory if not in contemporary practice. But its insistence on this point was more powerful than was the Nazis' harping on the same issue. The Baedeker divided up the world into national communities just as systematically as the National Socialists did, but it always presupposed that individual traveler-collectors operated somewhere underneath and between the lines of political (and racial) divisions. The National Socialist travel culture had no real match for this fierce individualism, which could appear anywhere—in hotel rooms and restaurants, in trains and automobiles, in clothing stores and ski resorts—where leisured displacement 'happened.'

Yet the Baedeker was no longer the platform from which to preach modern leisure travel's individualizing message. The firm was economically damaged and ideologically compromised. It was now less than the sum of the parts made up by its vast distribution of guidebooks to all parts of the world. The defeat of National Socialism in a war of unprecedented violence made it possible to reassemble the fragments of the Baedeker heritage, though in a new format with different cultural and geopolitical coordinates. From this act of reassembling would also come new definitions of the individual traveler and the German nation as a tourist unity.

# Chapter Four

# Fodor's Germany

## I

Americans touring Germany in the early 1950s had but one up-to-date and comprehensive English-language guidebook to help them plan their itineraries. It was published by the David McKay company in New York and edited by Eugene Fodor, founder of the now famous Fodor's Modern Guide series. A Hungarian who emigrated to London and later wrote in Paris and the US, Fodor began his career as a travel tycoon with a guide to Europe in the 1930s. The new postwar guide to Germany seemed to be an impossible task at first because, after tabulating the losses caused by the war, it was tempting to conclude 'there is nothing left to see,' according to the foreword. There were also terminological complications stemming from the political situation. Fodor defended the handbook's title, *Germany 1953*, arguing that both 'West Germany' and 'The German Federal Republic' were too cumbrous. And in any case, as the editor put it, 'it's a fairly safe bet that there isn't a great deal of pleasure travel going on, for tourists who speak any language, in the other Germany' (Fodor 1953, 7–8). Incorrect though this assumption was, it well reflected the then popular idea that the German Democratic Republic was a no-man's land for tourism—and for almost anything else having to do with Western notions of individual freedom. A map gave graphical expression to this idea. It depicted West Germany in white, with a dense traffic network and major cities, but the East appeared as a gray zone, with only Berlin, Leipzig, and Dresden identified, and only the major highways allowing Western access into the country outlined.

The guide began with the usual practical information on preparing the trip, traveling from North America to the Continent, and getting around by train and auto once in Germany. A major part of this introductory material was devoted to 'the German scene,' which included essays by American and English journalists and travel writers on food and customs as well as on 'national character' and history. An unsigned article entitled 'The Germans: What They Think and How They Act' offered a panorama, discussing German regions, occupation influences, education and family life, local traditions, relations between the sexes, and hobbies and sports. German society was revolutionized—or traumatized—by the war, and although Germans still showed great respect for hard work and authority, they now appeared

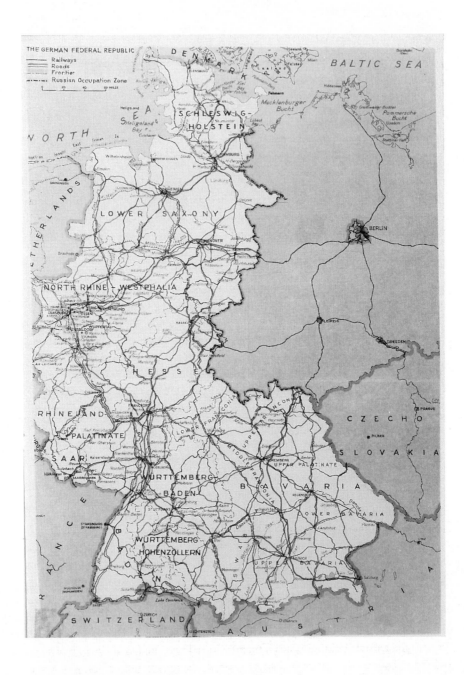

*Figure 16   Fodor's foldout map of Germany: Western tourist paradise versus Eastern no-man's land (Fodor 1953).*

*Figure 17*  'Simple pleasures can be simpler in Germany than almost anywhere else: a stein of beer, a funny hat, and the party's on' (Fodor 1953, photo opposite page 48).

to be relatively benign, even relaxed and jovial, in their enjoyment of simple pleasures. This same article took a long view of national character, beginning with Tacitus' account of Germanic tribes and then plummeting ahead to Beethoven, Wilhelm II, and Hitler. But this long history, so different than that of the country from which US travelers came, suggested a degree of identification between the two cultures. 'The monolithic façades of the Kaiser's and Hitler's Reichs have obscured the fact that through most of its history Germany has been diverse, disunited and unstable,' read the guide. 'It has accepted foreign influence, and been caught up in dynastic struggles and international storms. Germany has been a melting pot with new ingredients continually added and pressures and temperatures erratically changed' (ibid., 42).

One can forgive a tour book for using gastronomic metaphors; drinking and eating well are after all part of the travel experience. Even so, the use of the then still widely used American term 'melting pot' was extraordinary as a description of the country that less than a decade previously had been the radical Other to western liberal values. The term 'melting pot' was discredited in serious discussions of American identity in the 1920s, but it persisted in journalistic and popular usage and enjoyed a revival in academic discussion in the 1950s (Gleason 1980, 39–40). One could of course dismiss the language in a number of ways: as yet another chapter in the long history of touristic kitsch, for instance, or as the result of the postwar 'construction' or 'invention' of Germany. One could argue that the Fodor's guide was part of a larger project, evident in politics, culture, economics, education, and many other areas, in which the requirements of the Cold War transformed former German enemies into valued friends. The guidebook made this point directly, arguing that since 'the west is richer and more powerful for the addition of this new ally' it was 'all the more important . . . to cement these bonds with the personal experience of travel, in both directions' (Fodor 1953, 49). Scholars of national images would employ such material to consider how the tourist industry used Germany to repress a series of nasty 'heteroimages' (of German author-itarianism, for instance) with an 'autoimage' more palatable to Americans interested in things German. All these approaches have something to offer, but all are unsatisfactory in some respect as well, as I have argued elsewhere (forthcoming).

It is more useful here to discuss the Fodor guide in the context of the narrative of German travel cultures. It will be maintained that the Fodor guide appropriated the German nation as a touristic whole in a manner similar to that of the Baedeker guidebook of the pre-World War I era. (Recent scholarship has done a good job outlining how certain postwar German groups appropriated the symbols and objects of American culture [Maase 1999], but I am arguing that we also need to look at the way in which American culture appropriated Germany.) After the national–liberal travel culture was deformed from within; after modernist, socialist, and National Socialist travel cultures eviscerated the image of the German nation in efforts to create a new synthesis as an alternative to the failed Baedeker project; the Fodor worked as a new—and successful—reconstructive effort. In part, Fodor's accomplishment was the result of a learning process stretching back over the previous decades whereby Americans became acquainted with Germany as a tourist destination. But it was also a function of the utter defeat of Germany in the war, a defeat that allowed the American travel culture to step in and play a decisive role in reassembling the broken shards of tourist Germany. Above all, it depended not on a one-way street but an inter-societal transfer consisting of what Americans told themselves about Germany and what Germans told each other and Americans about themselves. More than ever before, the German travel culture rested on the movement of images and experiences across national borders or, in this case, across the Atlantic. As one reads the Fodor guide, it is important to follow what images arise in German tourist literature of the time, and what the relationship (or mis-relationship) between these images and those Americans had of Germany are. No less important is what was left out—about Germany in general and about the former German Communist state in particular—in this image migration across borders. Such a reading will enable us to understand the formation of a new American–German travel culture that was neither wholly American nor German, but something else.

## II

In understanding the evolution of postwar American perceptions of Germany, it is important to emphasize that there was continuity between World War II and its aftermath. At no time in World War II except in November 1944 did the share of Americans who saw 'the German people' as the enemy rise above 20 percent. Conversely, in Great Britain, despite a degree of sympathy for the Nazi regime earlier in the 1930s among some members of the British elite, the share of those who were hostile to the German people was as high as 50 percent. This hostility found expression in postwar tourist literature, as when a British travel guide declared that the German character, so often 'immersed in a sea of mysticism,' was 'unbalanced' (Cooper 1954, 72). At the end of the war, and after public knowledge of the concentration camps was widespread, only 13 percent of American respondents expressed support for the controversial Morgenthau plan to 'pastoralize' Germany. There was of course some contradictory evidence: in an August 1945 survey only 20 percent of the American respondents thought Germany could learn from World War II and give up its aggressive designs in world politics (Jarausch 1986, 16). But the overall flow of opinion indicated that the majority of Americans, perhaps more than two out of three of those polled, did not give voice to an intense hostility toward Germany. They took a long view stressing the possibilities of education and democratic transformation in a new postwar German state (Henke 1995, 75; Merritt 1995, 47). The title of a *Life* magazine editorial featuring Germany as the 'awakened giant' summed up this attitude: 'Furor Teutonicus: If History Can Change Character of a Nation, Germany's Is a Better Bet' (1954, 34).

The reasons for this comparatively liberal assessment are numerous. The German background of a significant part of the American population is one factor. Moreover, unlike British populations, Americans never experienced direct attack by German military forces. American popular culture played a significant role in shaping attitudes, and cinema in particular, even when it confronted the history of Nazi concentration camps in films such as *The Mortal Storm*, did more to minimize than to encourage public criticism of the Nazi regime. More than a conscious strategy, this tendency reflected Hollywood's commitment to a kind of entertainment that avoided overly disturbing 'realism' or controversial moral issues. Cinematic and touristic realities shared this characteristic. World War II also galvanized Americans' commitment to universal values of freedom of speech and democracy. Re-emphasizing a liberal American identity created the potential for a more open and tolerant view of other societies, even those that had attacked the United States and created political systems diametrically opposed to American traditions (Haack 1991; Gleason 1980, 48). Well before the rhetoric of globalization and the global community took hold of pundits and politicians, the American Nobel

Prize novelist Pearl Buck wrote that 'the world has become a neighborhood.' This proximity to the world meant that Americans had to take a direct interest in seeing to it that 'good people' prevail in Germany. Good Germans were ultimately not Germans at all, in Buck's eyes, just as Americans lost their national distinctiveness when they saw themselves in a 'natural brotherhood of the good among all peoples' (Buck 1946, 6). The era of liberality in American political culture may have passed by the early 1950s, at least for those many Americans who embraced Cold War rhetoric, but the sense of cross-cultural identity and universalism continued to have effect, shaping the American–German travel culture in the process.

German attitudes toward American occupiers were generally positive as well. This stemmed partly from the fact that a relatively small number of Germans ever got to know American military personnel very well, the public outrage over relations between GIs and German women notwithstanding. At first, the US military expected anything but good relations with the German people. A US serviceman's pocket guide to the country stated unequivocally that 'German hatred against America has been concentrated by education, propaganda, and the accuracy of the Allied Forces bombardment.' It advised GIs to 'keep your left out. Trust no one but your own kind' (Army Information Branch 1944, 7). Nonetheless, the German population took an understanding stance toward the behavior of American soldiers, and they believed that the 'Amis' were generally friendly toward Germans. Almost two-thirds of the respondents in the American occupation zone in a 1946 opinion poll gave positive traits for Americans when asked to characterize the occupiers. By the time the military government phase of the occupation ended, nearly three-quarters of opinion poll respondents who came into contact with American soldiers stated that soldiers' behavior toward Germans had been 'good' or 'very good.' Although Germans thought that British soldiers behaved more correctly toward the occupied population than American soldiers did, they still said that US troops did as well or better than German troops would have in a similar situation. The great exception to this attitude of acceptance was Germans' response to African American troops. The German population had generally negative perceptions of these soldiers, regarding them as a 'lower race' than whites. It might be added that Germans also denied that American troops in general were morally superior to Germans, and they denied that US soldiers were better military men than Germans had been. Still, the overall picture is one of tolerance if not acceptance (Merritt 1995, 252–60).

Once one moves beyond the realm of specific interactions between soldiers and the occupied population, the situation becomes more complex, although on balance German attitudes toward the United States were more positive than negative, and they became increasingly more positive as the 1950s wore on (Merritt 1995, 260). The history of German images of America is of course long and variegated. Germans regarded the United States as both a symbol of greater freedom and economic opportunity as well as a land of unlimited barbarism and vulgarity. The fruits of American economic and technological life were embraced and emulated, just as the power of US industry was feared. Germans reacted to every new American innovation, from the skyscraper to jazz, with a mix of awe and anxiety.

No generation of Germans grew up with a more positive attitude toward Americans than the children and teenagers of the first decade after World War II. Again, the US military did not anticipate German youth's welcome, informing GIs to 'be on guard particularly against young Germans between the ages of 14 and 28' (Army Information Branch 1944, 7). Having escaped both the influence of Nazism's intense anti-American propaganda during the war and longer bouts of Hitler Youth indoctrination, Germans born between 1935 and 1945 in particular defied official predictions by embracing things American. They rejected the tradition of racism toward blacks, making the African American soldier virtually the symbol not only of the occupation but also of America itself. (Interestingly, only a decade before, two African Americans, Jesse Owens and Joe Louis, were also among the best-known US public figures beside Franklin Roosevelt among Germans, although with quite different consequences [Van Til 1938, 85].) Generosity, friendliness, informality, even sexual prowess—all these traits seemed to converge in the symbol of the smiling black US serviceman. For schoolchildren, CARE (Cooperative for American Remittances to Europe) packages, US-organized youth centers, chewing gum, chocolates and a host of other material objects and sites added up to an ever growing web of positive American influences in daily life. By the time of the Fodor's publication, many West German teenagers had already begun to embrace American popular culture in clothing and hairstyles, cinema, and jazz music. The Fodor guidebook (1953, 48) remarked that 'the younger generation has taken to American ways in dress and language, in dancing and in outlook.' This embrace would become even stronger after the mid-1950s as American rock'n'roll worked its way through a receptive European teen culture (Maase 1992, 83–9).

It is important to avoid seeing this as a process of 'Americanization' forced from outside. West German teens, like their counterparts elsewhere in Europe, willingly appropriated American cultural and commercial influences, transforming them into what may be called a distinctive national style of Americanization (Maase 1992). To analyze this national style would take us far beyond the present discussion; it is enough for now to emphasize that the 'self-Americanization' of significant parts of German culture created a kind of two-way transmission belt through which Americans and Germans mutually created new inter-societal identities. Given that young people were the most avid travelers in postwar Germany, this process of appropriation and transformation of American influences has a direct bearing on the building of a new German travel culture.

The Fodor travel guide appeared at a propitious time in postwar Germany. Wars have always stimulated travel, but World War II may have done so even more not only because of its scope but because its outcome left the main defeated country thoroughly in the hands of foreigners. These foreigners were encouraged to travel to Germany by several institutions, not the least influential being the German Tourist Information Office, which opened in New York in 1950 and soon had branches in San Francisco, Chicago, and other North American cities (Titzhoff 1959, 526). Not only the war but the Cold War played its part as well. Growing antagonisms between the United States and the Soviet Union put a premium on getting to know one's potential (and later, real) German allies. More broadly, leisure travel appeared to be an antidote to mounting international tension. The Nagel Travel Guide series for Europe was available to tourists in English, French, German, Spanish, Italian, Swedish, and Danish. The preface to one of its guides pinpointed the idea of leisure travel as a counterbalance to political acrimony: 'The present widespread interest in travel and the manifold opportunities now available to tourists could . . . play an important part in dispelling the mistrust and enmity now afflicting mankind' (1956, v–vi). Germany was at the center of the storm of mistrust and enmity that blew over Europe soon after World War II ended.

The US military occupation brought almost 1 million American military personnel and their dependents, government agents, writers and journalists, and business representatives to the defeated country. They were fascinated by the destruction wrought by the war—a fascination one New York travel agency exploited by inviting Americans to see Germany in 1953 with the slogan 'last chance to see the ruins' (Eich 1963, 329–30). They gobbled up Nazi party paraphernalia and souvenirs—and sometimes much more, including works of art and artifacts that made their way into US soldiers' private collections back home or were sold on the black market in Germany. US servicemen used military guidebooks to direct them to the Nuremberg Altstadt, 'possibly the most awesome ruin in Germany,' and to help them find the way to Hitler's destroyed Bavarian villa, where they laughed at a sign reading 'Hitler doesn't live here any more' (Armed Forces Information 1951, 51, 55). In the immediate postwar period, some 30,000 US servicemen visited Hitler's Berchtesgaden retreat every month (Bach 1946, 45).

Soldiers, administrators, and their families lived much like tourists when they were in Germany. Housed in bases separated from the native population, US personnel often knew Germans only from afar, barely acquiring the minimal language skills to get by, and creating their own touristic islands, 'little Americas' within the German sea. But there were certainly many exceptions to this isolation, appropriately praised in the US military press or in publications back home, and these exceptions did much to build a new American–German travel culture (Healy 1952; Mayes 1952). This applies even more directly to those US soldiers of German heritage for whom World War II was a kind of Bildungsreise. They gained a clearer appreciation of the country from which their ancestors came during the war, and they returned to the Continent after 1945 as tourists, businessmen, students, and administrators. For those whose first exposure to Germany came during the occupation, a similar process of learning about their 'roots' took place.

Although the Fodor was the first comprehensive guide to Germany in English after the fall of Hitler, it was not the first postwar travel guide by any means. Military authorities issued a pocket guide for Germany as early as 1944, and they began issuing travel guides for soldiers in Berlin soon after the war's end. Often consisting of only schematic street plans and very general descriptions of mostly bombed-out landmarks, these guides were the first real introduction to the former German capital for many GIs. French occupiers could also get government-issued guides, one of which projected the city plan of Paris onto Hitler's destroyed capital to orient soldiers. Soldiers received tips on Berlin nightlife, and the French even got a guide to military uniforms in order to be able to distinguish the ranks of foreign soldiers they met in the city. Tourist literature from the Russian side was scantier. Russian authorities were hesitant to encourage tourism among rank and file soldiers, and so it was at first only officers and their wives who traveled to the western sectors of Berlin. Later the Russian military organized bus tours throughout the city for its soldiers (Poock-Feller and Krausch 1996, 105–7).

Berlin had been the most important tourist destination in Germany, and city authorities were hard-pressed to pick up on this tradition given the destruction all around them. But pick up on it they did, beginning with travel brochures. A significant problem was that advertising slogans could not very well return to the language of the Nazi period. Moreover, the slogans of the Weimar era were dated. 'Everyone at least once in Berlin' may have worked well when Berlin was the cultural and political capital, but Berlin had been decisively 'decentered.' And in any case, other West German cities, anxious to capture their share of the domestic and foreign tourist market, were fearful that the divided city would once again become the tourist magnet it was in better times. One of the earliest examples to break new ground in this genre in the English language came from the Berlin–Charlottenburg Travel Bureau for the Greater Berlin magistrate (Magistrat von Groß-Berlin 1947). Its motto was 'Berlin Lives, Berlin Calls.' It included scenes of how Berlin looked before the war—'that was once Berlin,' read the accompanying text—and how it looked in 1947, when rubble women cleared streets over which the hulking ruins of prewar architecture cast shadows. The message was that Berlin was rebuilding, both physically and emotionally. 'One will hardly recognize Berlin,' the brochure continued. 'Berlin's piles of rubble are gray—but Berlin life is colorful. Traffic flows again. Work is being done.' A map contained 42 sightseeing destinations, 29 of which were described as 'damaged' or 'destroyed.' Others were described as 'repaired' or in the process of being so.

169

The blockade of Berlin in 1948 put a quick end to efforts to treat the metropolis as a touristic whole. But just days after the blockade ended, the city tourist office was back at work, strengthened with a 30,000-mark advertising budget from the Berlin Senate. As the Cold War escalated, Berlin's fraught political situation was used as a tourist attraction. The Berlin travel bureau, founded in 1949, issued a publication in 1950 touting the occupied metropolis as 'the most interesting city in Europe.' 'In the last half-decade Berlin was one of the most-mentioned cities in the world,' it read. 'And today—really!—it is more interesting than ever . . . In Berlin West and East meet, the oppositions touch one another here.' Soon the contrast between the two Berlins would become even more strongly pronounced in tourist advertising issued by the West Berlin travel office. The Kurfürstendamm became the 'boulevard of desire,' its shop windows and attractive women visible markers of prosperity and bodily pleasure, while East Berlin's Friedrichstraße was said to 'look as if it lies in Asia' (Verkehrsamt 1950a, 1; Poock-Feller and Krausch 1996, 108, 110). Political conflict created geographical and cultural distance between entities that were literally just minutes away from each other. Another brochure carried the title in English: *Don't Miss Berlin, the International City Behind the Iron Curtain* (Verkehrsamt 1950b). Not incidentally, Berlin here appeared as a beauty queen, draped in the flags of the occupying powers.

But it was not only Berlin that received early and consistent attention in travel propaganda. And it was not only scenes of destruction, rubble clearance, and political division that carried the day. For American businessmen looking for profits, the Joint Export–Import Agency of the US Department of Commerce offered a handy guide to the combined British and American occupation zones (1949). It covered practical travel arrangements for hotels and car rentals but also gave detailed information on commercial regulations, the status of businessmen in the three Western zones, contracts, customs, and import licenses. As political and economic reconstruction proceeded, the Federal Republic's office for the Marshall Plan issued a travel prospect entitled 'The Door is Open to Germany.' The cover of this skillfully done booklet featured a wrought-iron gate opening out onto a country lane bordered by wildflowers and grass. The lane led down into a green valley where a small village and church steeple, modern highways, well-tended fields, and—off in the distance—industrial smokestacks co-existed. The picture depicted Germany as an industrial garden, in which the traveler felt like 'the child in a fairy tale. He doesn't know what he should wish for, or where he should go.' Germany—'heartland Europe'—offered something for the sports enthusiast, the music lover, the spa-goer, or the businessman. As befit a publication originating in Marshall Plan Germany, the text stressed growth and production: 'A reconstruction is taking place that has turned Germany into a beehive of hard work and productivity, a productivity as unprecedented as the destruction that came before it.' By contrast, in the East, one saw nothing but 'grayness,' high infant mortality

THE INTERNATIONAL CITY
BEHIND THE IRON CURTAIN

*Figure 18   A tourist brochure cover:* Don't Miss Berlin *(Verkehrsamt der Stadt Berlin, 1950b).*

rates, and tubercular young people. The door to Germany 'stood open,' even if a large part of the German people lived behind 'the iron curtain' (Bundesministerium für den Marshallplan 1951, 3, 11, 67).

The door stood open for many nationalities, but Americans were among the most favored visitors to the German garden. The share of American families with incomes exceeding $3,000 grew from 16 percent in 1941 to 50 percent in 1947. Although American tourists were a varied group, they came largely from families with incomes at or above this 'middle-class' level. It was estimated that in 1950 alone some 327,000 US 'dollar bearers' traveled to Europe in 1950, contributing $370 million dollars to OEEC (Organisation for European Economic Cooperation) countries. American tourists to Germany accounted for only about 2 percent of the total number of American travelers in Europe in 1948–9, down from 15 percent ten years earlier (Dulles 1964, 170–3; OEEC 1951, 11–26). But the early 1950s saw a rapid increase in Germany's attractiveness as a tourist destination for Americans. From 1951 to 1955, the number of overnight stays registered by travelers from the United States during the West German summer tourist season nearly tripled, reaching over 800,000 in 1955. This well exceeded the rate of increase for all overnight stays by foreign visitors to West Germany in the same period. Of all foreign guests in the Federal Republic in the 1955 travel season, only the Dutch registered more overnight stays than Americans did (Statistisches Bundesamt 1954, 364; 1956, 340). The high number of overnight stays was related in part to the fact that when US tourists traveled to Europe, they tended to stay longer than European tourists. No comprehensive comparative statistics on this matter were available for the postwar era, but the OEEC reported that on average American tourists stayed 63 days in Europe as compared with 52 days in 1937–8 (OEEC 1951, 21).

Not only was American travel to Europe and Germany recovering, but Germans themselves were back on the roads. World War II had done much to stimulate tourism, as German soldiers returned as tourists to places that they had first seen as conquerors. But this took time. The 'economic miracle' spread its benefits slowly and unevenly, as many working-class families subsisted on budgets that recalled the Depression and the war more than the prosperity that was to come (Wildt 1994). Just as a situation of more widespread consumption and confidence in the future did not take hold until the second half of the 1950s, the vaunted German propensity for foreign travel emerged only after a decade had passed since the currency reform of 1948. In fact, 1958 was a watershed, since it was the first postwar year in which more West Germans traveled abroad than foreigners visited the Federal Republic. Before this time, only about one-tenth of all West Germans had traveled outside their national borders. And the vast majority of those who traveled domestically usually did so within fairly constricted areas, venturing no more than 600 kilometers from home. Many still spent their vacations at home. In the first flush of postwar freedom, the disastrous social and economic conditions, to say nothing of disruptions in the transportation network and in hotels—only about 40 percent of prewar sleeping accommodations were available for tourist use in 1949—still made leisure travel the exception rather than the rule. And even if resources were available for such travel, Germans in the late 1940s and early 1950s considered parsimoniousness to be one of the most significant markers of good character. Combined with a great reluctance to go into debt—surveys showed that Americans were more willing to buy on credit or take loans than West Germans were—the culture of thriftiness meant that vacations away from home were either to be very modest or were to be foregone entirely. At the beginning of the 1950s the German tourist industry was only about one-third the size it had been in 1936 (Wildt 1996, 66; Schildt 1995, 183, 199, 200).

A massive public effort was one of the things required to get the tourist industry back on its feet. The provincial tourist bureaus and the nationally organized Association of German Travel Bureaus were re-established. The hotel industry banded together in a national interest group. German spas and resorts reorganized themselves in a national pressure group, as did the German Travel Agency (DER), a continuation of the earlier Central European Travel Agency (MER). In 1948 these and a host of other organizations representing the railway administration, the postal service, the municipalities, and chambers of industry and commerce allied in the German Agency for Tourism (*Deutsche Zentrale für Fremdenverkehr*, or DZF). The trade unions were also involved, joining some of the above-named organizations in the Association for Social Tourism and Travel Savings, which provided discounted tours for lower-income groups and encouraged savings accounts for vacations. The German railways modernized their tracks and wagons, and the German highways set up information booths at border crossings, and more telephones, restaurants, and rest stops along the way. In 1951, the Western occupation authorities transferred jurisdiction over passports to the Federal Republic, and in subsequent years the FRG stopped requiring visas and, in some select cases, passports for foreign nationals traveling in Germany. The Transportation Ministry of the Federal Republic became responsible for all matters relating to the tourist industry in 1949 (Titzhoff 1959, 520–1, 523–4, 527–8). Relatively soon after the war, the infrastructural requirements for getting tourism going again were in place.

The tourist industry took longer to recover than the economic system as a whole in the late 1940s—in contrast to the situation from 1952 to 1960—but conditions were variable, and regions such as Bavaria saw a faster growth rate in the tourist industry than did others. Around one-third of all overnight stays were accounted for by the southern German state in this period. Thanks to the efforts of the travel entrepreneur Carl Degener, the resort town Ruhpolding in Upper Bavaria became the mecca of inexpensive package tours for West Germans in the first postwar decade (Putschögl 1999, 50; Schildt 1995, 183, 195). It was unsurprising in this context to see the Baedeker firm produce some of its first fully reworked postwar German-language guidebooks for Bavaria and Munich. For the Bavarian capital, the Baedeker wanted 'to show, what was left after the terrible destruction of the unfortunate war, what was destroyed and what was saved, what was restored through the purposeful reconstruction of cultural landmarks and historic churches since 1945, and what part of [the city's] irrepressible spirit has reawakened' (1951, 5). Like the 1948 Baedeker to Leipzig, which was the first postwar Baedeker in any language, its goal was to enlighten both local people and the gathering crowds of tourists in the German south about what remained after the 'unfortunate' destruction of the war (1948, 5).

US occupation forces contributed to the gradual recovery of domestic German tourism when they promoted youth camping and other related activities as part of their re-education campaign. Labor negotiations helped to widen the sphere of leisure time as well, as by the end of the 1950s three weeks' vacation time became the rule rather than the exception for employed Germans (Schildt 1995, 182). Opinion surveys from 1950 indicate that only a little more than one-fifth of the respondents had taken a vacation in the previous year. But by 1953 West German hostels reached their prewar capacity, while resort and other vacation areas did the same in 1955. When in that year survey respondents were asked if they considered tourism a 'luxury good,' more than 80 percent replied in the negative. In 1953, more than half of all West German respondents placed travel ahead of all other leisure activities in importance, suggesting a willingness to sacrifice for tourism. Travelers reported they would often forego ordering drinks with their meals in order to have money for guided tours and other attractions while on vacation (Becher 1990, 196; Schildt 1995, 199). The 'typical' working-class family of four now began to devote ever larger amounts of the household income to vacation travel. In 1952 just 0.6 percent of household income was devoted to such purposes; ten years later the figure was 2 percent (Wildt 1996, 73). The recovery from the war and its aftermath accelerated; the age of mass tourism was on the horizon. Tourism—and this was the biggest difference between the 1950s and earlier moments in the history of leisure travel—was now a 'self-evident' expectation for the majority of the population rather than a still distant goal for which political and ideological struggle was necessary (Schildt 1995, 180).

Even so, in 1958, at the moment when cultural critic Hans Magnus Enzensberger derided leisure travel as a mass industry that cheapened *everyone*, only about one-third of West German adults took vacations away from home. Social disparities persisted, as those who were more educated, more urban, and financially better-off traveled more than manual workers, farmers, the partly employed or unemployed, or families with many children. Generational differences also existed, as those under 21 had the highest rates of travel while those over 70 had the lowest. When West Germans went on tour, important differences emerged in the amount of money they had to spend. More than half spent less than 200 marks during their vacations, well below the national average of 266. The alleged 'massification' and homogenization of unthinking hordes of tourists did not take place from this angle of perspective; social gradations continued to affect both the composition of those who toured and the behavior of tourists (Ganser 1996, 193; Schildt 1995, 189–90, 199; 1996, 69–73, 75).

A Nazi propaganda slogan once stated 'Wheels must roll for victory!' In 1957, a popular illustrated magazine did a pictorial on German tourism under the title 'Wheels roll into vacation' (Schildt 1995, 188). The political and cultural climate had changed dramatically between the times when these slogans carried the day.

But so too had the 'wheels' that carried German armies and German armies of tourists to their destinations. Increasing automobile ownership, the building of the Autobahns, the camping movement, and the promise of a 'people's car' contributed mightily to the expansion of tourism before World War II. In 1954, about one-fifth of all West Germans took their vacations with private autos, and many more took advantage of bus tours; more than half still used the railways for tourism. Seven years later, the train and the car were equally popular as a means of transportation for vacations, each accounting for about 40 percent of the types of transportation mentioned. (It would take until the 1960s before air travel became an accessible mode of tourist transportation for significant numbers of West Germans.) The availability of the automobile for private transportation and the widening of the highway network encouraged a more spontaneous approach to tourism, as weekend outings and day trips could be arranged with a minimum of planning. Not for nothing was the auto praised in the German press as a 'vehicle of freedom' for the traveling individual or family. Not only was more spontaneity possible, but once far-off tourist destinations were now within reach thanks to automobile travel. For West Germans of the 1950s, Austria was the most popular travel destination outside the Federal Republic, but Italy soon became a close second. Austria's popularity was due in part to cultural and linguistic ties but also to the fact that many Germans experienced hostility or suspicion in other European lands when they traveled in the decade after the war. Spurred by the automobile, the camping movement reached unprecedented proportions after growing modestly in the 1930s; around 3 million West Germans stayed in some 60,000 campgrounds annually by the end of the 1950s (Andersen 1997, 154–92).

The Fodor guidebook acknowledged the progress of the automobile, praising Germany as 'an ideal country for motor touring.' It had 'excellent roads and good garage service, while the number of interesting small localities makes travel through Germany more rewarding for the motorist, who can stop at will and vary his route as he wishes, than for the train traveler' (1953, 23). But there were disadvantages as well. 'Germans show an inclination to be demon drivers, however small and rattly their cars' read the guide. 'Their contempt for traffic signals and road courtesy is one of the least pleasant of a traveler's experiences' (ibid., 23, 49). That the critique could be made at all reflected the expanded use of the automobile in everyday life; that it pointed to questionable driving habits suggests that West Germany was still an immature nation with respect to automotive practice. But the car was in Germany to stay, and soon 'rattly' postwar automobiles gave way to solid Volkswagens and expensive BMWs.

Travel publishers aided motorized tourism by producing guides oriented entirely to the highway network. In one respect this was continuous with the practice of the 1930s. The Baedeker firm re-established its reputation for reliability and comprehensiveness in this genre, for example, issuing *Shell Auto Guides* for West

German regions. The editor was Oskar Steinheil, who also compiled automobile guides for Baedeker during the Nazi period. These guides led the travelers through a part of the 'beautiful German landscape,' suggesting automobile routes along the way. For the Rhine and Mosel edition of 1952, eight suggestions for short tours and ten major routes were offered, with an alphabetical description of the major cities and towns. The Shell Baedeker still offered much detail and cultural background, but it was less encyclopedic than its prewar predecessors. Cologne received less than four pages in the 1952 guide compared to 41 in the Rhenish guide of 1925 (Steinheil 1952, 2, 92–5). 'Auto-touristic' practice, to use a term of the time, made Baedeker 'thick description' obsolete.

This could not have been predicted from the beginning of the automobile's spread as a tourist vehicle. Proponents of auto-tourism had always insisted that the use of the car enabled the tourist to seek out sights and appreciate vistas the train traveler could not grasp. It enabled more detail rather than less, in this argument. Perhaps the loss of the encyclopedic gaze has more to do with the tourists themselves, who belonged to social groups that were less comfortably grounded in classical education and less attuned to the almost scholarly pace of nineteenth-century bourgeois tourism. In any case, the auto-tourist guides stressed individuality and a do-it-yourself spirit of the kind the Viaropa travel agency of Bielefeld provided in its contribution to motorized tourism. It offered Anglophone tourists a handy guide consisting of 'route-mapping-blocks.' Using the blocks, the tourist could decide what day to travel and what 'off-days' to take, and he could fashion his own tour through Germany relying on auto routes as well as train and air trips. Auto trips were central to the Viaropa system, which maximized flexibility and assured its customers 'you'll be absolutely independent' (Viaropa Tours, 1). This of course was thoroughly within the Baedeker tradition of freeing the tourist from unnecessary obstacles.

Turning to East Germany, Fodor's assessment of the new state as a Dark Continent of leisure travel was strikingly wrong. It is true that foreign travel for ordinary GDR citizens was ruthlessly restricted; only in 1954 were trips to other socialist countries allowed, and only in the late 1960s did such foreign travel become substantial. But in the Soviet zone soon after the war's end—and despite the great number of refugees—the Baltic Sea resorts were once again popular, attracting 24,000 guests in 1946 and 87,000 a year later. The Soviet military pledged paid vacations for all workers and employees, an idea taken up in 1951 in the constitution of the German Democratic Republic. In 1946, the Free German Trade Union Association (Freier Deutscher Gewerkschaftsbund, FDGB) sent 7,000 members to vacation homes, and in the following year it set up a program offering financial aid for vacations for big families and trusted 'activists.' FDGB resorts and hotels and inns expropriated by the Soviets were widely used for such purposes. The first Baedeker licensed in the Soviet zone focused on Leipzig, which in comparison to many other German cities experienced relatively minor damage. Yet like other cities, Leipzig was also overflowing with refugees who needed orientation and guidance as they got to know their new Heimat (Baedeker 1948, 4, 5; Koshar 2000, 143–6). Like the Allied occupying forces, the East German state mobilized youth for the political cause by promoting tourism and hiking in the early 1950s. 'Every young pioneer and student should be a tourist,' stated the Free German Youth publication *Young Tourists*. Hiking and backpacking with other members of the Communist youth group was supposed to enhance the 'collective spirit' and willingness to fight for socialism on the part of the participants (Zentralrat 1955, 3).

Berlin played a special role in GDR officials' attempts to encourage travel, as it did in the West. A massive reconstruction effort in the heart of Berlin, the Stalinallee was an important symbol of Berlin's role not only as the capital of the German Democratic Republic but also the westernmost outpost of Communist Europe. After the first phase of the Stalinallee's construction was completed in 1952, tours for both foreign and East German guests became important for demonstrating the new state's accomplishments (Spode 1996, 15–16; Poock-Feller and Krausch 1996, 110–12). As the 1950s wore on, tourist advertising for East Berlin became more comprehensive, partly in recognition of the fact that the state had exploited the city's potential as a tourist magnet only to a limited degree. One result was the availability of more attractive and informative guidebook literature. The *Little Berolina Series*, issued by the Berolina travel agency under the direction of the East Berlin city magistrate, was an example. It published short guidebooks to the Berlin city hall, the Brandenburg Gate, the giant Soviet memorial in Treptow, the Friedrichshain, and other important sites. The descriptions, given in several languages including English, were predictable. The introduction to the Treptow memorial guide read: 'The people of the new democratic Germany honor here with grateful hearts the people of the Soviet Union and their heroic army, because their struggle was responsible for the defeat of fascism' (Berlin-Werbung Berolina 1961, 7). Yet the guides were done well, comparable to West German publications in terms of their production values, and they pointed to the more sophisticated elaboration of official guidebook literature in years to come.

Not only was there much more leisure travel in East Germany than the Fodor guide assumed; there was also much more individual travel as well. Reliable figures for the first postwar decade are unavailable, but Hasso Spode (1996, 20) has asserted that there was in fact more 'unorganized' tourism, including camping, than collectively organized tourism over the life of the GDR. Even within the context of tourism organized by the state or its official agencies, such as the FDGB, individualistic—or, perhaps, individualizing—motifs were prevalent, just as they were in the socialist travel culture of the Weimar Republic and in Nazi travel culture. When the FDGB published a handbook to resorts and spas in the German

Democratic Republic, it made no mistake about its collective goals. 'Life should be more beautiful and valuable for all workers,' read the introduction. 'Joy in life, happiness, and a feeling of well-being should bring all workers vigor and the enjoyment of being' (Freier Deutscher Gewerkschaftsbund 1959, 5). Similarities between Nazi and East German uses of the 'joy' motif are unmistakable. Also, numerous photographs throughout the book suggested collective leisure: workers discussing travel plans after receiving 'vacation checks,' beach-goers submitting to the sweaty rigors of group calisthenics, GDR citizens at an outdoor theater, and children playing under the watchful eye of the teacher-state in an FDGB camp. Yet the photos also depicted many rather middle-class-looking couples enjoying romantic moments strolling by the seaside or relaxing languidly in an idyllic resort hotel. Their pictures would have been at home in a travel guide or brochure in any Western country. Even more striking is the number of photographs of young, attractive, and presumably single women, sometimes in pairs or groups of three, often in bathing suits, both of a one-piece and two-piece variety, and usually in a scenic natural landscape. The FDBG was making its publication more appealing to the male heterosexual gaze in much the same way that travel propaganda did in the West. Yet it is also difficult to overlook the impression of youthful individuality—perhaps a degree of *Eigen-Sinn*, or 'sense of one's own,' to use Alf Lüdtke's apt term (1989, 262–5)—in these pictures. They suggest that the strong individualizing impulse of modern leisure travel, its unremitting drive toward subjectivization and personalization, persisted even when it was channeled into collectivist streams organized by a Communist dictatorship.

### III

The revival of American tourism in West Germany depended on the provision and improvement of accommodations. In the early postwar years, tourists were highly uncertain as to the availability and quality of hotels and hostels. The 1947 brochure for Berlin discussed above went out of its way to note that 'even in difficult conditions hotels and inns provide for the good accommodation of guests in Berlin.' But the brochure did not say that most intact hotel rooms were being used by the military and long-term renters, or that pleasure travelers often took rooms in private homes or dark bunker 'hotels' (Magistrat von Groß-Berlin 1947; Poock-Feller and Krausch 1996, 107). With economic recovery, West Germany began making great strides in the hotel industry. The Fodor guide praised the wide availability, cleanliness, and inexpensiveness of German hotels, stating that 'you can put it down pretty confidently as a fact that even in frequented resorts and big cities, there are always good rooms available at six marks' (1953, 24).

*Figure 19   Communist tourism: An East German woman on the beach looks much like
her Western counterpart (Freier Deutscher Gewerkschaftsbund 1959, 109).*

   More than simply pointing to the convenience of West Germany as a land of
leisure travel, this statement also situated tourism in a larger cultural matrix. Many
observers of German culture, from novelists to anthropologists, had identified
cleanliness as an enduring German trait. Some saw an overbearing attachment
to cleanliness as symptomatic of distorted emotional relations manifested in
authoritarian family structures and extremist political movements (Freese 1990,
121–2). This attitude was reinforced by the experience of Nazism and World War
II, and in North America in particular many journalistic and academic careers
were now being made putting the German nation on the social–psychological
couch. But the image of (often perverse) German cleanliness was hardly arbitrary

as it found concrete expression in postwar Germany well before Fodor tourists set foot on the Continent. In one of the most informative early journeys through the American occupation zone, the American journalist Julian Bach noted that US soldiers had positive first impressions of Germany based on their bad memories of fighting initially in France. Aside from Paris, which continued to capture the imagination of Americans abroad, the towns and villages of rural France appeared muddy, dirty, and run-down to US soldiers. By contrast, where Allied bombers had not done their work, houses and villages in Germany were well-built and clean, the roads in good shape, and sanitary conditions more like those the servicemen were accustomed to in the United States. In comparison to France, wrote Bach, the GI 'smelled less manure in the countryside, and found more sidewalks in the cities. As the highest praise that most Americans feel like bestowing on anything foreign is, "It's clean!" he was surprised and pleased with Germany's physical plant' (1946, 271).

Bach's account was based on nearly two years of reporting on American troops in the European theater. He was able to watch American servicemen who fought in Europe arrive and stay in Germany until as late as December 1945, and he was there when a new wave of soldiers without prior experience of European combat arrived by the thousands in an occupied country. No friend of Germany, Bach nonetheless strove for accuracy and fair mindedness. Although critics saw his book as 'neither very well written nor very profound,' its observations on the middle and lower echelons of military government and on the attitudes of American servicemen were regarded as 'on the whole sound and useful' (Sweezy 1946, 586).

Bach's observation on US soldiers' first impressions is noteworthy partly because it reminds us that ruin and destruction were not the only or even the dominant images many formed when they first encountered Germany in the last days of the war and the first postwar years. Their views of Germany were more touristic than military. In addition, it suggests that such heteroimages gain a large part of their resonance not only from comparisons between one's home and a foreign country but also between other foreign countries. Germany was 'not France,' and that was almost as important as the character of Germany itself. American soldiers in the Rhineland after 1918 reacted similarly, making invidious comparisons between their 'frigid, medieval' billets in France and their relative comfort in Koblenz, headquarters of the American occupation army (Franck 1920, 25, 52). Significantly, German nationalist rhetoric, from criticisms of French occupying troops after World War I to Nazi racist propaganda during the Saar campaign, also contrasted 'dirty' France and 'clean' Germany (Bürckel 1934). In World War II, German soldiers wrote home about the filthiness of Galicia, Poland, Ukraine, and other parts of the Balkans and Soviet Union. They contrasted these places with a notionally 'clean' Germany, and often contrasted 'clean' parts of Eastern Europe, such as

Bulgaria, with 'dirty' regions (often, not coincidentally, regions with large Jewish populations). In the context of service on the Eastern Front, too, France appeared to be 'clean' to Wehrmacht soldier-travelers (Latzel 1995, 448–51).

Most important is the fact that relative cleanliness, as it was being defined, was a significant element of the bodily memory of US soldiers. Sight, smell, and tactile experiences of the physical environment were as important to the inter-cultural negotiations taking place between Americans and Germans as army propaganda was. Reflecting broader tendencies in the burgeoning postwar tourist industry, Fodor's handbook exploited this sense of cleanliness as a key switching point, a moment of significant inter-societal transfer, between Americans and Germans. Clean hotel rooms were imbricated in a larger set of memories and experiences that operated quite literally close to the skin, and which American travelers could draw on as they traversed postwar Germany. That the trope of cleanliness was also deeply historical, in the sense that it suggested a more urban and 'middle-class' sense of the term as it was used in both journalistic and tourist accounts, should also be noted. If Americans and Germans effectively had the same understanding of cleanliness, they participated in a broader cultural matrix that was not specifically national but rather transnational in character and oriented largely to Anglo-American and Northern European standards (Monaco 1990, 176). The boundaries of this particular understanding were not confined to America and Germany alone.

Bach argued that cleanliness was linked in the minds of US soldiers with qualities such as modernity, orderliness, and industriousness. These too were enduring elements of the public imagery of Germany. We have noted that this impression was deeply rooted in the minds of pre-1914 American travelers, who saw the Baedeker guide itself as a product of a typically German sense of organization. The popular assessment also derived from direct experience after World War II. US soldiers were interested in getting things done and they often expressed admiration for the way in which Germans began quickly rebuilding roads, schools, offices, factories, and architectural landmarks. Military personnel in Germany received an official pocket guide to the country that began with a short account of how Germans 'picked their way through the wreckage of their cities and of their pride to the beginning of a new phase in their history' (Armed Forces Information 1951, 5). One could argue that the imagery of a kind of self-made nation literally 'rising from nothing,' as popular German rhetoric of the time put it (Zentner 1954), appealed to Americans' autoimage as 'self-made men,' who with hard work and a bit of guile 'made' something of themselves. Germans understood 'success,' argued Bach, and US soldiers always admired success. Again, the Franco-German comparison was important, as Bach said US soldiers considered the French to be lazy while Germans were seen as willing workers. The continuity with the Nazi period should not be overlooked either, as postwar images of German productivity picked up on National Socialist attempts to place *Leistung,* or 'performance,' at the center of the Volksgemeinschaft (Koshar 1998a, 152–70).

This American heteroimage gained additional strength in Fodor guide descriptions of partially rebuilt German cities. These often expressed a degree of wonder at what had been accomplished in Berlin, Cologne, and other badly bombed towns. In an introductory essay by the journalist and radio commentator Richard C. Hottelet, Fodor tourists could read prose virtually humming with the rhythm of rebuilding. 'Roads and railroads were repaired, bridges rebuilt. Blasted cities were cleaned up and restored. More than 1 million dwellings were built in the first three years of the Adenauer government' wrote Hottelet (Fodor 1953, 39). Hottelot referred to 'phenomenal Berlin' in another part of his essay, and in the description of the city later in the guidebook a similarly admiring stance was adopted. 'Berlin faced a reconstruction effort which might have crippled a city established on a fundamentally sounder economic basis,' read the guide, 'Yet she has risen triumphantly from her ruins' (ibid., 313). The technical process of reconstruction itself was often the source of fascination—not a surprising observation given Americans' pragmatic and technically minded perspective on things. For Frankfurt am Main, Fodor travelers were encouraged to visit the 'unique spectacle' of the 'ruins processing facility' in the eastern part of the city, where daily thousands of blocks and other building materials were efficiently manufactured from the Hessian metropolis's war rubble (ibid., 120). The guidebook conceded openly that Frankfurt had little to offer tourists looking for medieval architecture due to the air raids of the war. But technology could compensate for history. The tourist could view the transformation of 12,000 tons of rubble, half of all the rubble in Hesse, into a modern metropolis, then sit at the rebuilt Hauptwache, the main traffic node in the central city, and 'watch the traffic jams' (ibid., 126).

The German propensity for work was the subject of a satirical introductory essay in the Fodor guide by the Hungarian-born British writer George Mikes, who adapted the piece from his travelogue, mischievously titled *Über Alles: Germany Explored* (1953). Mikes casually noted that foreign observers, having seen the material wellbeing already achieved in the early 1950s in Germany, wondered how they might get their countries to lose a war to America. He recounted the then well-known joke about two Israeli visitors to the Kurfürstendamm. After marveling at the riches displayed on this West Berlin avenue, one Israeli comments that the solution to his country's problem is to declare war on America, ensuring that the US would spend millions of dollars on the defeated country after war's end. The other thinks it over, but decides against this option. 'Why not?' his puzzled companion asks. 'What if we beat America?' replies the other (ibid., 53–6). Mikes was convinced that the key to the new German prosperity was not to be found in Marshall Plan aid. Rather, 'it was the amazing and staggering energy of the Germans which performed the miracles' (ibid., 54). The sense of wonder at German reconstruction quickly became a leitmotif of other tourist guidebooks as even the understated Baedeker guide to northern Bavaria, published in a new English-language edition, wrote of Germans' 'indestructible energy' in rebuilding the country (1951, 5).

The link with Germans' perception of what they were about should not be overlooked. Moving, neatly piling up, and re-using the mountains of rubble left by the war constituted an important source of collective identity on both sides of the German–German border. Leisure travel in the ruins was one of the ways in which Germans informed themselves about the scope of destruction and the status of rebuilding efforts. Such travel could take the form of a relatively informal family outing, or it could be folded into a more extended visit to a city or region (Koshar 1998a, 227–9). Such experiences also furthered tourism's interest in the spectacle. Just as battlefield tourism had impressed the traveler looking for the sublime, the piles of rubble and seemingly endless rows of bombed-out buildings referred the traveler to something truly otherworldly, beyond representation. As the 1950s wore on, *not* removing the rubble became a source of embarrassment, especially to the East Berlin authorities, who eventually banned the popular 'rubble tours' to the East organized by entrepreneurial Western bus companies (Poock-Feller and Krausch 1996, 111). Travel guidebooks often pointed out what had been destroyed, what had been rebuilt, and what was an entirely new structure. It was of course not the first time that an 'economic miracle' became a tourist attraction. The Nazi regime had used the Autobahn building program to stimulate tourism by making the process of construction itself the center of attention, and early Baedeker tourism marveled at the roads, bridges, and factories of the industrial revolution.

The perception of German industriousness ramified throughout the relations between Germany and America. It had an impact on both high-level industrial relations between the two countries and on Allied policy toward the Germans. It enabled a 'complex process of interaction between the two industrial cultures,' as Volker Berghahn demonstrates (1995, 73). The symbiosis between US and German firms, which Berghahn discusses from the German side, also depended on American business's regard for German colleagues and the expectation of future German productivity. One should not overlook how American attitudes mirrored those of German manufacturers. Since early in the century they had admired (not always without doubt) American business methods and efficiency, and much more than French businessmen, they regarded the US economy as a positive if not entirely transferable model (Nolan 1994; Schmidt 1997, 138–53). The failures of de-Nazification in all three Allied zones may be attributed in part to the fact that, as relations between the Soviet Union and the United States deteriorated, expectations of German industriousness put a premium on using experts who could get the job done. Individuals' prior involvement in the Nazi party was a secondary matter. This was a controversial subject, taken up by journalists such as William Shirer, a vitriolic critic of Germany who bitterly attacked American troops' less than activist approach to de-Nazification of industrial management and big manufacturers (1947, 306–7).

In the tourist industry, the trope of German industriousness also shaped American travelers' consumption habits and promoted shared understandings of the meaning and nature of commercial culture. German industry had been based not only on extensive mass production, but also on a reputation for manufacturing high-quality goods marked by taste and technological excellence. For many Germans, such high-quality production values symbolized an antidote both to the alleged shoddiness of US-style mass-produced goods and, later in the 1950s, to the appearance of cheap manufactured products from East German industry. Modern production values that had not lost touch with artisan tradition represented a 'third way' between the alternatives of full-scale capitalism and socialist industrialization. As Frank Trommler argues, German national identity also derived a good part of its resonance from the status attributed to skilled labor and quality work (1998). The revival of the nylon stocking (Perlon) industry in West Germany was based precisely on this kind of hybridity: an acceptance of modern values of consumerism folded into German traditions of 'quality work.' West German industry ensured through its propaganda efforts that only one of the postwar Germanys was allowed to call this value its own (Carter 1997, 164–70).

For postwar American travelers, such symbolism had a similar meaning. The Fodor guidebook included an essay on shopping in Germany by the American writer Nan Robertson, who also wrote a column on fashion and shopping for the Armed Forces Edition of the *New York Herald Tribune*. She advised tourists to avoid gift shops with English-language signs, arguing they 'are run by tradesmen who offer vulgar junk or souvenirs under the misconception that this is what Americans or Britons want' (Fodor 1953, 83). The wise foreign traveler sought out shops where one could find high-quality antiques, Bavarian handicrafts, 'clothes from the Dirndl belt,' beer steins, binoculars, cameras, candles, clocks, dolls, figurines, *Lederhosen* and loden cloth, porcelain and silver, steelware, and toys. On the landscape of such artifacts and goods, Americans and Germans established a symbiotic relationship grounded simultaneously in a critique of mass production and an embrace of 'elite' forms of consumption. This reflected a more general tendency of leisure travel in the postwar period. Ellen Furlough writes that 'mass tourism's success and appeal from the middle of the twentieth century was due to its ability both to be popularly accessible and to express social distinction and cultural difference' (1998, 248).

Germany had not yet entered the first age of mass tourism, and thus one is tempted to argue that the synthesis of popular and elite elements was somewhat premature (or prefigurative) by German standards. Yet we have noted that the tradition of 'distinction through travel' was part of the national–liberal travel culture.

It would be accurate to argue that in the 1950s an older tradition was adapted to wider audiences and an expanded repertoire of tourism. For Americans, the age of mass travel started well before this time, if not necessarily for travel to Europe. Moreover, American identity was so thoroughly associated with mass production techniques and industrial discipline that the distinction afforded by consumption of high-quality goods represented a sharper critique of American tradition for US tourists and soldiers than the insistence on 'quality work' and craft production did for Germans. For the latter, the traditions of distinction through travel and elitist consumption simultaneously popularized and gave a new home to pre-existing values after World War II. So often seen as a moment of the one-way imposition of American values on Europe, the postwar period also included significant movements in the other direction as Americans embraced, or adapted to, 'European' values and representations. Pells (1997) offers an informative if diffuse account of this process from the European side.

German industriousness and success at rebuilding consumer culture were not regarded as unequivocally positive characteristics. George Mikes' satirical Fodor essay expressed a degree of discomfort with the 'strange mixture of ruins and luxury' one found in Munich. 'Shop windows, furnished with exquisite taste and packed with alluring treasures delight your eyes,' wrote Mikes, 'but you know that a few corpses must be still buried under the ruins, just a few yards from the handbags, jewelry and toys' (1953, 53–4). Much has been written about German reconstruction as a compensatory act enabling a society to avoid full confrontation with its violent history. This was also a recurring theme in travel narratives of the postwar era. For the Italian writer Carlo Levi (1962), Germans' almost maniacal efforts at rebuilding hid a deeper flight from history. Germans lived in a 'two-fold night,' argued Levi, one brought on by Nazism, the other by the absence of a full confrontation with the horrors of the regime. The alleged German 'inability to mourn' (Mitscherlich and Mitscherlich 1975)—and the corresponding tenacity with which the Federal Republic grasped for prosperity—became clichés of postwar historical and social–psychological discourse. Conservative observers were also anxious about German forgetting, but of a different kind. They were shocked that the new travel and consumer culture diminished not a critical memory of atrocity but respect for national history and tradition. One illustrated history of Germany's 'rise from nothing' showed a photograph with a casually dressed young woman, back toward the viewer, looking at a war monument made up of a simple cross on which a German army helmet was placed. The caption reads: 'In shorts and Bikini blouse, the mobile, much-traveled omnibus tourists fall upon the sites with great enthusiasm. Reverence, distance, and a feeling for dignity escape them, as this picture from the Salzburg Cathedral shows' (Zentner 1954, 2:47).

Yet it can be argued that Mikes' discomfort and related German criticisms were rooted in a realization that the juxtaposition of ruins and luxury was also the product

*Figure 20   Tourism disrespects tradition: 'In shorts and Bikini blouse, mobile, much-traveled omnibus tourists fall upon the sights with great enthusiasm. Reverence, distance, and a feeling for dignity escape them, as this picture from the Salzburg Cathedral shows' (Zentner 1954, 2: 47).*

of an Atlantic understanding. It was not only Germans who looked to the promises of future prosperity as a balm for the past (Willett 1989, 121, 127). Americans too, having experienced economic depression, the social unrest of the 1930s, and the war, viewed consumption and travel as redemption from a past marked by austerity and want. It was not that the past should be forgotten entirely, but the quest for 'normalcy' and prosperity were now more important. The Fodor guidebook did not fail to mention Dachau in its section on excursions from Munich. For many Americans, Dachau, liberated by the US army in 1945, had come to stand for the Holocaust, just as Bergen–Belsen symbolized Nazi atrocities for English audiences much more than Auschwitz did (Kushner 1996). Dachau, according to the Fodor text, 'was notorious for the concentration camp east of it, where a monument to its victims now stands, but before the Nazis provided it with an evil reputation it was a pleasant old town . . . much frequented by landscape painters, for the beauty of its scenery.' 'It is also a gayhearted place,' the commentary continued, 'with a mid-August festival in local costumes and races, not of horses, but of cattle' (1953, 253–4). Touristic value trumped historical significance in this account, just as the luxury items in Munich shop windows deflected the (not quite extinguished) public memory of nearby corpses.

The Dachau quote reflects the lack of specificity with which the Fodor guidebook treated such sites. No mention could be found of how the concentration camp originated, what it was used for, how it came to house thousands of sick and starving refugees from death camps in the East, and so forth. The identity of the victims— Catholics, Jews, political dissidents—received no attention at all. It was even worse for other Holocaust sites. The Fodor overlooked Bergen–Belsen entirely, even though by 1950 it had been cleared of its huge population of displaced persons and contained a number of memorials and moving mass graves of victims of Nazi terror (Puvogel 1987, 395–7). One need only remember the silence with which German travel guidebooks of World War II passed over the sites of genocide. Forgetting the nature and extent of industrial mass killing was already a well-established pattern of modern leisure culture, a pattern the Fodor continued without hesitation.

To be fair, the sites of Nazi crimes received only sporadic attention in German public life for most of the postwar era until the 1970s (Young 1993). The same could be said for American and English memory of Nazi atrocities. The public impact of the Nuremberg war crimes trial was relatively short lived. Tourist guidebook information on such sites on either side of the Atlantic was virtually non-existent in the first two decades after the war. The best the US military pocket guide of 1944 could do with respect to the problem of genocide was a sentence stating that the Nazis 'herded hundreds of thousands of innocent people into concentration camps.' The 1951 army guide made no reference to the camps at all (Army Information Branch 1944, 19; Armed Forces Information and Education Division 1951). Accessible tourist information on the phenomenon of Nazism itself was hard to come by as well. When the postwar English-language Baedeker to Munich appeared, it included a paragraph on the rise of Adolf Hitler in the Bavarian capital (1950, 17). But the text was in small print, a Baedeker convention indicating information of secondary importance, designed only for the traveler who needed additional explanation.

Jewish travel guides were an exception to this general inattention, but they were very understated in their references to the Holocaust, and they were aimed at an audience that sought little general recognition in public consciousness of the time. They included excerpts of speeches by West German President Theodor Heuss and Berlin mayor Ernst Reuter, both acknowledging Jewish victimhood but also using a universalizing rhetoric of mankind's need for rebirth in the face of trauma. More troublesome because of their possible associations with the Nazi period were a tourist map to 'romantic Germany' and an advertisement for Mercedes auto-mobiles in one such tour book (*Jüdischer Reiseführer* 1954, 4–8, 10–19, 33, 79). In general, the 'real' Jewish travel guides to Europe offered virtual travel only, in the form of memorial books (*yizker-bikher*), popular folk ethnographies of once thriving Jewish communities compiled by emigrés and Holocaust survivors (Kugelmass and Boyarin 1983; Kugelmass 1993, 400). In Israel, where many survivors of the Nazi camps settled, memory of the Holocaust was uneven despite the state's commitment to commemoration. There is also the fact that many of the camps were either destroyed or re-used for other purposes, and that the historio-graphy of the perpetrators was not yet developed (Koshar 2000, 198–221). The Baedeker tradition showed that travel guidebook literature could incorporate serious subjects of historical significance without losing focus on the enjoyment of leisure travel. American travelers in Europe were fascinated with the history of World War II and the Hitler regime. Yet there was something different about the Holocaust. Public memory of Nazi crimes—and the tourism that would later nurture it—faced unusual obstacles because unspeakable horrors were almost impossible to represent so soon after they happened. All this makes it understandable that the Fodor guide devoted so little attention to the subject. The Holocaust was not yet an important switching point of American–German identity, as it would be after the 1970s.

## IV

The emergent American–German travel culture was also characterized by a particular attitude toward gender relations. Without the slightest embarrassment, the Fodor guidebook noted that Tacitus had found women of the Germanic tribes to be unusually chaste and incorruptible. But Tacitus might have raised his eyebrows by estimates that West Germany now had a 10 percent illegitimacy rate. Elsewhere the guide alluded to the problem of so-called fraternization between US soldiers and German women. It noted Germans' 'anger and shame at the spectacle of German women giving themselves for chocolate bars and companionship' in the first years after the war, but it also pointed out that such intense feelings had receded with improved economic conditions. It allowed that although Germany was still very much 'a man's country,' German women were now 'far removed from the braided Gretchen type, fecund and docile, which was the old ideal of the German male'(1953, 38, 48).

Such comments should be understood against the background of an American–German conversation about sexual relations that began immediately as US soldiers set foot on German soil. The term 'fraternization' quickly came to symbolize a broad range of interactions between GIs and Germans in general, and GIs and German women in particular. It was not a new term by any means, as American occupation soldiers in Germany after World War I also had orders not to fraternize with the local population. Then too, Americans and Germans found ways to get around the ruling (Franck 1920, 52–67). Still, the situation was treated with great moral and political gravity in World War II. A 1944 pocket guide to Germany for US servicemen set a high standard: '*There must be no fraternization. This is absolute!*'(Army Information Branch 1944, 2, italics in original). This did not mean there would be no contact, but rather, unless otherwise permitted, US military personnel would not be allowed into German homes or to associate with Germans 'on terms of friendly intimacy.' It did not mean that American troops were to be rude or discourteous: 'This warning against fraternization doesn't mean that you are to act like a sourpuss or military automaton,' the guide gently explained. 'At home, you had minor transactions with many people. You were courteous to them, but never discussed intimate affairs . . . Let that behavior be your model now' (ibid.).

Not that many American soldiers acted like 'sourpusses' toward their German hosts, it appears, for the American military's non-fraternization policy was implemented in part as a reaction to the scope and intensity of contact between US soldiers and the German populace. The policy was a disastrous failure with regard to heterosexual relations, as anywhere between 50 and 90 percent of male soldiers went 'frattin'' with German women. By 1946 more than 2,000 marriages between American soldiers and German women had taken place, and by the mid-1950s more than 7,000 West German women married occupation soldiers annually (Bach 1946, 75–6; Heineman 1996, 381; 1999, 95–107; Henke 1995, 185–204). Fraternization became a well-known theme in American commercial culture, stimulated by cinematic representations such as Billy Wilder's 1948 film *A Foreign Affair* (Willett 1989, 28–44). It was a theme in illustrated magazines such as *Life*, whose sometimes shocked readers found information on how the American military fought sexually transmitted diseases by publicizing a 'VD Hall of Fame' featuring only infected German women rather than American soldiers. Readers were told that American servicemen were more 'victims than culprits' in the spread of venereal diseases ('Occupied Germany' 1947, 91).

The Germans most likely to get to know Americans were not younger women but 'men in the upper and middle socioeconomic strata,' according to opinion polls. Moreover, only two in five Germans polled agreed in principle with non-fraternization, leaving a much larger proportion of respondents who were tolerant toward or indifferent to contact between soldiers and women (Merritt 1995, 252, 254). Nonetheless, one should not underestimate the moral outrage expressed by

American military elites and public opinion leaders about fraternization between soldiers and German women. Nor should one forget that for many Germans, US soldiers' relations with German women not only appeared to defile women but also represented the larger degradation of national culture at the hands of the occupation. In developing this narrative, Germans forgot that widespread promiscuity and short-term liaisons were frequent in the last years of the war, not just during the occupation. Furthermore, Germans' sense of degradation, which quickly evolved into a fear of 'national rape' in the earliest months of the occupation, resulted in part from the continued effect of Nazi racist propaganda depicting Slavs and US blacks defiling Germany (Heineman 1999, 96; Niethammer 1983, 22–34).

Yet it is equally important to point out that soldiers were responding to a German female sexuality that in many ways seemed more 'American' than that which they had encountered in England or France. Once again, the journalist Julian Bach is a good source for understanding the kind of intercultural identity being formed. His argument may be summarized: Americans come from an overly sexualized culture, and they were not only more intensely attracted to women, but women were more attracted to them. Yet American soldiers, still Puritans at heart, liked German women partly because, in comparison to French women, they seemed more respectable. French women seemed 'fast,' while German women would say 'no.' American soldiers criticized unusually promiscuous German women just as much as Germans did. American soldiers wanted little to do with talk of politics or recent history, and they found willing companions among German women, who, according to Bach, were among the most politically immature individuals he encountered. Political immaturity aside, neither American soldiers nor their German female companions were unaware that their relationships were rooted in a universal human right. 'However sordid love over a chocolate bar and a box of salt water taffy may be,' wrote Bach, 'it does represent the right of two human beings freely to pick their own associates' (1946, 71–83, 235, 268–9). It would stretch matters to say that Bach emphasized the 'oppositional' nature of fraternization for both American soldiers and German women. But given the degree to which the US military and the German police violated the civil rights of German women in its attempt to control sexually transmitted diseases through 'vice raids' and other actions, fraternizers' liaisons with US soldiers did have a kind of contestatory quality (Heineman 1999, 102–3). In any case, to the considerable degree (in Bach's mind) that German women understood their right to choose a partner, they had moved in the direction of accepting an important tenet of individualism and democracy.

For its part, the Fodor guide had hit on a particular mix of 'chastity,' sexuality, and growing independence to characterize the German women American tourists were likely to encounter. Bach's discussion suggests that this characterization was rooted in a series of intercultural relations and sexual understandings over which elites in both national cultures had little control and which continued to operate once the political twilight of occupation gave way to the more settled 1950s. The recurrent Franco-German comparison in Bach's analysis also reinforced a long tradition emphasizing the sexual license and immorality of French society. This same stereotype could be found not only among American journalists but among tourists in France as well (Levenstein 1998, 198–203). In the interwar era, American tourist literature pinpointed German sexual excess, to be sure (Milton 1935, 65–6). But the themes of German morality and female respectability always seemed to come through more strongly.

How did German-language travel literature represent German women vis-à-vis foreign audiences in this context? We may turn once again to the material published by the Berlin Tourist Bureau for a partial answer. The first point to be made is that the travel literature assumed there was an essential 'Berlin woman,' the *Berlinerin*, who could be found only in the scarred metropolis. This was an important argument because soldiers from each of the four occupation zones appeared to have a different impression of Berlin women. In one article from a 1950 Travel Bureau magazine, versions of Berlinerin appeared in four different photographs depicting traits each of the Allies recognized in the females of their zones (Magistrat von Groß-Berlin 1950, 24–5). The photograph of the 'Berlinerin à la England' depicted a plain-looking woman with a blouse buttoned all the way to the top and little makeup. There was also the Berlin woman as seen by the Soviets, a sturdy-looking figure standing in a cornfield. 'To the Soviet,' read the caption, 'she appears so robust, that she is capable of drinking huge amounts of Vodka and singing hymns of praise to Stalin.' In the French occupation zone, by contrast, the Berlinerin was elegantly dressed and heavily made up—a woman 'who has understood how to appropriate the charm of French women.' As for the American-style Berlinerin, a photograph showed a smiling, attractive young woman tying her headscarf. She, the reader is told, is 'a progressive representative of "old" Europe' in the eyes of Americans. Disparate views notwithstanding, Berlinerin, according to the article, 'have not changed despite their openness to the world.' The same attributes applied now as 20 years earlier, when the writer Carl Zuckmayer, according to the magazine, characterized the Berlinerin as 'the woman, who works, creates, fights, marches, pushes forward, calm, brave, tough, full of energy, full of the future.' Accompanying these lines was a large photograph, the fifth in the article, portraying the Berlinerin 'as she really is'—a young woman photographed in profile, dressed fashionably in a sweater and tartan print skirt, striding forward confidently with a bright smile on her face.

Without stating the matter directly, the article saw the Berlinerin of occupied Germany as the New Woman of the 1920s adapted to the post-1945 world of deprivation and want. Where the Fodor saw transformation in German women, the Berlin Travel Bureau saw continuity. Perhaps it is only a matter of the Fodor guide's broadly German focus and the Bureau's concentration on Berlin. We do not know how the guidebook treated the trope of the Berlinerin because no mention was made of her. Yet the contrast may be qualified somewhat by considering another Travel Bureau magazine from 1951 (Verkehrsamt der Stadt Berlin 1951, 2:38–9). Written in both English and German, the article carried the subtitle 'Berlin girls and women fend for themselves.' Here again, photography was deployed to portray different female 'types' in West Berlin. The idea of this article was that Berlin women faced obstacles in the postwar world that their sisters in West German cities never experienced. The West Berlinerin's story was one of triumph: 'neither frightful air-raids, nor death in battle, neither conquest nor hunger, neither cold nor blockade have succeeded in breaking their tenacious attachment to life.' Portraits of 'five Berlin girls' who aspired to careers in the arts followed, each taken from a single postwar year, each demonstrating some aspect of that 'indomitable energy' the Allies had come to respect. There was Susanne Erichsen, victim of a 'painful pilgrimage through Soviet concentration camps,' but now not only Germany's best-known model but also Miss Germany of 1950 (ibid., 38). There was Anna-Elisabeth Riehl, 17 years old in 1946, orphaned and forced to care for her brothers and sisters, starving, but also determined to study stage directing, which she takes up in 1948. There is Christa Nehrling, who by 1947 had two years of acting school behind her and who passes the entrance exam to the Academy of Arts in Berlin, where she wants to study painting. But poverty forces her 'to wield not only the brush, but the trowel too, which she uses clearing up rubble.' The photograph depicts her smiling as she stands working in front of a pile of bricks.

And so forth. These individualized portraits, moving though they were, were manipulated by the Tourist Bureau to demonstrate the tenacity not only of Berlin women but also of the (West-) German nation. This was one of countless renditions of the 'hour of the woman,' which, as Elizabeth Heineman shows (1996; 1999), obscured the specific stories of postwar German women in favor of a general portrait of national rebuilding. It was difficult to think of the defeated German male as a symbol of reconstruction; the German woman was another matter. And yet, the German woman had to remain a woman in such cultural–political propaganda. The Travel Bureau magazine hit the nail on the head: 'Still, amidst surrounding hardships, [the Berlinerin] are very feminine in these pictures: they smile. Their invincible joy of living transcends all the hardships that have assailed them' (Verkehrsamt der Stadt Berlin 1951, 2:39). These unmistakably feminine paragons of hard work and joy fit quite closely with the Fodor guide character-ization of the new German women, whose mixture of conservative sexuality, European charm, and independence befitting the partner of a 'self-made man' seemed perfectly in line with American heterosexual male fantasies. Perhaps this was what was meant in the 1950 photograph of the 'Berlinerin à la USA,' the 'progressive representative of "old" Europe.'

## V

No trope was more important to the Fodor guide's sense of Germany than regional diversity (1953, 42–3). 'Anyone who moves around Western Germany is bound to be most strikingly impressed by the regional differences,' read the guide. These differences could be seen not only in the landscapes and towns, but also in the physical characteristics of the people, which ranged 'from the small, brown haired, brown eyed Alpine people of the south to the flaxen haired, rawboned, blue eyed northerners.' This diversity struck the guide as rather American insofar as Bavarians detested the Prussians as much as Alabamans or Georgians disliked Yankees. Geographical markers were as distinct in Germany as in America: 'The Main River is a sort of Mason–Dixon line in Germany, and those who live north of it consider themselves more cosmopolitan, more liberal, and harder working.' Although this passage characterized German attitudes, it nonetheless also reversed a long-standing American discourse in which southern Germany was viewed as the 'good' Germany and northern Germany as the Prussianized, militarized 'bad' part of the country (Freese 1990, 115–19). The destruction of Prussia may have made it possible to consider northern Germany independently of the heritage of Prussian militarism after World War II.

The Fodor's focus on regional peculiarities had a folkloristic ambience. Touring the Swabian mountains, the editors highlighted the inscrutability of the inhabitants. 'The peasants, shut up in their mountain villages, live in an isolation which has hardly changed for centuries,' read part of the description. 'Even the other Germans find something mysterious about the Swabians, especially the Swabians of these mountains.' The guide went on to stress the somber hues of Swabian peasents' dress and the sternness of the Swabian demeanor, which it also linked to the historical spread of the Reformation. 'The soul searching of these peasants continues so intensively even today,' stated the guide, 'that you still find sub-divisions and subsubdivisions of Protestantism which have become so minute that some cults are confined to a single tiny hamlet.' Such observations gave rise to ethnographic comparisons: 'The people to the south, on Lake Constance, are Catholic, and much gayer than the mountain Swabians; as for the Rhinelanders, they are even more Catholic and even gayer' (Fodor 1953, 191).

It is unsurprising to find a tour guide using the geographical and cultural vernacular of its readers to enlighten them and make foreign lands more comprehensible. But once again there was something more going on in such passages. Regional diversity was of course a significant trope of American identity even before the founding of the nation. Ethnicity played a major role in the formulation of regional characteristics. The consideration of 'racial groups' and 'national character' was an important part of both scholarly and public discourse on both sides of the Atlantic in the 1930s and 1940s. The American Guide Series published by the Work Projects Administration—an extraordinary record of one nation's attempt to represent itself to its citizens and employ starving humanists at the same time—often included a section devoted to 'racial elements.' The 1941 guide to the state of Michigan is a good example (Michigan State Administrative Board 1941, 103–12). This sort of social delineation would have been well understood in Continental Europe between 1919 and 1945, and it persisted after the war as well. Military life during the Occupation was seen by some as a melting pot in miniature, and hence a key element in the continued evolution of an 'American character' built out of diverse ethnicities and regions (Gleason 1980, 47–8). The fundamental question of American identity, the dialogue between unity and multiplicity, could in this context be easily transposed onto German soil.

Yet this was more than a simple transposition. With reference to the US, Eric Hobsbawm states: 'Paradoxically, the most democratic and, both territorially and constitutionally, one of the most clearly defined nations faced a problem of national identity in some respects similar to imperial Germany' (1983, 279). Americans were 'made' out of immigrants who, especially after the middle of the nineteenth century, could not be counted on to have the same customs and values held by the largely Anglo-Saxon populations who no longer constituted the majority of the population. For its part, the German nation had to be mobilized not mainly from immigrant groups but from populations with well-established territorial, linguistic, social, and religious traditions rooted in a broad though largely undefined national–cultural identity. More than Americans, Germans defined themselves existentially, a point Hobsbawm does not mention in his analysis. Yet the lack of political and territorial unity in Germany resulted in a situation in which both existential and ideological elements, both ethno-cultural and civic definitions, interacted. In both cases, an intense dialogue between dispersed and focused identities, between multiplicity and unity, between 'the many' and 'the one,' was constitutive of nationality. This dialogue, which at moments turned into bloody conflict, also gave each nation a constant sense of newness, of discontinuity and malleability, that was perhaps less salient in other national traditions. This in turn implied the corresponding need for tradition, ethnic texture, and history, of which there was an abundant supply in Germany—and for which American tourists and soldiers searched in their travels throughout Europe.

German-language guidebook literature of the postwar period also represented the German nation with an eye to regional and ethnic coordinates even though the racist vocabulary of wartime Woerl and Baedeker guides was gone. Cuisine had always been an important means for pinpointing such divisions, and it remained so in the 1950s, when food not only gave badly needed nourishment but also symbolized economic recovery. The 'eating wave' of the early Federal Republic played a role in tourism, as hotels and restaurants offering a wide range of culinary selections demonstrated the country's reemergence as a favored destination. The Baedeker Shell auto guides regularly carried information on regional cuisine, as the Baedeker handbooks of earlier decades did. In the gastronomic tourism of the 1930s, German cooking was regarded as 'simple, strong, and rich with variation' (Steinheil 1938, xxv). In the postwar era, a somewhat more differentiated—and chastened—message was evident. The delights of Rhine wine, Sauerbraten, *Heringstipp* (potatoes with herring bits), and trout came in for praise in the Baedeker Rhine–Mosel guide (Steinheil 1952, 13). For Eastern Bavaria, beef dishes were favored, although the guide pointed out that postwar shortages of meat forced the people to rely more on vegetable dishes than in the past. The Baedeker was entirely accurate on this score, as statistics showed that only in the course of the 1950s did meat consumption return to its prewar level. This was not attributable to a wave of vegetarianism but rather to the fact that the devastated meat industry took years to restore its capacity to meet consumer demand (Andersen 1997, 39). The Baedeker noted that 'Bavarian cooking offers many dishes that are not very well-known in northern Germany, and is rich in expressions from the local dialect.' Among the most favored dishes were veal knuckles (*Kalbshaxen*) with potato salad, stuffed white sausage (with veal, pork, tripe, and liberal amounts of parsley), and Bavarian dumplings, or *Klöße*. Even so, lamented the guide, 'due to the population mixing of the last decade, much in this area has been assimilated to general language usage' (Steinheil 1953, 12).

For its part, the Fodor guidebook did not hesitate to criticize German cuisine. It complained that Germans used lard for cooking, that 'everything which *can* be served with dumplings *is* served with dumplings,' and that the food portions were too large. 'Don't assume you are likely to grow thinner in Germany,' it opined. This statement may be attributed in part to the American tendency to see Germans as voracious eaters and drinkers whose love of order and cleanliness was counterbalanced by their overwrought culinary habits (Freese 1990, 119–21). The Fodor made the same point the Baedeker did about a decline in regional variety, noting the spread of various local dishes throughout the country (Eich 1963, 261; Fodor 1953, 62–4). But it was not as perspicacious as the Baedeker in attributing a part of this shift to the population movements of the war and the postwar decade. Despite voicing such criticism, the guide was not without appreciation of German food. It praised German beer, wine (not as various as the French but just as high in quality), rye bread and Westphalian pumperknickel ('if you call instead for white bread, you deserve to get it'), and herring. In the case of the latter, it could be had in especially plentiful amounts in Emden, where 'they'll give you a whole herring lunch, with hors d'oeuvre, main dish and salad all provided by this protean fish' (1953, 64, 67). Throughout the Fodor guide, finally, one found additional information on regional and local dishes, although overall the language was usually restrained or at times ambivalent. Frankfurt had only a 'respectable culinary tradition,' for example, despite the frankfurter (a 'sausage made from every part of the pig'), pigs' knuckles nested in sauerkraut, *Brenten* (almond cookies flavored with rum or rose-water), apple wine, and a special quince paste (ibid., 117–18).

The most radical 'regional' difference was of course to be seen along what the Fodor called the 'East–West Axis' dividing Berlin. Here political–military conflict gave rise to what became an etched-in cultural difference. Many of the themes we have stressed in the foregoing reappeared in two essays on the German metropolis, one by the foreign correspondent James Wakefield Burke, also the author of a forgettable novel about the Soviet occupation of the city entitled *The Big Rape*. No stranger to historical irony, Burke was quick to point out that whereas Prussia's Berlin had once symbolized authority and militarism, the new Berlin of the West was 'an island of freedom' (ibid., 312). This recapitulated the argument of much of the advertising that emanated from the West Berlin travel agency from 1949. But Burke's history was also inaccurate. He referred to Berlin as 'a capital artificially created by Bismarck' (ibid., 312), thereby ignoring not only the contributions of Prussian monarchs but also the Iron Chancellor's wariness about giving Berlin too much authority in the newly created Reich of 1871.

Burke picked up on the prevailing American–German travel culture in another way by using the tropes of light and dark to characterize the contrast between to the two Berlins. He was rather sophisticated, eschewing the obvious identification of West Berlin with brightness or illumination, and the East with darkness. Instead, light and dark had different metaphorical and literal meanings on the two sides of the border. 'As your plane drones in from Hamburg or Frankfort, you will see the western half of the city below you, with hundreds of thousands of brilliant lights winking up in a diapered pattern,' he wrote. '[A]nd then, as your plane swings lower and banks about for a landing, you will find yourself suddenly over a somber darker city. Here and there a new building will be shining under floodlights, picked out by them from the obscurity which surrounds them' (ibid., 313). The contrast between the dark East and the brightly-lit West was predictable, but on the East side, the lights that shone were from the buildings of the Soviet military authorities. Otherwise, the Eastern part of the city was dim. On the Western side, meanwhile, another relationship between light and dark unfolded. The bright lights of shop windows, 'filled with high-quality merchandise,' recalled the identification between West Germany and the burgeoning consumer culture of the postwar world. But 'blazing neon lights herald once more the animation of her night life,' wrote Burke, making it clear that Berlin 'does not look like a has-been' (ibid., 313).

Elsewhere, Burke elaborated, stating that Berlin nightclubs had once again retained their 'notoriousness.' The visitor could find any number of out-of-the-way clubs where 'small smoke-filled rooms, minute bars, barmaids with plunging necklines, [and] three-piece bands' were regular fare. The Ballhaus Resi was no smoke-filled dive but a more elaborate establishment. Here some 800 guests could use telephone and message chutes at each table to 'pick the member of the opposite sex of your choice, and invite the lucky nominee, orally or in writing, for a dance, a drink, or what have you.' At Remde's St. Pauli am Zoo, customers were provided with fishing rods. These reflected the maritime décor of the club, but they were also functional: 'When a young lady charitably described as a dancer appears in a costume consisting of a large number of loosely attached odds and ends of clothing, the guests are encouraged to use the rods to fish off her clothes.' At Rancho Dancing in Charlottenburg one could see 'beauty dancers.' A beauty dancer, wrote Burke, 'is a well built girl who can't dance and proves it in the nude.' At the Kelch bar in the Kurfürstendamm district, one found a 'rendezvous for men dressed as women' (ibid., 319–20).

The symbolism of Berlin nightlife cut in a number of directions in 1953. On the one hand, it should be seen in the context of that American–German sexual culture created by the US occupation. Yet Burke's reference to the re-animation of Berlin night life also gave it an important point of issue to the city's past as a capital of 'naughty' delights, a place where one 'amused' oneself, with all the connotations that term carried. We are dealing here partly with an element of persistence, and partly with discontinuity with the past. Persistence could be found in the continuation of cabarets, nude reviews, and other elements of the heterosexual and modernist travel culture charted in comprehensive form in Moreck's interwar guide to the city. It may be seen to a degree even in the repressed homosexual subculture of SA tourism at the end of the Weimar Republic and during the Nazi period. Berlin remained very much identified with sexualized tourism even if its more obvious, politically liberal, or 'alternative' variations retreated into the anonymity of local clubs during Hitler's rule, if they were not destroyed altogether in the concentration camps (Hauser 1939, 18–19; Schlör 1991, 261–5).

In contrast, the reference to a reanimated night life could be nothing more than a pale attempt to ignore the fact that the sexualized travel culture of modernist Berlin as it existed in the 1920s could never be re-established in West Berlin of the 1950s. Naughty Berlin in its time was a revolutionary departure from what existed before, a phenomenon closely associated with a cultural modernism seeking radical expression wherever it turned. But naughty Berlin in the 1950s was like the modernist architecture that began to appear all over the occupied Western zones. The product of a once revolutionary impulse, modern architecture now fell under the influence of 'no-frills modernism,' a lethargic functionalism that undercut the shocking or unprecedented qualities of the earlier architecture (Relph 1987, 198–201). In this new context, Berlin sexuality was less 'theological' in tone, to borrow Kracauer's evocative word, less aimed at testing the borders of the Baedeker version of bourgeois identity, than its Weimar predecessor was. It was now more thoroughly tied to the consumerist desires fed by the Allied occupation and the neo-liberal ideology of prosperity. It was imbricated in an American–German sexual culture that moderated or even repressed the most outrageous or challenging aspects of Weimar experimentalism. This is not to say that the theological aspects of tourism had been destroyed in postwar Germany or Berlin, but rather that they were no longer to be found in sexual experimentation in the modernist key.

On the other side of the East–West axis, illumination and darkness had another metaphorical significance. Many East Germans who took vacations sponsored by the FDGB would travel through Berlin on their way to a Baltic Sea resort, a tourist spot in the Harz mountains, or an idyllic retreat in the Thuringian forest. They were invited to get to know the 'democratic sector of Greater Berlin,' as a FDGB publication put it. The 'wonderful hours' passed strolling along the Stalinallee or marveling at the new apartment blocks of East Berlin were certain to convince the tourist of the progress made by the state 'after the insane destruction of the Anglo-American air war.' These travelers were invited not only to spend the day 'on the sunny side of Berlin,' but also to commit ideologically to East Germany and avoid the seductions of the other sectors. 'Do not forget,' read the FDGB guide, 'that within Berlin the freedom camp and the war-mongering camp touch each other directly; so stay on the sunny side of Berlin, stay in the democratic sector! Be class-conscious representatives of the German Democratic Republic!' (Freier Deutscher Gewerkschaftsbund 1959, 63).

The remainder of the Fodor's Berlin section took the reader around the city, starting with the Kurfürstendamm, now the center of West Berlin for Allied soldiers and tourists. This section once again contained errors or oversights. It erroneously stated that the Reichstag originally housed the Prussian rather than German parliament. It failed to point out that the gargantuan Victory Column, raised in 1873 to commemorate German victory in the Franco-Prussian War, was moved by the Nazis from its spot in front of the Reichstag to the place where it stood now. Standing at the Potsdamer Platz and looking East, the guidebook mistakenly referred to the GDR as the 'Popular Democratic Republic of Germany.' It also continued to use the coinage of ethnic character, stating that 'Teutonic peoples are fond of zoos,' and finding this a good reason for the fact that the Berlin Zoo was a pleasant place to visit not only for its animals but for its food and entertainment. The animals themselves were important personalities in this account, since they were 'individual heroes . . . who survived the air raids [and] are known by name throughout Germany.' This was not an exaggeration, since newspapers and other media throughout Germany had publicized the survival of Shanti the elephant, Knautschke the hippopotamus, Nina the chimpanzee, Schorsch the polar bear, and Schwips the brown bear—all duly mentioned in the Fodor text. One could even have a photograph taken with a brown bear at the zoo, a fact that would play a political role in the Fodor text later on in the Berlin section. A healthy amount of irony again helped to capture Berlin humor: the hulking ruin of the Kaiser Wilhelm Memorial Church was said to be an improvement over the original building (1953, 323–5).

But the exploration was really about contrasting the two Berlins once again, picking up on the theme signaled in Burke's prelude. From the Potsdamer Platz, the reader was invited to peer over into the 'Soviet paradise,' which was not very paradisiacal at all but, in contrast to the West, 'a nightmare city of ruins which the war left behind' (ibid., 326). The guidebook did note that the East Germans had a tougher time of rebuilding since they inherited the most congested and less well-off sections of the city. The reader was informed that 'unlike Paris and London, Berlin had no slums' in the prewar era, and that Berlin 'workers were housed in solid, clean buildings, big apartment houses surrounding central courts. But they were crowded together, and when the bombs and shells fell upon them, thousands of buildings were converted into ruins' (ibid.). Students of Berlin would of course find the statement on the absence of slums to be a strange account of the city's interwar social history. But they could have agreed with the guidebook's characterization of the congested living quarters to which Allied bombing laid waste. Even more curious was the reference to the 1953 workers' uprising in East Berlin. Here the guidebook was vague, stating only that the Potsdamer Platz was where 'the stonings and the fighting of which you may have read in the papers' took place (ibid., 326).

The Brandenburg Gate offered one of the most propitious opportunities for exploiting the touristic potential of the East–West divide. The guidebook gave a brief account of the monument's history, emphasizing that the former Prussian Arch of Triumph now lay in the Russian sector. In front of the Brandenburg Gate the Russians erected a 'Victory Monument' of their own, but it was in the British sector. This monument was less consequential for the fact that it was 'one of those massive tasteless structures for which they [the Russians] have a gift' than that Red Army sentinels kept constant guard over it. This photo opportunity could not be passed up. 'This is certainly the only place in the world where you can with impunity have your picture taken with a Soviet soldier holding a submachine gun,' read the guidebook (ibid., 326–7). The guards were not permitted to fire their weapons since they were on British territory:

> So step beside him, if you wish, and let a friend snap the picture. There is no guarantee that the guard will stay there. The rules don't oblige him to do that. Some of them pretend not to notice you, others grin, still others look sheepish, much as a guard in a similar position might at home, and a few snarl and walk away. But you may want to try, especially if you have previously succumbed to the blandishments of the photographer in the Zoo. The Tiergarten is the place where you can be snapped with a brown bear at one end and with the Red bear at the other (ibid., 327).

Along the East–West tourist axis, pictures of Red Army guards were souvenirs and brown bears stood for freedom. Meanwhile, the traditional symbol of the city, the Berlin bear, had become a leitmotif of the municipal travel office in the West. Such connections reinforced a world of symbols that Fodor tourist readers helped to build as they trudged from site to site.

Those same tourists were instrumental in building the American–German travel culture for which Berlin was an important center. After visiting the zoo and having their picture snapped with a Red Army guard, they were encouraged to move south along the Martin-Luther-Straße to 'the seat of Berlin's government and the symbolic citadel of the democracy of which Berlin is the most advanced outpost' (ibid., 327). The guide referred here to the Schöneberg city hall, one of the finest official buildings in the city, now the headquarters of the Berlin Senate and the political center of West Berlin as a whole. In its belfry hung a replica of the American Liberty Bell, and in a wooden chest there were stored 16,000,000 signatures of American citizens who subscribed to the motto carved on it: 'I believe that all men derive the right to freedom equally from God.' The trip to Berlin thereby turned into a pilgrimage. The varied sites of the evolving American–German travel culture crystallized finally around the Schöneberg town hall, where American and postwar West German values meshed in a seamless fabric of democracy, freedom of the individual, and liberty. Earlier guidebooks always confirmed the general German sense, built up from comparing the German metropolis to some hypo- thetically typical US standard, that Berlin was the 'most American' of German urban centers. That view now had more than metaphor to sustain it.

## VI

Scholars debate whether national and ethnic images are constantly in flux or if they endure for long stretches of time even when the conditions that produced them change or disappear. It is worthwhile suggesting that the issue cannot be reasonably discussed without referring to certain constitutive moments in the history of national images. Such moments rarely create the possibility for a radical departure from previous understandings—a sociologist would argue they are 'path-dependent'—but they do lend themselves to important recastings and reformulations. The decade after World War II was certainly one of these moments in the history of cultural exchange between Americans and Germans. American heteroimages of German cleanliness, industriousness, artisan production values, history, female sexuality, and regional tradition were in many important ways confirmed as US military government gave way to West German statehood, and as soldiers were joined by an increasing number of American tourists, exchange students, academics, and businessmen. Yet the moment was also unprecedented in the history of American–German relations. Without being able to provide full supporting evidence, one may argue that the sheer quantity of interactions resulted in a qualitative shift. It was not that the 'binational perception process,' to use a term from Nagler (1997, 146), that characterized such relations in the past merely continued. Rather this process resulted in a more intense, sustained, and deliberate interaction that gave rise to a hybrid form. This was not a relationship between two bounded national entities, but a series of emergent, experiential inter-cultures operating 'to the side,' as it were, of military government, business corporations, and national states. These inter-cultures created new modes of understanding and new sites of inter-societal transfer that worked more like tactical maneuvers than strategic interventions for those who were involved in them. Harold James argues correctly that the Americanization of postwar Germany 'was generally not a conscious process' (1989, 188). Postwar interactions between Americans and Germans should not be confused with (although they were undoubtedly related to) a very different and strategic 'transnationality' promoted, for example, by major multinational business corporations and (not least) the tourist industry. The 1953 Fodor guide was not only a significant artifact of the inter-societal transfers on which the new cultural understanding was based; it also helped to shape that understanding by directing, advising, and stimulating those who crossed the Atlantic divide.

One should also note the counter-movements. It is easy to find numerous and one-sided criticisms of German society by American and British observers during and after World War II. Representing a 'hard' or punitive policy toward Germany, they became less strident as the occupation developed, but they could still be heard (Lach 1945). The history of American reactions to what was perceived to be a German inability to feel guilty about the Holocaust provides many examples in this area (Barnouw 1996; Bourke-White 1946). But so too does popular culture, especially when tourist guidebooks and travelogues dramatized efforts to 'descend into the depths of the German character' (Mikes 1953, 7). From the other side, anti-American thought in Germany, nurtured by 12 years of Nazi propaganda, continued well after Hitler left the scene. Many Germans regarded Americans and Russians as roughly the same: childish, barbaric, naïve, and incapable of under-standing the profundity of German culture (Diner 1993, 124). The juvenile behavior of American servicemen themselves often did little to promote 'the American way of life,' as research by Gimbel (1961, 69–70) and others shows, and American tourists provided more than enough ammunition for anti-American sentiment not just in Germany but throughout Europe. It was a dubious comment on Americans' stature abroad when a 1960 *Time* article stated with a note of pride that West Germans had replaced Americans as the most unloved foreign travelers in Italy (Schildt 1995, 201).

A tiny minority of intellectuals in postwar Germany hoped for a renascent Prussianism espousing a high-cultural and universal tradition of austerity equidistant from both American consumerism and Soviet Communism. This perspective had deep roots in German culture as it looked back to nineteenth-century debates among German historians and philosophers, who tried to unite a sense of Prussia's historical singularity with a 'cosmopolitan' worldview (Iggers 1968). In this argument, stated most controversially in the immediate postwar years by journalist Heinrich Hauser (1945), a new 'melting pot' made up of occupation forces, displaced persons, refugees, and Germans nested in newly rediscovered and valued homelands was forming in Germany. This hybrid community of 'new German thought' would sever forever the bonds that had grown between America and Europe. Hauser's quirky political metaphysics, developed in part during the author's stay in the United States during the war, was ultimately closer to the ideas of the failed conservative resistance to Hitler than to the sentiments of those who encountered Americans in daily life, as Michael Ermarth (1993, 126–8) notes. On the ground, meanwhile, the interchanges Hauser wanted to end once and for all were evolving with a force and intensity that could hardly be stopped. Hauser himself admitted that Germans and Americans still had many traits in common even as he predicted the opening of an unbridgeable chasm between Europe and the United States.

The Fodor guidebook not only disagreed philosophically with Hauser's outlook and predictions; it also worked to ensure that Hauser's view of a reemergent German 'special path' would not see the light of day. The American–German travel culture had the cumulative force of circumstances behind it, while Hauser's thought operated at a considerable distance from reality. On the winning side of history, Fodor's vision also suggested a broader narrative of the development of tourism on German soil. Not Baedeker's world of nationally oriented liberalism; not the interwar theologies of sex, class, and race; but a new Atlantic synthesis now gave form and meaning to the travel culture in which Americans, West Germans, and (by their ever-present absence) East Germans took part.

# Conclusion

The modern tourist seeks 'elsewherelands,' writes Orvar Löfgren, whose history of vacationing charts a search for transcendence lying at the heart of leisure travel. For Löfgren, it is the longing for a 'great personal experience' that constitutes the Holy Grail of tourism and the motivation that makes tourists begin planning for their next trip before they finish with the one they are on (1999, 282). In one respect, the argument is indisputable, even mundane; tourism is by definition something that takes us away from the everyday. This applies not only to the vacationer who just wants to see the sights but also the 'sophisticated traveler' of *New York Times* vintage, whose erudite search for something interesting or unprecedented supposedly distinguishes her or him from the great mass of tourists. Nonetheless, I have argued that the traveler's desire to 'get away from it all' is in fact an attempt to read (and thereby understand) a central moment of modernity: incessant movement and displacement. To tour for pleasure is not primarily a design for being elsewhere, in the non-spatial meaning of the term, but rather for experiencing and deriving meaning from that sense of movement that grips every modern, bringing each one of them into contact with a world of peripatetic strangers. Moving voluntarily and for recreation between home and away, between sessility and displacement, is not a search for something divorced from daily routines, but a cultural practice that intentionally puts the tourist at the heart of things, in the 'here and now.' It is a cultural practice that requires and, to varying degrees, instantiates, a hermeneutics of tourism based on the interpretation of a multiplicity of texts and markers, all oriented to producing knowledge of Self and Other.

This is more than a metaphorical relationship, as the evidence presented in this book demonstrates. Even when they sought out isolated coastal resorts or the darkest recesses of the forests, German tourists often did so with the latest means of transportation and in large numbers. They marveled at the wonders of modern rail transportation and the automobile, and they were aware of the pleasure they took in their amazement. Hardly seeking disengagement from social interaction, they compared themselves to their hosts as well as to other tourists, a point Löfgren himself makes with admirable clarity. Socialist and Communist campers as well as Nazi youth group members often regarded collective experience, the sense of solidarity that came from direct and comradely interaction, as the highest value, even when they explored seemingly isolated natural environments. Many did not even embrace the illusion of solitude or isolation; instead they gravitated to the crowds, whether at the bourgeois spa, the streets of Berlin nightlife, the conquered cities of World War II, or the tourist ruins of postwar Germany. Even when they traveled far from home, they 'brought' their *mentalité* with them, as when American tourists embraced Germany after Hitler as a 'melting pot.' These tourists were not 'elsewhere' at all, even when they sought release and relaxation, even when they searched for the ideal country lane or the quiet, narrow street of a scenic historical district. Rather, they were self-consciously at the center of historically specific traveling cultures the complex itineraries of which required interpretation if they were to be understood.

If the idea of elsewhereness is troublesome, or at the very least misleading, Löfgren's emphasis on the individuality of travel and the quest for personal experience is more convincing. One of the central problems of much scholarship on leisure travel is that it has treated tourists as malleable dupes cowed by the commercialized itineraries of a burgeoning tourist industry. One does not have to look for long in the history of tourism to find numerous examples of mindless conformity and unthinking consumption. Yet Löfgren's study as well as work by Urry (1990; 1995) and others make it clear that tourism's popularity depends to a great degree on the innumerable individual experiences and resources it generates. It has been the contention of the foregoing discussion that the travel guidebook offers us a useful tool for exploring some of the dimensions of this multifaceted and individuating practice we call tourism. Regarded as the first great synthesizer (and manipulator) of the tourist experience in the modern age, the Baedeker guidebook appears here as a facilitator of individual choice, a tourist text or marker that enabled responsible and creative reading of an array of other 'texts' encountered on the trip well-taken. The tremendous dilation of tourist markets and guidebooks throughout the last 150 years only confirms the idea of leisure travel as an individuating and knowledge-creating phenomenon with virtually limitless possibilities—and limitless ways of ruining the natural environment, appealing to baser human instincts, and creating bad relations between hosts and guests.

Even when historically specific travel cultures looked for ways to confirm collectivizing political ideologies such as socialism or Nazism, they ultimately failed to dam that deep stream of individuality that buoyed the tourist. Modern tourism is the product of an age of liberalism, and the Baedeker was its most authoritative, if not its first, primer. Baedeker liberal individualism runs throughout the history of modern travel cultures like a red thread, even at those points in the past where the little red book lent itself to racist ideologies opposed to everything for which the original, emancipatory movement stood. Moreover, although this individualism was initially closely tied to the values and interests of the property-owning middle strata—and particularly to the male heads of households within those strata—it had an impact far beyond these social groups. Although it was based initially on a sense of public morality and critique, as analyzed in Jürgen Habermas' study of the bourgeois public sphere (1962), it could be appropriated for more privatized (though never entirely 'non-public') uses. It became a 'classless' (and genderless?) discourse available, in theory if not always in practice, to a broad array of leisure travelers from many points on the social spectrum and, once the Baedeker became an international standard, to many nationalities. In German historiography, the failure of middle-class liberalism and the corresponding rise of illiberal political projects that issued into Nazism are key themes. But in the history of tourism, it is the triumph and durability of a changing Baedeker liberalism, stamped initially by the experiences and perspectives of the nineteenth-century German Bürgertum, marketed for international audiences but always indexed in complex ways to German conditions, that provides the more convincing leitmotif.

About what kind of individual does it make sense to talk? An answer to this question has been implicit rather than explicit in the narrative presented here. It is necessary to extrapolate from the evidence to suggest the outlines of a response. The individuating tradition of leisure travel does not lead one to posit the existence of a bounded, unitary personality even if this was the ideal to which the Baedeker guidebook initially aspired. Rather, my narrative has followed the interaction of multiple tourist selves, capable of devastating conflict as well as conciliatory amalgamation, and contained not only in the language of collective travel cultures but also in the personalities and actions of individual travelers. The Baedeker guidebook's prose style aimed for transparency of communication and the unambiguous representation of tourist sites. Yet even when its austere prose seemed to simplify and 'decode' the tourist's world, it necessarily put the traveler in an environment of ambiguity, conflict, and uncertainty. The nineteenth-century Baedekerite could move between middle-class identity and national allegiance, or between a focus on the national state and the international coordinates of a modern leisure culture. Such identities could overlap and reinforce one another, but they could also clash, depending on historical circumstances. The tourist's desire for modesty responded to a fundamental contradiction of (not just) German society, namely that commercial development had given rise not to widespread prosperity but to excessive consumption among some social groups. The Baedekerite often regarded women as being especially susceptible to overconsumption. Yet the rhetoric of the 'modest pedestrian' was also directed at the male bourgeois traveler; this rhetoric served as a guide to balanced leisure practice as well as a warning against profligacy. For their part, female consumers embraced leisure travel, and although they may have appeared as 'typical' shoppers or as objects of male desire in guidebook representations, they too could adopt tactics that gave them space for individual autonomy through travel—but that also forced them to make difficult choices. Caught by the riveting male heterosexual gaze of the Weimar Republic's sexualized culture, women also potentially returned the gaze when it was regulated by ideas and itineraries such as those laid out in Moreck's tour guide to 'depraved' Berlin.

Tourists on the former battlefields of World War I oscillated between reverence and a commercialized self-indulgence that bordered on the macabre. The socialist traveler of the interwar years embraced a collective ideology of workers' solidarity and leisure, but she or he was not immune to the blandishments of a sophisticated tourist industry offering pure pleasure rather than ideological zeal. The SA tourist warrior appeared to be the adjunct of a totalizing ideology, but what ill feelings did he harbor toward the Nazi regime as he realized how his guided tour through Berlin's realms of memory reflected his marginality within the National Socialist polycracy? And what of German Wehrmacht personnel in World War II, who were invited to enjoy far-off cities not only as conquerors but also as ordinary tourists? The same question could be posed to the Baedeker travelers of the Eastern Front. Beneficiaries of a racist war of extermination, they were encouraged to take in 'Jew-free' Polish cities as normal tourist sites. I have argued that they may have done so with an essentially nineteenth-century vision of Germany's relationship to Eastern Europe in their heads. The mental and political coordinates that regulated their actions may have had more to do with the national–liberal travel culture of the prewar era than with Nazi ideology. West German and American tourists came from different worlds after World War II, but they interacted in a cultural space that was a hybrid of travel cultures from both nations. When Americans adopted the melting pot metaphor to envision Germany, they created a cultural bridge over which complicated inter-societal transfers of dreams, images, and practices occurred. For West Germans, the new situation demanded it own set of antinomies, necessitating the presence of an American Other within German culture while also calling for the present absence of the 'other Germany.' All leisure travelers operated within a spectrum of available cultural strategies through which either social distinction or conformist identification with the broad mass of tourists could be expressed. The examples could be increased, and indeed the careful reader will no doubt find instances in my narrative where the opportunity to 'complexify' the picture of multiplicity, crosscutting influences, hybrid formations, contradictions, and dissonance was overlooked.

The 'success' of tourism may be measured by the degree to which such complexities are arranged or resolved by individual travelers. Leisure travel may facilitate the building of a strong personal identity because it exposes individuals to new experiences, places, and peoples. Even the most well-organized group tour has the potential for genuine novelty and surprise even if its participants try to control the unpredictability of interaction in contact zones. In a world where geographical, cultural, and personal borders are traversed with unprecedented intensity, the successful tourist learns to negotiate boundaries freely chosen and encountered. However, unpredictability may also force a retreat into pre-existing prejudices and reactions. Unable to reassemble their experiences in new constellations, or unwilling to embrace the creative destruction brought about by traversing unexpected cultural paths, the tourist falls back on tried and true formulas. These formulas may reinforce extant national, class, and gender hierarchies. The travel guidebook has operated on either side of this divide. It has been one of the devices tourists have used to minimize risk, but this minimization could have different functions. It could enable the traveler to mark out a set of cultural templates for choosing between hitherto unknown alternatives, thereby facilitating self-organization and creative orientation. Used in this way, the travel handbook worked as an important vehicle through which the 'tactics of leisure' (Mackaman 1998) could be articulated and applied, and the creation of a new cultural competence ensured. 'Reason' could emerge from 'mere' consumption. But the guidebook could also help tourists to stick unthinkingly to the beaten track, where so many others had gone before them, and to see the same sights everyone else has seen. It could be used to deny the necessity of a hermeneutics of travel, and to deny the potentially creative effects of displacement.

The notion of identity underlying this study is that of the modern, rather than the postmodern, self. Theorists of modern identity once posited an innate and essential self that could be discovered and developed by individuals as they came to know themselves and others through a process of education and interaction with society and nature. But theorists of the modern such as Nietzsche, Heidegger, and Sartre also developed a more dynamic model in which identity is 'a construct and a creation from available social roles and material' (Kellner 1992, 143). In this perspective, personal identity is destabilized by transiency and change, by a sense that 'all that is solid melts into air.' Yet this does not preclude the possibility of getting the individual parts of a personal self to add up to a whole, if only temporarily and with great anxiety, and of using social interaction (including autoimages and heteroimages) to situate oneself successfully in a wider cultural context. This interpretation is not blind to the often overpowering ways in which existing political forces shape or even define the created self, and it is certainly not without an awareness of how authoritative discourses of class and gender exert their dominance. But it does posit a moment of self-construction for all individuals (at least those touched by Western modernity) regardless finally of their class or gender positions.

In contrast, postmodern theories of identity take the 'constructivist' version of modern identity and radicalize it, denying the possibility of even temporary stability, arguing that personal identity ultimately does not exist outside a destabilizing and superficial role-playing in which every individual is forced to engage. There is

207

good reason to be suspicious of the postmodern theorization of the self, in my opinion, although this is not the place to develop a full argument on that subject. From the perspective of this study, the mere existence of tourist guidebooks suggests that the postmodern argument of the self's unremitting instability and lack of depth is too one sided. As orientation manuals to the beaten track, tourist guidebooks reflect the continuing patterns and choices tourists have made in their journeys between home and away. The continued existence (or creation) of traditions and widely accepted modes of social interaction do not sit well with a postmodern reading of identity's unrelenting uncertainty. The existence of such cultural paths and markers may seem to be a sign of deadening conformity for some, but there is no law that forces leisure travelers to follow guidebook itineraries. Within the patterns of departure, approach, and return that guidebooks synthesize, there is much room for individual variation and decision making.

Moreover, the existence of alternative guidebooks, whether those of the sexual topographies of Berlin or of paramilitary violence, suggest that tourism helps individual subjects to resolve (or try to resolve) the social contradictions embedded in 'mainstream' tourism. By literally seeking out the experiences left unmapped in Baedeker's world, many Germans sought depth and meaning from the knowledge gained by interacting with new places and peoples, and they tried to establish new patterns of meaning that looked to a more hospitable and humane future. That in Nazi Germany this search for alternatives could result in dangerous and even genocidal acts of cruelty (or inattention to such acts) should not keep us from recognizing the larger point. It should not lead us to accept uncritically Walter Benjamin's statement: 'The most European of all accomplishments, that more or less discernible irony with which the life of the individual asserts the right to run its course independently of the community ... has completely deserted the Germans' (1986 [1928], 73). The history of tourism indicates that not even Nazi tribalism could extinguish entirely that sense of individuality (which is by no means always to be equated with humane actions) that Benjamin valued.

In this sense, my argument stresses that German travelers had much in common with their counterparts in other Western nations. The evidence for the irreducibility of personal subjectivity, the fact that seeing the sights was always finally gauged to personal experience, indicates that in leisure travel there was no German 'special path' through time. All German travel cultures, regardless of their relationship to particular political camps, shared this loyalty to the individual subject, though they often defined that subject in contrasting ways. The well-known story of deep and irreversible *political* conflict in Germany history appears in need of qualification when placed against the narrative of leisure travel sketched out in the preceding pages. Political conflict indeed left its footprint on the history of tourism, but that footprint became more indistinct through the riverine workings of German travel cultures.

Patterns of collective experience as they apply to tourism played a role in stabilizing or reconstructing personal identities. In the preceding pages, various travel cultures worked to give potentially contradictory cultural selves a degree of coherence by formulating predictable and easily recognizable horizons of expectation and experience. The national–liberal travel culture was a constitutive element in a process whereby the individual tourist experience was articulated with a collective sense of self. National identity in the Baedeker key was the great mediating factor in this relationship. My narrative charts a story in which the national–liberal travel culture gained hegemony in German tourism but then became increasingly brittle as new groups clamored for an updated hermeneutics of leisure travel. The varied challenges to Baedeker's world presupposed new images of the German nation, new patterns of class relations, new gender roles, and new modes of racial hierarchy. Yet elements of the national–liberal culture persisted. The individuating dynamic of the national–liberal perspective, the necessity that all versions of the collective passed through the personal, proved to be particularly influential in other travel cultures, even those that rejected the Baedeker sense of identity. After World War II, this continuity made it possible for a new, 'Fodorian' travel culture to integrate what was left of the Baedeker tradition in an American–German identity shaped by the exigencies of Cold War cultural politics. Throughout these changes, though individuals may have experienced the depthlessness and lack of fixed identities that postmodern theory posits, they continued to choose identities that offered respite and relative stability. The 'modest pedestrian' of Baedeker travel, the 'sober' tourist of interwar modernism, the socialist wanderer, the paramilitary SA tourist, and the 'American–German' user of the Fodor guidebook—all represented new, though related, versions of collective identity through which individual subjects operated as active participants in historical change.

If much of my discussion has emphasized the interaction of travel cultures oriented to national identity, the international or transnational coordinates of the modern tourist self also remain important. The Baedeker guidebook was an appropriate model in this context because it gained its ascendancy by being marketed internationally before it determined the boundaries and content of the national–liberal travel culture in Germany. It created a recognized standard that, once translated into various national idioms, created an international canon of tourist destinations. Working within this tradition, the Fodor guidebook performed an analogous act of cultural labor, but it did so with a more specific focus on American–German relations. Even so, it is the national species of collective identity that has assumed priority in the preceding narrative. This is attributable neither to the peculiarities of German culture nor to German nationalism, but rather to the nature of collective existence in the twentieth century. Despite unremitting exchange of images, ideas, goods, and people across national borders in the past century, there is much evidence that national loyalties remain strong. Moreover, despite the 'global' character of modern culture and economy, the pull exerted by the nation on its peripatetic subjects persists. This too suggests that the modernist reading of collective and personal identity has more to offer than a postmodernist reading does. A set of persistent patterns and emulations, oriented around the national community in its multiform versions, continues to help moderns make sense of themselves and others as they experience a global displacement that only seemingly makes strangers of us all. My account is neither a defense of the national state nor a claim that leisure travel always reinforces existing national prejudices and identities. But it does recognize the insistence with which the national past situates the present, even under conditions of radical change and intense cross-border migrations.

That process of situating the present ultimately leads us back to the individual with whom Löfgren's analysis of elsewhereness begins. For national or trans-national identities stem finally from the temporal and spatial markers that individuals use to create a meaningful cosmos. It is worth recalling a general point: the modern national state, despite its record of violence and war, has been the single most consistent 'container' for the advance of individual rights (including the right to leisure). Concepts of the nation and the individual subject are closely linked in Western modernity, for better or for worse. The nation has produced the individual, just as the individual has produced the nation. Even so, I would argue that collective and personal identities are ultimately the products not primarily of social interaction but of individual efforts, as Friedrich Nietzsche, who took modernist conceptions of the self about as far as they could go, so rightly insisted. These individual efforts cannot be understood outside concrete social contexts, but they are not fully determined by those contexts either. The philosopher Charles Taylor makes a relevant point here, arguing that although the modernist sensibility may be 'transpersonal,' access to it 'can only be within the personal' (1989, 481).

Hardly appearing to be a likely subject for such lofty musings, the tourist nonetheless has engaged in an array of 'identity-producing' activities, perhaps most often in spite of him- or herself. Much current theory regards tourism as yet another example of the play of surfaces and superficialities that transforms contemporary society into a commodified iron cage. The meaninglessness of it all delights viewers, as corporations, states, and advertisers bombard people with unrelenting images bringing commodification into the most intimate spaces of daily existence. In the postmodern tourist gaze, even blighted urban landscapes and wrecked automobiles 'gleam with some new hallucinatory splendor,' argues the neo-Marxist literature scholar Fredric Jameson (1991, 32–3) in his critique of the 'cultural logic of late capitalism.' Yet the historical tourist with whom my narrative is concerned most often consulted a guidebook with the intent of 'reading' that which was seen. The tourist wanted to 'produce' new meanings, and demonstrated a willingness to experience that temporary instability, that liminal existence between sessility and displacement, which gives leisure travel its appeal. The tourist accepted the guidebook as a necessary tool, but did not pursue a totally predetermined or unthinkingly chosen route. The tourist guidebook was not a mechanism of closure but one of controlled possibility, of situated freedom. The leisure traveler had all the limitations we would expect from an individual ill-equipped to take a fully reflexive perspective on the self and society; was at times also a disturbing reminder that the individual was capable of unspeakable cruelty—and could enjoy that cruelty as entertainment. But the tourist's presence 'out there' in an environment of transiency and flux was itself an indicator of higher (if sometimes frighteningly misdirected) intentions.

The history of tourist guidebooks helps us to map those higher intentions. It charts the passages and places that have drawn the tourist in search of meaning. If scholarship has done a too diligent job of analyzing the historical (and contemporary) tourist's baser motivations, let us conclude with a brief discussion of a 'tourist' whose experiences and ideas may suggest, rather unexpectedly, the upper limits of leisure travel's possibilities. The famous German sociologist Max Weber, still recovering from a series of mysterious psychosomatic ailments that had plagued him for years, came to the United States in 1904 on a tour that took him from Boston and New York City to Chicago, Oklahoma, and the deep South (Diggins 1996, 17–44). Weber had professional obligations and research goals, but he and his wife did not fail to act like tourists as they marveled at New York City's skyscrapers and enjoyed the unbounded spaces of the American Midwest. We do not know if he used Baedeker's guide to the United States, available for the first time in 1893 and in a third, revised, edition in the year he made his trans-Atlantic voyage. Weber's American experience sharpened his sense that deep within American culture lay a buried historical treasure, the idea of ethical character based on Puritan religious experience. Humans chose the great ideas with which they lived their lives, argued the sociologist, but they did so with a heroically constructed 'inner core' of existence from which they ventured out into the world of nature and social interaction. This inner core incarnated 'life-world' relations, to be sure, but once established, it also worked as a defining and orienting moment for the individual subject. For Weber, the idea of ethical character was central to his conception of 'vocation' or 'calling.' A bureaucratized world where the higher meaning of productive labor was debilitated, where work became compulsion and leisure functioned as a shelter from daily routine, needed to revitalize and rethink the approach to work. Armed with a meaningful calling, individuals could strengthen their inner core of existence, engaging modernity with that degree of tenuous certainty provided by ethical character.

The tourist with which we have been dealing seems worlds away from Weber's conception of modern identity. Indeed, much of modern leisure culture would have strengthened the sociologist's sense that labor was a debilitated experience for which activities such as tourism could only inadequately compensate. Yet there is good reason to suggest that ethical character, the idea of a personal inner core, however much a product of modernity's corrosive changes, also includes the need for leisure and entertainment, not as compensations but as primary and constitutive activities. Sweeping historical characterizations that see 'labor-oriented' societies transformed into 'leisure societies' overlook the degree to which plain hard work remains both necessary and desirable for Western culture. Yet ethical character, less vested in publicly resonant authorities and more oriented toward consumption than Weber could have envisioned, now draws sustenance and creates a fuller life experience not only from a calling but also from a more engaged commitment to informed 'distraction.'

Tourists too may have constructed and reconstructed their inner core of existence by placing themselves in the liminal environment of leisured displacement. The tourist experience consisted of a leisure itinerary linking an 'inner' and an 'outer' (or social) core of existence, the latter shaped in no small part by interactions with unknown environments and peoples. We noted in the introduction that Horne (1984, 10) refers to tourist guidebooks as the 'devotional' texts of contemporary society's chief pilgrims. This is a compelling metaphor when considered in relation to Weber's desire to reassert ethical character as a central moment of modern identity. A modern ethical character requires its guides and catechisms, its sacred texts and rituals, not to enact a new orthodoxy, but to equip individuals with the resources needed to comprehend the transiency of modernity. The tourist guidebook thereby appears as a serious artifact of modern culture, and a symbol of desire for emancipatory meaning. If now as in the past it most often falls short of its ambitious goals, its failure is a function of the social contradictions that produced it in the first place, and of the limitations of its all too human users.

# Bibliography

## I Travel Guidebooks and other Primary Sources

Altenberg, Margo. 1932. Urlaub. *Garçonne* 13:1.

Armed Forces Information and Education Division. 1951. *A Pocket Guide to Germany.* Washington D.C.: U.S. Government Printing Office.

Army Information Branch, Army Service Forces, United States Army. 1944. *Pocket Guide to Germany.* Washington D.C.: U.S. Government Printing Office.

Arnold, Karl. 1938. Vorbereitungen für Urlaub und Reise. *Simplicissimus* 43:294–5. 26 June.

Auch der Arbeiter soll reisen. 1928. *Sozialistische Republik.* 31 May–1 June.

Austellungs-, Messe- und Fremdenverkehrs-Amt der Stadt Berlin. 1928. *Offizieller Führer für Berlin und Umgebung und Potsdam und seine Schlösser.* Berlin: Rotophot.

Das Auto von vorn bis hinten. 1936. *Allgemeine Automobil Zeitung* 3:13. 18 January.

Bach, Jr., Julian. 1946. *America's Germany: An Account of the Occupation.* New York: Random House.

Baedeker, Karl. 1872. *Deutschland und Österreich. Handbuch für Reisende.* 15th edn. Koblenz: Karl Baedeker.

——. 1883. *Mittel- und Nord-Deutschland, Westlich bis zum Rhein. Handbuch für Reisende.* 20th edn. Leipzig: Karl Baedeker.

——. 1889. *Berlin und Umgebungen. Handbuch für Reisende.* 6th edn. Leipzig: Karl Baedeker.

——. 1895. *Italy: Handbook for Travelers.* Pt. 1, *Northern Italy.* 10th edn. Leipzig: Karl Baedeker.

——. 1896. *The Rhine from Rotterdam to Constance. Handbook for Travelers.* 13th edn. Leipzig: Karl Baedeker.

——. 1904. *The United States with an Excursion into Mexico. Handbook for Travelers.* 3rd edn. Leipzig: Karl Baedeker.

——. 1910. *Berlin und Umgebung. Handbuch für Reisende.* 16th edn. Leipzig: Karl Baedeker.

——. 1911. *Austria–Hungary. Handbook for Travellers.* 11th edn. Leipzig: Karl Baedeker.

——. 1913a. *Deutschland in einem Bande: Kurzes Reisehandbuch.* 3rd edn. Leipzig: Karl Baedeker.

——. 1913b. *Northern Germany as far as the Bavarian and Austrian Frontiers.* 16th edn. Leipzig: Karl Baedeker.

——. 1923. *Berlin and its Environs: Handbook for Travelers.* 6th edn. Leipzig: Karl Baedeker.

——. 1924. *Paris and its Environs with Routes from London to Paris. Handbook for Travelers.* 19th edn. Leipzig: Karl Baedeker.

——. 1925. *Northern Germany, Excluding the Rhineland. Handbook for Travelers.* 17th edn. Leipzig: Karl Baedeker.

——. 1927. *Berlin und Umgebung. Handbuch für Reisende.* 20th edn. Leipzig: Karl Baedeker.

——. 1938. *Tirol: Voralberg, Westliches Salzburg, Hochkärnten. Handbuch für Reisende.* 40th edn. Leipzig: Karl Baedeker.

——. 1942. *Das Elsass. Strassburg und die Vogesen. Reisehandbuch.* Leipzig: Karl Baedeker.

——. 1943. *Das Generalgouvernement. Reisehandbuch.* Leipzig: Karl Baedeker.

——. 1948. *Leipzig. Ein neuer Führer.* Leipzig: Bibliographisches Institut.

——. 1950. *Munich and its Environs. Handbook for Travellers.* Hamburg: Karl Baedeker; Munich: Richard Pflaum Verlag.

——. 1951. *München und Umgebung.* 2nd edn. Hamburg: Karl Baedeker; Munich: Richard Pflaum Verlag.

——. 1978 [1849]. *Rheinreise von Basel bis Düsseldorf.* Reprint. Dortmund: Harenberg Kommunikation.

Berlin-Werbung Berolina, ed. 1961. *Das sowjetische Ehrenmal.* Die kleine Berolina-Reihe. East Berlin: Berlin-Werbung Berolina.

*Das Berliner Nachtleben! Beschreibung und Führung durch das elegante Berlin.* 1920. Berlin: Im Werner-Verlage.

Bertarelli, L.V. 1924. *Guida D'Itália del Touring Club Italiano: Itália Centrale.* Vol. 1. Milan: Touring Club Italiano.

Besucht das fröhliche Deutschland. 1938. Advertisement of Deutsche Lufthansa in *Deutsche Werbung* 6.

Bierbaum, Otto Julius. 1903. *Reisegeschichten. Yankeedoodle-Fahrt. Eine empfindsame Reise im Automobil.* Rev. edn. Munich: Georg Müller.

Bissing-Kraftwagenbetrieb Braunschweig, ed. 1910. *Fahrpläne der Kraftomnibuslinien im Harz für den Sommer 1910.* Braunschweig: Bissing-Kraftwagenbetrieb.

Bourke-White, Margaret. 1946. *'Dear Fatherland, Rest Quietly': A Report on the Collapse of Hitler's 'Thousand Years'.* New York: Simon & Schuster.

*Braunbuch über Reichstagsbrand und Hitlerterror.* 1978 [1933]. Facsimile edition. Frankfurt am Main: Röderberg-Verlag.

Buck, Pearl S. 1946. Letter to Germany. *Common Ground* VI, 2:3–10.

Bund Deutscher Verkehrsverbände, ed. 1933. *Heidelberg und Umgebung.* Deutschland-Bildheft 41. Berlin: Universum Verlagsanstalt.

——. 1933. *Frankfurt (Oder) und Umgebung.* Deutschland-Bildheft 75. Berlin: Universum Verlagsanstalt.

Bundesministerium für den Marshallplan, ed. 1951. *Das Tor ist offen nach Deutschland.* Bonn: Verlag für Publizistik.

Bunsen, Marie von. 1914. *Im Ruderboot durch Deutschland: Havel, Werra, Weser und Oder.* Berlin: Fischer Verlag.

Bürckel, Josef, ed. 1934. *Kampf um die Saar.* Stuttgart: Verlag Friedrich Bohnenberger.

Centralstelle für den Fremdenverkehr Groß-Berlins, ed. 1915. *Kriegszeit-Programm für einen Besuch Berlins an einem, drei oder sieben Tagen.* Berlin: Verlag der Centralstelle für den Fremdenverkehr Groß-Berlins.

Cooper, Gordon. 1954. *Your Holiday in Germany.* London: Alvin Redman.

Crockett, William Day, and Sarah Gates Crockett. 1933. *A Satchel Guide to Europe.* 52nd edn. London: George Allen & Unwin.

# Bibliography

Dawson, William Harbutt. 1901. *German Life in Town and Country*. New York: G. P. Putnam's Sons.

Dehn, Paul. 1895. Moderne Reiselust. *Stangen's Illustrierte Reise- u. Verkehrs-Zeitung* 2: 54–6. March.

Deutscher Kongress für Innere Medizin, ed. 1916. *Ärtztlicher Führer durch Warschau*.

Dietz. 1932. *Arbeiter-, Reise- und Wanderführer: Ein Führer für billige Reise und Wanderung*. Berlin: Verlag J.H.W. Dietz Nachfolger.

Döhling, Kunrat [Willy Hoffmeister]. 1933. *Mit leichtem Gepäck durch Süddeutschland*. Göttingen: Ernst Große.

Eckert, Erwin. 1932. An der Riviera der Arbeiter und Bauern. *Sozialistische Republik*. 21 May.

Ehrler, Hans Heinrich. 1930. *Meine Fahrt nach Berlin: Erlebnisse eines Provinzmanns*. Stuttgart: Verlagsanstalt Greiner & Pfeiffer.

Engelbrechten, J.K. von, and Hans Volz. 1937. *Wir wandern durch das nationalsozialistische Berlin. Ein Führer durch die Gedenkstätten des Kampfes um die Reichshauptstadt*. Munich: Zentralverlag der NSDAP, Franz Eher Nachf.

*Erinnerung an Paris 1940. Kleiner Führer durch Paris für Deutsche Soldaten*. 1940. Paris: Dompol's Editions.

Ernst, Paul. 1907. *Der Harz*. Stuttgart: Carl Krabbe Verlag.

Esser, Hermann. 1938. Introduction. In *Germany*, edited by Reich Committee for Tourist Travel, 5:4. January.

Feldeinheit 22 444. 1942. *Kurzer Führer durch Warschau*. Warsaw: Frontsammelstelle, Feldeinheit 09436.

Fetridge, W. Pembroke. 1884. *Harper's Hand-Book for Travelers in Europe and the East*. Vol. I, *Great Britain, Ireland, France, Belgium, and Holland*. New York: Harper & Brothers.

Fischer, Heinrich. 1914. *Rechts und Links der Eisenbahn!* Vol. 1, *Berlin–Frankfurt a. M. über Eisenach*. Gotha: Justus Perthes.

Fodor, Eugene, ed. 1953. *Germany 1953*. Fodor's Modern Guides. New York: David McKay.

Fontane, Theodor. 1929. Der Tower. *Reisen und Schauen. Reiseblätter der 'Kulturwille'* 6:11–12. April.

Foster, G.G. 1850. *New York by Gas-Light. With Here and There a Streak of Sunshine*. New York: Dewitt & Davenport.

Franck, Harry A. 1920. *Vagabonding through Changing Germany*. New York: Harper & Brothers.

Freier Deutscher Gewerkschaftsbund, ed. 1959. *Urlaub, Erholung, Genesung durch den Freien Deutschen Gewerkschaftsbund*. Berlin: Tribüne.

Furor Teutonicus: If History Can Change Character of a Nation, Germany's Is a Better Bet. 1954. *Life*. 10 May: 34.

Gemeinnützige Berliner Ausstellungs-, Messe- und Fremdenverkehrs-GmbH. 1936. *Deutschland: Amtlicher Führer durch die Ausstellung, Berlin 1936, 18. Juli bis 16. August, Ausstellungshallen am Funkturm*. Berlin: Verlag und Anzeigen-Verwaltung, ALA Anzeigen-Aktiengesellschaft.

Gleason, Arthur H, and Helen Hayes Gleason. 1916. *Golden Lads: A Thrilling Account of How the Invading War Machine Crushed Belgium*. New York: A. L. Burt.

Goethe, Johann Wolfgang von. 1982. *Italian Journey (1786–1788)*. San Francisco: North Point Press.

Grieben. 1926. *Eisenach, Wartburg, and Umgebung*. 14th edn. Grieben Reiseführer, vol. 83. Berlin: Grieben-Verlag.

——. 1936a. *Berlin and Potsdam*. 8th edn. Grieben's Guide Books, vol. 108. Berlin: Grieben-Verlag; London: 'Geographia.'

——. 1936b. *Berlin und Umgebung. Kleine Ausgabe*. 70th edn. Grieben Reiseführer, vol. 25. Berlin: Grieben-Verlag.

——. 1939. *Deutsche Ostmark*. 2nd edn. Grieben Reiseführer, vol. 219. Berlin: Grieben-Verlag.

Hamburg-American Line. 1930. *Through Germany*. Hamburg: Hamburg-American Line.

Happ, Alfred. 1938. Attractive Stations for German Railways. In *Germany*, edited by Reich Committee for Tourist Travel, 5:20–3. January.

Hare, Augustus J.C. 1894. *Walks in London*. 2 Vols. 6th edn. London: George Allen.

Hare, Augustus J.C., and St. Clair Baddeley. 1923. *Walks in Rome*. 21st edn. London: Kegan, Paul, Trench, Trubner & Co.

Hartmann, Hans. 1929. Reise nach Frankreich. *Reisen und Schauen. Reiseblätter der 'Kulturwille'* 6:20–1. July/August.

Hauser, Heinrich. 1939. *Battle against Time: A Survey of the Germany of 1939 from the Inside*. New York: Charles Scribner's Sons.

——. 1945. *The German Talks Back*. New York: Henry Holt & Company.

Häussler, Gustav. 1932. *Auf nach Berlin!* Mit Rucksack und Nagelschuh, vol. 9. Berlin: Triasdruck.

Healy, Nancy Lee. 1952. We Live in a Glass House. *Information Bulletin: Monthly Magazine of the Office of US High Commissioner for Germany*. January: 27–9.

Hemstreet, William. 1875. *The Economical European Tourist: A Journalist Three Months Abroad for $430*. New York: S.W. Green.

Hessel, Franz. 1984 [1929]. *Ein Flaneur in Berlin*. Berlin: Das Arsenal.

Heydenreich, F. 1932. Berliner Ausflüge und Spaziergänge. In *Was die Frau von Berlin wissen muß. Ein praktisches Frauenbuch für Einheimische und Fremde*, 239–44. 2nd edn. Berlin: Herbert S. Loesdau Verlagsbuchhandlung.

Hirschfeld, Ludwig. 1927. *Das Buch von Wien*. Munich: R. Piper Verlag.

Holitscher, Arthur. 1925. *Der Narrenführer durch Paris und London*. Berlin: Fischer Verlag.

Huret, Jules. 1908. *En Allemagne. De Hambourg aux Marches de Pologne*. Paris: Bibliotheque-Charpentier.

*Illustrierter Führer durch die Gauhauptstadt Posen und Umgebung mit Einschluß von Gnesen*. 1940. 5th edn. Woerl's Reisehandbücher. Leipzig: Woerl's Reisebücher-Verlag.

*Das Internationale Reiseführer*. 1920–1. Berlin: Verlag Karl Schultz.

Jahn, Friedrich Ludwig. 1991. *Deutsches Volkstum*. Berlin: Aufbau Verlag.

Joint Export–Import Agency. 1949. *The Businessmen's Guide to the Combined US/UK Area of Germany*. Washington D.C.: U.S. Department of Commerce.

*Jüdischer Reiseführer. Das jüdische Leben in Deutschland*. 1954. Stuttgart: Paneuropäische Edition.

Kahl, Werner. 1940. *Der deutsche Arbeiter reist*. Berlin: Deutscher Verlag.

Kaiserliches Deutsches General-Gouvernement, ed. 1915. *Belgien: Land, Leute, Wirtschaftsleben*. Berlin: Ernst Siegfried Mittler und Sohn.

Kapitän Nemo [pseud.]. 1936. Gedanken eines Ausländers. *Allgemeine Automobil Zeitung* 8:12–15. 22 February.

Kästner, Erich. 1993 [1931]. *Fabian: The Story of a Moralist*. Evanston: Northwestern University Press.

Kessler, Harry Graf. 1935. *Gesichter und Zeiten: Erinnerungen*. Vol. 1, *Völker und Vaterländer*. Berlin: Fischer Verlag.

Kiesel, Karl A., ed. 1933. *Passing through Germany*. 9th edn. Berlin: Terramare Office.

Klemperer, Victor. 1998. *I will Bear Witness: A Diary of the Nazi Years, 1933–1941*. New York: Random House.

Knyrim, August. 1900. *Wohin gehen wir nächsten Sonntag? Illustrierter Führer für Spaziergänge und Ausflüge in die nähere und weitere Umgebung Frankfurt's*. Vol. 2, *Ganze Tagestouren*. Frankfurt am Main: Verlag J. Braner-Hub.

Königliches Unterrichtsministerium. n.d. *Die Siegesallee. Amtlicher Führer durch die Standbildergruppen*. Berlin: Verlag Martin Oldenbourg.

Küke, Heinz A. 1934. Deutschland, das Land der Motortouristik. In *Deutschland*, edited by Reichsausschuss für Fremdenverkehr, 1:23–5.

——. 1938. International Automobile and Motor Cycle Exhibition in Berlin. In *Germany*, edited by Reich Committee for Tourist Travel, 5:4–5. February.

Kunter, Karl. 1910. *Reisealmanach. Praktisches Handbuch für Ferien-, Erholungs-, Bade-Reisende und Touristen*. Halle a. S.: C.A. Kaemmerer & Co.

Laughlin, Clara E. 1930. *So You're Going to Germany and Austria!* Boston: Houghton Mifflin.

Levi, Carlo. 1962. *The Two-fold Night: A Narrative of Travel in Germany*. London: The Cresset Press.

Magistrat von Groß-Berlin. 1947. *Berlin Lebt. Berlin Ruft*. Berlin: Verkehrsamt Berlin-Charlottenburg.

Magistrat von Groß-Berlin. Verkehrsamt. 1950. Die Berlinerin wie die anderen sie sehen, und wie sie wirklich ist. In *Berlin: Treffpunkt der Welt*, 24–5. Berlin: Verkehrsamt.

Mayes, Martin. 1952. Cultural Integration. *Information Bulletin: Monthly Magazine of the Office of US High Commissioner for Germany*. June: 11–16.

Michigan State Administrative Board, ed. 1941. *Michigan: A Guide to the Wolverine State*. American Guide Series. New York: Oxford University Press.

Mikes, George. 1953. *Über Alles: Germany Explored*. London: Allan Wingate.

Milton, Arthur. 1935. *Berlin in Seven Days: A Guide for People in a Hurry*. New York: Robert McBride & Co.

Moes, Eberhard. 1935. German Workers Make a Cruise. In *Germany*, edited by Reich Committee for Tourist Travel, 6:26–7.

Moreck, Curt. 1931. *Führer durch das 'lasterhafte' Berlin*. Leipzig: Verlag moderner Stadtführer; reprint, 1996: Berlin: Nicolaische Verlagsbuchhandlung.

Muirhead, Findlay, ed. 1920. *Belgium and the Western Front*. The Blue Guides. London: Macmillan and Co.

Müller-Gaisberg, G., ed. 1936. *Volk nach der Arbeit*. Berlin: Verlag Richard Carl Schmidt & Co.

Murray, John. 1858. *A Handbook for Travellers on the Continent: Being a Guide to Holland, Belgium, Prussia, Northern Germany, and the Rhine from Holland to Switzerland*. 12th edn. London: John Murray.

*Nagel's Germany*. 1956. The Nagel Travel Guide Series. Geneva: Nagel Publishers.

Nitsch, Harry. 1926/7. Das englische 'Week-end' auf dem Kontinent. *Das Reisebüro* 6/7. 20 November, 5 December, 20 December 1926; 5 January 1927.

North German Lloyd Steamship Co. 1898. *Guide through Germany, Austria-Hungary, Switzerland, Italy, Belgium, Holland, France and England*. Berlin: J. Reichmann & Cantor.

Norton, Minerva Brace. 1889. *In and around Berlin*. Chicago: A. C. McClurg and Co.

Occupied Germany: *Life* Presents a Progress Report on the U.S. Zone. 1947. *Life*. 10 February.

# Bibliography

Orr, J. Edwin. 1937. *Such Things Happen. 100,000 Miles around the Globe*. London: Marshall, Morgan & Scott.

Ostwald, Hans. 1905/07. *Das Berliner Dirnentum*. 2 vols. Leipzig: Walther Fiedler.

Pasewaldt, C.W.A. 1938. Aus der Werbearbeit für die KdF-Reisen. In *Deutsche Werbung* 7:508–10. April.

Petersen, Jen. 1938. *Our Street: A Chronicle Written in the Heart of Fascist Germany*. London: Victor Gollancz.

*Pharus-Buch. Berlin mit Vororten. Wegweiser auf Schritt und Tritt*. 1906. Berlin: Pharus-Verlag.

Piehler, H.A. 1933. *England for Everyman*. London: J. M. Dent & Sons.

Pitman, Marie J. [Margery Deane]. 1882. *European Breezes*. Boston: Lee and Shepard Publishers; New York: Charles T. Dillingham.

Reichsausschuss für Sozialistische Bildungsarbeit, ed. 1930. *Bedingungen für die Teilnahme an den Reisen 1930*. Berlin: Reichsausschuss für Sozialistische Bildungsarbeit.

Reichsbahnzentrale für den Deutschen Reiseverkehr, ed. 1934. *Driving your own Car in Germany*. Berlin: Reichsbahnzentrale für den Deutschen Reiseverkehr.

——. n.d. *Vom Deutschen Menschen und Seiner Art*. Berlin: Reichsbahnzentrale für den Deutschen Reiseverkehr.

Reichsfremdenverkehrsverband, ed. 1938. *Reichs-Handbuch der Deutschen Fremdenverkehrsorte. Wegweiser durch Deutschland für Kur, Reise und Erholung. Ostmark-Band*. Rev. 10th edn. Berlin: Reichs-Bäder-Addressbuch-Verlag.

Reichsverband der Automobilindustrie e.V. 1937. *Internationale Automobil- und Motorrad-Austelllung Berlin 1937*. Berlin: Reichsverband der Automobilindustrie.

*Reiseführer. Deutsche Demokratische Republik*. 1981. 9th edn. Berlin and Leipzig: VEB Tourist Verlag.

Reisen und Wandern–Jahresschau Dresden 1929. 1929. *Gewerkschafts-Zeitung*. 3 August.

Reismann, Otto. 1939. The Motorists' Paradise. In *Germany*, edited by Reich Committee for Tourist Travel, 2:4–7. February.

Review of *Meyers Reisebücher: Dresden, Sächsische Schweiz, Böhmische Schweiz, Oestlisches Erzgebirge, Böhmisches Mittelgebirge, Prag*. 12th edn. Leipzig: Verlag Bibliographisches Institut. 1930a. In *Archiv für den Fremdenverkehr* 3:142. October.

Review of *Meyers Reisebücher: Riesengebirge, Isergebirge. Breslau*. 21st edn. Leipzig: Verlag Bibliographisches Institut. 1930b. In *Archiv für den Fremdenverkehr* 3:142. October.

Review of series *Was nicht im Baedeker steht*. 1931a. In *Archiv für den Fremdenverkehr* 1:31. April.

Review of Karl Baedeker, *Leipzig, Nordbayern, Franken, Oberpfalz, Niederbayern, Bayerischer und Böhmer Wald, Böhmische Grenzgebiete*. 2nd edn. Leipzig: Karl Baedeker. 1931b. In *Archiv für den Fremdenverkehr* 2:64. July.

Richter. 1915. *Berlin und Umgebung*. Richters Reiseführer. Hamburg: Richters Reiseführer-Verlag.

Riehl, Wilhelm Heinrich. 1929. Drei Wunder von Kevelaar. *Reisen und Schauen. Reiseblätter der 'Kulturwille'* 6:27–8. July/August.

Roellig, Ruth Margarete. 1928. *Berlins lesbische Frauen*. Leipzig: Bruno Gebauer Verlag für Kulturprobleme.

Rolfe, J.W. 1899. *A Satchel Guide for the Vacation Tourist in Europe: A Compact Itinerary of the British Isles, Belgium and Holland, Germany and the Rhine, Switzerland, France, Austria, and Italy*. Boston: Houghton, Mifflin and Co.

# Bibliography

Sargent, Henry Winthrop. 1870. *Skeleton Tours through England, Scotland, Ireland, Wales, Denmark, Norway, Sweden, Russia, Poland, and Spain.* New York: D. Appleton.

Schaffner, Jakob. 1936. *Volk zu Schiff: Zwei Seefahrten mit der 'KdF'-Hochseeflotte.* Hamburg: Hanseatische Verlagsanstalt.

Schauffler, Robert Haven. 1910. *Romantic Germany.* New York: The Century Co.

Schlachtfeld-Piraten. 1929. *Reisen und Schauen. Reiseblätter der 'Kulturwille'* 6:21. July/ August.

Schloemp, Felix, ed. 1913. *Berliner Bummel. Ein lustiger Bärenführer durch das amüsante Berlin.* Berlin: Verlag der 'Lustigen Blätter' (Dr. Eysler & Co.).

Schramm, Albert. 1935. *Der innere Kreis: Aufzeichnungen eines Artztes.* Tübingen: Rainer Wunderlich.

Schulz-Luckau, Karl, ed. 1937. *Mit KdF in den Urlaub.* Vol. 2, *Berlin.* Berlin: Wehrverlag Joseph Bercker.

Seelig-Stanton, R. 1914. *Reiselust und Reisekunst. Plaudereien und allerlei Wissenwertes.* 2nd edn. Richters Reisebücher. Hamburg: Verlagsanstalt und Druckerei-Gesellschaft.

Shirer, William L. 1941. *Berlin Diary: The Journal of a Foreign Correspondent, 1934–1941.* New York: Alfred A. Knopf.

———. 1947. *End of a Berlin Diary.* New York: Alfred A. Knopf.

Siemsen, Anna. 1927/8. Baedeker. *Urania: Kulturpolitische Monatshefte über Natur und Gesellschaft* 4:249–52.

Der Sportwagen—wie unsere Leser ihn sehen. 1936. *Allgemeine Automobil Zeitung* 1:11–14. 4 January.

Stangen, Carl. 1888/9. *Stangen's Illustrierter Führer durch Berlin, Potsdam, und Umgebungen.* 6th edn. Berlin: Fischer.

Stedman, Edmund C., and Thomas L. Stedman. 1909. *The Complete Pocket Guide to Europe.* New York: William R. Jenkins Co.

Stein, Irmgard von. 1936. Kosmetik des Automobilisten. *Allgemeine Automobil Zeitung* 3:26–7. 18 January.

Steinheil, Oskar. 1938. *Baedekers Autoführer. Offizieller Führer des Deutschen Automobil-Clubs.* Vol. 1, *Deutsches Reich.* Leipzig: Karl Baedeker.

———. 1952. *Baedekers Shell-Autoführer.* Vol. 3, *Rhein und Mosel.* 2nd edn. Stuttgart: Baedekers Autoführer-Verlag.

———. 1953. *Baedekers Shell-Autoführer.* Vol. 6, *Ostbayern.* Stuttgart: Baedekers Autoführer-Verlag.

A Summary. 1939. *Die Reichshauptstadt* 11:1–3. 14–20 March.

Szatmari, Eugen. 1927. *Das Buch von Berlin.* Munich: R. Piper Verlag.

Taylor, Bayard. 1914. From Bonn to Mayence. In *Seeing Europe with Famous Authors.* Vol. 5, Pt. 1, *Germany, Austria–Hungary, and Switzerland,* edited by Francis W. Halsey, 4–7. New York and London: Funk & Wagnalls Co.

Temple, Edward Lowe. 1898. *Old World Memories.* Boston: The Page Co.

Thero [pseud.]. 1937. Die Globetrotter treffen sich. *Allgemeine Automobil Zeitung* 34:1026–8. 21 April.

Touring Club Italiano. 1939. *Guida Breve d'Italia.* Vol. 2, *Italia Centrale.* Milan: Consociazione Turistica Italiana.

United States Army. Mediterranean Theater of Operations [MTOUSA]. 1945. *A Soldier's Guide to Rome.* Information and Education Section, Headquarters, MTOUSA.

Usikota. 1938. *Zulu in Germany: The Travels of a Zulu Reporter amongst the Natives of Germany.* London: Victor Gollancz.

Van Til, William. 1938. *The Danube Flows through Fascism: Nine Hundred Miles in a Fold-Boat*. New York: Charles Scribner's Sons.

Verein zur Förderung des Fremden-Verkehrs in Hamburg, ed. 1903. *Wegweiser durch Hamburg und Umgebung*. 3rd edn. Hamburg: Verlag des Verein zur Förderung des Fremden-Verkehrs.

Verkehrsamt der Stadt Berlin. 1950a. *Berlin. Die interessanteste Stadt Europas*. Berlin: Verkehrsamt der Stadt.

———. 1950b. *Don't Miss Berlin, the International City behind the Iron Curtain*. Berlin: Verkehrsamt der Stadt.

———. 1951. Die Berlinerin fällt aus dem Rahmen und ist doch immer im Bilde/Berlin girls and women fend for themselves. In *Berlin: Treffpunkt der Welt*. Vol. 2, *Das ist Berlin*, 24–5. Berlin: Verkehrsamt der Stadt.

Viaropa Tours. n.d. *Guide through Germany*. Bielefeld: Viaropa Tours of Ferienreise GmbH.

Der Wagen für die Autobahn—im Spiegel unserer Leser. 1936. *Allgemeine Automobil Zeitung* 38:8–13. 19 September.

Warum, Dr. 1927. Wochenendfahrt nach Helgoland. *Rheinische Zeitung*. 16 July.

Waxman, Francis Sheafer. 1912. *A Shopping Guide to Paris and London*. New York: McBride, Nast & Co.

*Weimarer Land*. 1932. Meyers Reisebücher. Leipzig: Verlag Bibliographisches Institut.

Weka [Willy Pröger]. 1930. *Stätten der Berliner Prostitution. Von den Elends- und Absteigequartieren am Schlesischen Bahnhof und Alexanderplatz zur Luxusprostitution der Friedrichstraße und des Kurfürstendamms*. Berlin: Auffenberg Verlagsgesellschaft.

Werner, A. n.d. *Führer durch Kassel und das hessische Bergland*. Kassel: Verlag von Max Brunnemann.

Woerl, Leo. 1898. *Führer durch München und Umgebung*. 24th edn. Woerl's Reisehandbücher. Leipzig: Woerl's Reisebücherverlag.

Woon, Basil. 1927. *The Frantic Atlantic*. New York: Alfred A. Knopf.

Yorickson [Umberto Ferigni]. 1909. *Da Firenze a Firenze*. Florence: Stab. Tip. Del 'Nuovo Giornale.'

Zeddies. Adolf, 1937. *Unbekanntes Deutschland: Wanderungen durch verborgene Schönheiten deutscher Gaue*. Bad Homburg: Siemens-Verlags-Gesellschaft.

Zentner, Kurt, ed. 1954. *Aufstieg aus dem Nichts: Deutschland von 1945 bis 1953. Eine Soziographie in zwei Bänden*, 2 vols. Cologne: Kiepenheuer & Witsch.

Zentralrat der Freien Deutschen Jugend, ed. 1955. *Junge Touristen*. Berlin: Verlag Junge Welt.

Zimmermann, Gustav A. 1889. *Eine Ferienreise durch Frankreich, die Schweiz und Deutschland. Reisebriefe*. Milwaukee: Verlag von Georg Brumder.

## II  Secondary Literature

Allen, Esther. 1996. 'Money and the Little Red Books': Romanticism, Tourism, and the Rise of the Guidebook. *LIT* 7:213–26.

Amerikanische Erholungsreisen im Jahre 1930. 1931. In *Archiv für den Fremdenverkehr*. 3:91–3. October.

Andersen, Arne. 1997. *Der Traum vom guten Leben: Alltags- und Konsumgeschichte vom Wirtschaftswunder bis heute*. Frankfurt am Main: Campus.

# Bibliography

Applegate, Celia. 1990. *A Nation of Provincials: The German Idea of Heimat.* Berkeley: University of California Press.

Ashworth, G.J., and P.J. Larkham, eds. 1994. *Building a New Heritage: Tourism, Culture, and Identity.* London: Routledge.

Baird, Jay. 1990. *To Die for Germany: Heroes in the Nazi Pantheon.* Bloomington: Indiana University Press.

Baranowski, Shelley. 2000. Strength through Joy: Tourism and National Integration in the Third Reich. In *Tourism, Commercial Leisure and National Identities in 19th and 20th Century Europe and North America*, edited by Shelley Baranowski and Ellen Furlough. Ann Arbor: University of Michigan Press.

Baranowski, Shelley, and Ellen Furlough, eds. 2000. *Tourism, Commercial Leisure and National Identities in 19th and 20th Century Europe and North America.* Ann Arbor: University of Michigan Press.

Barclay, David, and Elizabeth Glaser-Schmidt, eds. 1997. *Transatlantic Images and Perceptions: Germany and America since 1776.* Cambridge: Cambridge University Press.

Barnouw, Dagmar. 1996. *Germany 1945: Views of War and Violence.* Bloomington: Indiana University Press.

Barthes, Roland. 1972. *Mythologies.* New York: Hill and Wang.

———. 1982. *Empire of Signs.* New York: Hill and Wang.

Bartov, Omer. 1996. *Murder in our Midst: The Holocaust, Industrial Killing, and Representation.* Oxford: Oxford University Press.

Baudrillard, Jean. 1988. *America.* London: Verso.

Baumgarten, Peter. 1978. Nachwort. In *Rheinreise von Basel bis Düsseldorf*, edited by Karl Baedeker [1849], 377–86. Reprint. Dortmund: Harenberg Kommunikation.

Bausinger, Hermann. 1987. Bürgerlichkeit und Kultur. In *Bürger und Bürgerlichkeit im 19. Jahrhundert*, edited by Jürgen Kocka, 121–42. Göttingen: Vandenhoeck & Ruprecht.

———. 1991. Grenzenlos . . . Ein Blick auf den modernen Tourismus. In *Reisekultur: Von der Pilgerfahrt zum modernen Tourismus*, edited by Hermann Bausinger, Klaus Beyrer, and Gottfried Korff, 343–53. Munich: C.H. Beck.

Bausinger, Hermann, Klaus Beyrer, and Gottfried Korff, eds. 1991. *Reisekultur: Von der Pilgerfahrt zum modernen Tourismus.* Munich: C.H. Beck.

Becher, Ursula A.J. 1990. *Geschichte des modernen Lebenstils. Essen-Wohnen-Freizeit-Reisen.* Munich: C.H. Beck.

Becker, Rolf. 1983. Der Aufbruch in die Moderne im Spiegel der Baedekerschen Reisehandbücher. Am Beispiel des Wuppertals und der Ruhrgebietsstädte Dortmund, Essen und Oberhausen dargestellt. *Romerike Berge* 4:1–13.

Benjamin, Walter. 1969 [1931]. Unpacking my Library: A Talk about Book Collecting. In *Illuminations: Essays and Reflections*, edited by Hannah Arendt, 59–67. New York: Schocken.

———. 1986 [1928]. One-Way Street (Selection). In *Reflections: Essays, Aphorisms, Autobiographical Writings*, edited by Peter Demetz, 61–94. New York: Schocken.

———. 1992 [1950]. Berliner Kindheit um Neunzehnhundert. Auswahl. In *Städtebilder*, by Walter Benjamin, 77–106. Frankfurt am Main: Suhrkamp Verlag.

Berghahn, Volker R. 1995. West German Reconstruction and American Industrial Culture, 1945–1960. In *The American Impact on Postwar Germany*, edited by Reiner Pommerin, 65–81. Providence: Berghahn Books.

Berman, Marshall. 1988. *All that is Solid Melts into Air: The Experience of Modernity.* New York: Penguin.

# Bibliography

Bernard, Paul B. 1978. *Rush to the Alps: The Evolution of Vacationing in Switzerland.* Boulder: East European Quarterly.

Blackbourn, David. 1998. *The Long Nineteenth Century: A History of Germany, 1780–1918.* New York: Oxford University Press.

Blackbourn, David, and Geoff Eley. 1984. *The Peculiarities of German History: Bourgeois Society and Politics in Nineteenth-Century Germany.* New York: Oxford University Press.

Blackbourn, David, and Richard Evans, eds. 1991. *The German Bourgeoisie.* London: Routledge.

Boberach, Heinz, ed. 1984. *Meldungen aus dem Reich: Die geheimen Lageberichte des Sicherheitsdienstes der SS 1938–1945.* 17 vols. Herrsching: Pawlak Verlag.

Boissevain, Jeremy, ed. 1996. *Coping with Tourists: European Reactions to Mass Tourism.* Providence: Berghahn Books.

Boorstin, Daniel J. 1961. *The Image: A Guide to Pseudo-Events in America.* New York: Harper & Row.

Bormann, Artur. 1932. Der Deutsche im Fremdenverkehr des europäischen Auslands. In *Archiv für den Fremdenverkehr* 3:68–87.

Böröcz, József. 1992. Travel-Capitalism: The Structure of Europe and the Advent of the Tourist. *Comparative Studies in Society and History* 34:708–41.

———. 1996. *Leisure Migration: A Sociological Study on Tourism.* Oxford: Elsevier Science.

Bosworth, R.J.B. 1997. The *Touring Club Italiano* and the Nationalization of the Italian Bourgeoisie. *European History Quarterly* 27:371–410.

Bourdieu, Pierre. 1984. *Distinction: A Social Critique of the Judgement of Taste.* Cambridge, Massachusetts: Harvard University Press.

Boyer, M. Christine. 1994. *The City of Collective Memory: Its Historical Imagery and Architectural Entertainments.* Cambridge, Massachusetts: MIT Press.

Boyle, Laurence. 1986. Hans Baedeker. *Reiseleben* 13:2–6.

Bracher, Karl Dietrich. 1970. *The German Dictatorship: The Origins, Structure, and Effects of National Socialism.* New York: Praeger.

Breckman, Warren G. 1990. Disciplining Consumption: The Debate about Luxury in Wilhelmine Germany, 1890–1914. *Journal of Social History* 24:485–505.

Brendon, Piers. 1991. *Thomas Cook: 150 Years of Popular Tourism.* London: Secker & Warburg.

Brenner, Peter, ed. 1989. *Der Reisebericht: Die Entwicklung einer Gattung in der deutschen Literatur.* Frankfurt am Main: Suhrkamp.

———. 1990. *Der Reisebericht in der deutschen Literatur: Ein Forschungsüberblick als Vorstudie zu einer Gattungsgeschichte.* Tübingen: Max Niemeyer.

Browning, Christopher R. 1992. *Ordinary Men: Reserve Police Battalion 101 and the Final Solution in Poland.* New York: HarperCollins.

Buzard, James. 1993. *The Beaten Track: European Tourism, Literature, and the Ways to Culture, 1880–1918.* Oxford: Clarendon.

Carter, Erica. 1997. *How German Is She? Postwar West German Reconstruction and the Consuming Woman.* Ann Arbor: University of Michigan Press.

Cavazza, Stefano. 1993. Tradizione regionale e rieusumazioni demologiche durante il fascismo. *Studi storici* 34:625-55.

Clifford, James. 1997. *Routes. Travel and Translation in the Late Twentieth Century.* Cambridge, Massachusetts: Harvard University Press.

Confino, Alon. 1997. *The Nation as a Local Metaphor: Württemberg, Imperial Germany, and National Memory.* Chapel Hill: University of North Carolina Press.

———. 1998. Tourismusgeschichte Ost- und Westdeutschlands: Ein Forschungsbericht. *Voyage* 2:145–52.

Corbin, Alain. 1994. *The Lure of the Sea: The Discovery of the Seaside in the Western World, 1750–1840*. Berkeley: University of California Press.

Cross, Gary. 1989. Vacations for All: The Leisure Question in the Era of the Popular Front. *Journal of Contemporary History* 24:599–621.

———. ed. 1990. *Worktowners at Blackpool. Mass-Observation and Popular Leisure in the 1930s*. London: Routledge.

Culler, Jonathan. 1981. Semiotics of Tourism. *American Journal of Semiotics* 1:127–40.

Debord, Guy. 1973. *Society of the Spectacle*. Detroit: Red & Black.

De Certeau, Michel. 1984. *The Practice of Everyday Life*. Berkeley: University of California Press.

De Grazia, Victoria. 1981. *The Culture of Consent: Mass Organization of Leisure in Fascist Italy*. Cambridge: Cambridge University Press.

De Grazia, Victoria, and Ellen Furlough, eds. 1996. *The Sex of Things: Gender and Consumption in Historical Perspective*. Berkeley: University of California Press.

De Lauretis, Theresa. 1984. *Alice doesn't: Feminism, Semiotics, Cinema*. Bloomington: Indiana University Press.

De Seta, Cesare. 1997. Before Photography. In *Le Grand Tour in the Photographs of Travelers of the 19th Century*, by Italo Zannier, 9–11. Venice: Canal & Stamperia Editrice.

Diggens, John Patrick. 1996. *Max Weber: Politics and the Spirit of Tragedy*. New York: Basic Books.

Diner, Dan. 1993. *Verkehrte Welten: Antiamerikanismus in Deutschland. Ein historischer Essay*. Frankfurt am Main: Eichborn.

Dulles, Foster Rhea. 1964. *Americans Abroad: Two Centuries of European Travel*. Ann Arbor: University of Michigan Press.

During, Simon, ed. 1999. *The Cultural Studies Reader*. 2nd edn. London: Routledge.

Eich, Hermann. 1963. *Die unheimlichen Deutschen*. Düsseldorf: Econ-Verlag.

Eichberg, Henning. 1992. Join the Army and See the World. Krieg als Touristik—Tourismus als Krieg. In *Reisen und Alltag. Beiträge zur kulturwissenschaftlichen Tourismus-forschungen*, edited by Dieter Kramer and Ronald Lutz, 207–28. Frankfurt am Main: Institut für Kulturanthropologie und Europäische Ethnologie der Universität.

Ein Jahr deutsche Verkehrswerbung in Amerika. 1926. *Das Reisebüro* 5:11.

Eksteins, Modris. 1989. *Rites of Spring: The Great War and the Birth of the Modern Age*. New York: Doubleday.

Endy, Christopher. 1998. Travel and World Power: Americans in Europe, 1890–1917. *Diplomatic History* 22:565–95. Fall.

Enzensberger, Hans Magnus. 1964. Eine Theorie des Tourismus. In *Einzelheiten I. Bewußtseins-Industrie*, by Hans Magnus Enzensberger, 179–205. Frankfurt Am Main: Suhrkamp.

Erdmann, Wulf, and Klaus-Peter Lorenz. 1985. *Die grüne Lust der roten Touristen: Das fotografierte Leben des Arbeiters und Naturfreundes Paul Schminke (1888–1966)*. Hamburg: Junius Verlag.

Ermarth, Michael. 1993. *The German Talks Back*: Heinrich Hauser and German Attitudes toward Americanization after World War II. In *America and the Shaping of German Society, 1945–1955*, edited by Michael Ermarth, 101–31. Providence: Berg Publishers.

Europas Flugzentrale. 1926. *Das Reisebüro* 6:10.

# Bibliography

Falkenberg, Regine. 1991. Reisespiele—Reiseziele. In *Reisekultur: Von der Pilgerfahrt zum modernen Tourismus*, edited by Hermann Bausinger, Klaus Beyrer, and Gottfried Korff, 286–90. Munich: C.H. Beck.

Feifer, Maxine. 1985. *Going Places: The Ways of the Tourist from Imperial Rome to the Present Day*. London: Macmillan.

Fiske, John. 1989. *Understanding Popular Culture*. London: Unwin Hyman.

Freese, Peter. 1990. Exercises in Boundary-Making: The German as the 'Other' in American Literature. In *Germany and German Thought in American Literature and Cultural Criticism*, edited by Peter Freese, 93–132. Essen: Die Blaue Eule.

Das Fremdenverkehrszahlungsbilanz der Vereinigten Staaten von Nordamerika. 1931. 1933. *Archiv für den Fremdenverkehr* 2:61–7.

Frevert, Ute. 1989. *Women in German History: From Bourgeois Emancipation to Sexual Liberation*. Oxford and New York: Berg Publishers.

Fritzsche, Peter. 1994. Vagabond in the Fugitive City: Hans Ostwald, Imperial Berlin and the *Grossstadt-Dokumente. Journal of Contemporary History* 29:385–402.

Frühauf, Helmut. 1992. *Das Verlagshaus Baedeker in Koblenz, 1827–1872*. Koblenz: Rheinische Landesbibliothek.

Frykman, Jonas, and Orvar Löfgren. 1987. *Culture Builders: A Historical Anthropology of Middle-Class Life*. New Brunswick: Rutgers University Press.

Furlough, Ellen. 1998. Making Mass Vacations: Tourism and Consumer Culture in France, 1930s to 1970s. *Comparative Studies in Society and History* 40:247–86.

Fussell, Paul. 1980. *Abroad: British Literary Travelers Between the Wars*. New York: Oxford University Press.

Ganser, Armin. 1996. Zur Geschichte touristischer Produkte in der Bundesrepublik. In *Goldstrand und Teutonengrill: Kultur- und Sozialgeschichte des Tourismus in Deutschland 1945 bis 1989*, edited by Hasso Spode, 185–200. Berlin: Verlag für universitäre Kommunikation.

Gatzke, Hans W. 1980. *Germany and the United States, a 'Special Relationship?'* Cambridge, Massachusetts: Harvard University Press.

Gay, Peter. 1984. *Education of the Senses*, Vol. 1 of *The Bourgeois Experience: Victoria to Freud*. New York: Oxford University Press.

Geese, Sabine. 1989. Konrad Haemmerling. In *Literatur Lexicon: Autoren und Werke deutscher Sprache*, 4:458. Gütersloh.

Giddens, Anthony. 1991. *Modernity and Self-Identity*. Cambridge: Polity.

Gilbert, James, 1991. *Perfect Cities: Chicago's Utopias of 1893*. Chicago: University of Chicago Press.

Gimbel, John. 1961. *A German Community under American Occupation: Marburg 1945–52*. Stanford: Stanford University Press.

Gleason, Philip. 1980. American Identity and Americanization. In *Harvard Encyclopedia of American Ethnic Groups*, edited by Stephan Thernstrom, 31–58. Cambridge, Massachusetts: Harvard University Press.

Gleber, Anke. 1989. Die Erfahrung der Moderne in der Stadt. Reiseliteratur der Weimarer Republik. In *Der Reisebericht: Die Entwicklung einer Gattung in der deutschen Literatur*, edited by Peter J. Brenner, 463–89. Frankfurt am Main: Suhrkamp.

——. 1999. *The Art of Taking a Walk: Flanerie, Literature, and Film in Weimar Culture*. Princeton: Princeton University Press.

Graf, Johannes. 1995. *'Die notwendige Reise': Reisen und Reiseliteratur junger Autoren während des Nationalsozialismus*. Stuttgart: Verlag für Wissenschaft und Forschung.

# Bibliography

Gretton, John R. 1993. Introduction. In *A Bibliography of Murray's Handbooks for Travelers*, by W.B.C. Lister, i–xxv. Dereham: Dereham Books.

Grewal, Inderpal. 1996. *Home and Harem: Nation, Gender, Empire, and the Cultures of Travel*. Durham: Duke University Press.

Grossmann, Atina. 1995. *Reforming Sex: The German Movement for Birth Control and Abortion Reform, 1920–1950*. New York: Oxford University Press.

Grünthal, A. 1931. Bericht über die Wirtschaftslage im deutschen Fremdenverkehr für die Zeit vom 1. Januar bis 31. März 1931. *Archiv für den Fremdenverkehr* 2:50–6.

Guttsman, W.L. 1990. *Workers' Culture in Weimar Germany: Between Tradition and Commitment*. Oxford: Berg Publishers.

Haack, Dietmar. 1991. The Mortal Storm: Stereotypical Frames. In *Mediating a Foreign Culture: The United States and Germany. Studies in Intercultural Understanding*, edited by Lothar Bredella, 93–107. Tübingen: Gunter Narr.

Habermas, Jürgen. 1962. *Strukturwandel der Öffentlichkeit: Untersuchungen zu einer Kategorie der bürgerlichen Gesellschaft*. Neuwied: Hermann Luchterhand Verlag.

Hall, C.M., and S.J. Page. 1999. *The Geography of Tourism and Recreation: Environment, Place, and Space*. London: Routledge.

Harp, Stephen L. 1999. Touring the Trenches: Michelin Guides to the World War I Battlefields and Interwar French Tourism. Unpublished paper, American Historical Association annual meeting, Washington D.C.

Haubner, Barbara. 1998. *Nervenkitzel und Freizeitvergnügen. Automobilismus in Deutschland 1886–1914*. Göttingen: Vandenhoeck & Ruprecht.

Heer, Hannes, and Klaus Naumann, eds. 1995. *Vernichtungskrieg: Verbrechen der Wehrmacht 1941–1944*. Hamburg: Hamburger Edition.

Hein, Dieter, and Andreas Schulz, eds. 1996. *Bürgerkultur im 19. Jahrhundert: Bildung, Kunst und Lebenswelt*. Munich: C.H. Beck.

Heineman, Elizabeth D. 1989. Gender Identity in the *Wandervogel* Movement. *German Studies Review* 12:249–70.

———. 1996. The Hour of the Woman: Memories of Germany's 'Crisis Years' and West German National Identity. *American Historical Review* 101:354–95.

———. 1999. *What Difference does a Husband Make? Women and Marital Status in Nazi and Postwar Germany*. Berkeley: University of California Press.

Henke, Klaus-Dietmar. 1995. *Die amerikanische Besatzung Deutschlands*. Munich: Oldenbourg.

Hermand, Jost. 1983. Die touristische Erschließung und Nationalisierung des Harzes im 18. Jahrhundert. In *Reise und soziale Realität am Ende des 18. Jahrhunderts*, edited by Wolfgang Griep and Hans-Wolf Jäger, 169–87. Heidelberg: Carl Winter.

Hewitt, Andrew. 1996. *Political Inversions: Homosexuality, Fascism, and the Modernist Imaginary*. Stanford: Stanford University Press.

Hinrichsen, Alex, ed. 1988. *Baedeker-Katalog. Verzeichnis aller Baedeker-Reiseführer von 1832–1987 mit einem Abriß der Verlagsgeschichte*. Holzminden: Ursula Hinrichsen.

———. 1991. *Baedeker's Reisehandbücher 1832–1990*. Bevern: Ursula Hinrichsen.

Hobsbawm, Eric. 1983. Mass-Producing Traditions: Europe, 1870–1914. In *The Invention of Tradition*, edited by Eric Hobsbawm and Terence Ranger, 263–307. Cambridge: Cambridge University Press.

Hohorst, Gerd, Jürgen Kocka, and Gerhard A. Ritter, eds. 1975. *Sozialgeschichtliches Arbeitsbuch. Materialien zur Statistik des Kaiserreichs 1870–1914*. Munich: C.H. Beck.

Horne, Donald. 1984. *The Great Museum: The Re-Presentation of History*. London: Pluto.

Huck, Gerhard, and Jürgen Reulecke, eds. 1978. . . . *und reges Leben ist überall sichtbar! Reisen im Bergischen Land um 1800*. Neustadt an der Aisch: Ph.C.W. Schmidt.

Iggers, Georg G. 1968. *The German Conception of History: The National Tradition of Historical Thought from Herder to the Present*. Hanover: Wesleyan University Press.

James, Harold. 1989. *A German Identity, 1770–1990*. New York: Routledge.

Jameson, Fredric. 1991. *Postmodernism, or, The Cultural Logic of Late Capitalism*. Durham: Duke University Press.

Jarausch, Konrad. 1986. Das amerikanische Deutschlandbild in drei Jahrhunderten. In *Das Deutschland- und Amerikabild. Beiträge zum gegenseitigen Verständnis beider Völker*, edited by Klaus Weigelt, 10–20. Melle: Verlag Ernst Knoth.

Jelavich, Peter. 1993. *Berlin Cabaret*. Cambridge, Massachusetts: Harvard University Press.

Kaschuba, Wolfgang. 1988. Deutsche Bürgerlichkeit nach 1800. Kultur als symbolische Praxis. In *Bürgertum im 19. Jahrhundert. Deutschland im europäischen Vergleich*, edited by Jürgen Kocka (with Ute Frevert), 3:9–44. Munich: Deutscher Taschenbuch Verlag.

———. 1991. Die Fußreise. Von der Arbeitswanderung zur bürgerlichen Bildungsbewegung. In *Reisekultur. Von der Pilgerfahrt zum modernen Tourismus*, edited by Hermann Bausinger, Klaus Beyrer, and Gottfried Korff, 165–73. Munich: C.H. Beck.

Keitz, Christine. 1989. Zwischen Kultur und Gegenkultur. Baedeker und die ersten Arbeitertouristen in der Weimarer Republik. *Reisen und Leben* 19:3–17.

———. 1992. Organisierte Arbeiterreisen und Tourismus in der Weimarer Republik: Eine sozialgeschichtliche Untersuchung über Voraussetzungen und Praxis des Reisens in der Arbeiterschicht. 3 vols. Dissertation, Freie Universität Berlin.

———. 1993. Die Anfänge des modernen Massentourismus in der Weimarer Republik. *Archiv für Sozialgeschichte* 33:179–209.

———. 1997. *Reisen als Leitbild: Die Entstehung des modernen Massentourismus in Deutschland*. Munich: Deutscher Taschenbuch Verlag.

Kellner, Douglas. 1992. Popular Culture and the Construction of Postmodern Identities. In *Modernity & Identity*, edited by Scott Lash and Jonathan Friedman, 141–77. Oxford: Blackwell.

Kirshenblatt-Gimblett, Barbara. 1998. *Destination Culture: Tourism, Museums, and Heritage*. Berkeley: University of California Press.

Knebel, Hans-Joachim. 1960. *Soziologische Strukturwandlungen im modernen Tourismus*. Stuttgart: Ferdinand Enke.

Kocka, Jürgen (with Ute Frevert), ed. 1988. *Bürgertum im 19. Jahrhundert. Deutschland im europäischen Vergleich*. 3 vols. Munich: Deutscher Taschenbuch Verlag.

Kohut, Thomas. 1991. *Wilhelm II and the Germans: A Study in Leadership*. New York: Oxford University Press.

König, Gudrun M. 1996. *Eine Kulturgeschichte des Spazierganges. Spuren einer bürgerlichen Praktik 1780–1850*. Vienna: Böhlau Verlag.

Koonz, Claudia. 1987. *Mothers in the Fatherland: Women, the Family, and Nazi Politics*. New York: St. Martin's.

Koshar, Rudy. 1998a. *Germany's Transient Pasts: Preservation and National Memory in the Twentieth Century*. Chapel Hill: University of North Carolina Press.

———. 1998b. 'What ought to Be Seen': Tourists' Guidebooks and National Identities in Modern Germany and Europe. *Journal of Contemporary History* 33:323–40.

———. 2000. *From Monuments to Traces: The Artifacts of German Memory, 1870–1990*. Berkeley: University of California Press.

——. Forthcoming. 'Germany has Been a Melting Pot': American and German Intercultures, 1945–1955. In *Being Present in the Other Culture*, edited by Frank Trommler and Elliot Shore. New York: Berghahn Books.

Kracauer, Siegfried. 1995. Travel and Dance. In *The Mass Ornament: Weimar Essays*, by Siegfried Kracauer, 65–73. Cambridge, Massachusetts: Harvard University Press.

Kramer, Dieter. 1984. Arbeiter als Touristen: Ein Privileg wird gebrochen. In *Mit uns zieht die neue Zeit: Die Naturfreunde. Zur Geschichte eines alternativen Arbeiterkulturbewegung*, edited by Jochen Zimmer, 31–65. Cologne: Pahl-Rugenstein.

Krasnobaev, B.I., Gert Robel, and Herbert Zeman, eds. 1980. *Reisen und Reisebeschreibungen im 18. und 19. Jahrhundert als Quellen der Kulturbeziehungsforschung*. Berlin: Verlag Ulrich Camen.

Kugelmass, Jack. 1993. The Rites of the Tribe: The Meaning of Poland for American Jewish Tourists. *YIVO Annual*, Vol. 21, *Going Home*, edited by Jack Kugelmass, 395–453. Evanston: Northwestern University Press.

Kugelmass, Jack, and Jonathan Boyarin, eds. 1983. *From a Ruined Garden: The Memorial Books of Polish Jewry*. New York: Schocken.

Kunsthistorisches Institut der Universität Tübingen, ed. 1981. *Mit dem Auge des Touristen: Zur Geschichte des Reisebildes*. Tübingen: pagina.

Kushner, Tony. 1996. The Memory of Belsen. *New Formations* 30:18–32.

Lach, Donald F. 1945. What They would Do about Germany. *The Journal of Modern History* 17:227–43. September.

Lamb, Stephen, and Anthony Phelan. 1995. Weimar Culture: The Birth of Modernism. In *German Cultural Studies: An Introduction*, edited by Rob Burns, 53–99. Oxford: Oxford University Press.

Lambert, R.S. 1935. *Grand Tour: A Journey in the Tracks of the Age of Aristocracy*. London: Faber and Faber.

Latzel, Klaus. 1995. Tourismus und Gewalt. Kriegswahrnehmungen in Feldpostbriefen. In *Vernichtungskrieg: Verbrechen der Wehrmacht 1941–1944*, edited by Hannes Heer and Klaus Naumann, 447–59. Hamburg: Hamburger Edition.

Lauterbach, Burkhart. 1989. Baedeker und andere Reiseführer: Eine Problemskizze. *Zeitschrift für Volkskunde* 85:206–34.

Leed, Eric J. 1991. *The Mind of the Traveler: From Gilgamesh to Global Tourism*. New York: Basic Books.

Lehnert, Uta. 1998. *Der Kaiser und die Siegesallee: Réclame Royale*. Berlin: Reimer.

Lepowitz, Helena Waddy. 1992. Pilgrims, Patients, and Painters: The Formation of a Tourist Culture in Bavaria. *Historical Reflections/Reflexions Historiques*, 18:121–45.

Lethen, Helmut. 1970. *Neue Sachlichkeit 1924–1932: Studien zur Literatur des 'Weissen Sozialismus.'* Stuttgart: Metzler 1970.

Levenstein, Harvey. 1998. *Seductive Journey: American Tourists in France from Jefferson to the Jazz Age*. Chicago: University of Chicago Press.

Lidtke, Vernon. 1985. *The Alternative Culture: Socialist Labor in Imperial Germany*. New York: Oxford University Press.

Liebersohn, Harry. 1998. *Aristocratic Encounters: European Travelers and North American Indians*. Cambridge: Cambridge University Press.

Lister, W.B.C. 1993. *A Bibliography of Murray's Handbooks for Travellers*. Dereham: Dereham Books.

Lloyd, David W. 1998. *Battlefield Tourism: Pilgrimage and Commemoration of the Great War in Britain, Australia and Canada*. Oxford and New York: Berg Publishers.

# Bibliography

Löfgren, Orvar. 1999. *On Holiday: A History of Vacationing*. Berkeley: University of California Press.

Lowenthal, David. 1985. *The Past is a Foreign Country*. Cambridge: Cambridge University Press.

——. 1996. *Possessed by the Past: The Heritage Crusade and the Spoils of History*. New York: The Free Press.

Lüdtke, Alf. 1989. Wo blieb die 'rote Glut'? Arbeitererfahrungen und deutscher Faschismus. In *Alltagsgeschichte. Zur Rekonstruktion historischer Erfahrungen und Lebensweisen*, edited by Alf Lüdtke, 224–82. Frankfurt am Main: Campus Verlag.

Lütgens, Annelie. 1997. The Conspiracy of Women: Images of City Life in the Work of Jeanne Mammen. In *Women in the Metropolis: Gender and Modernity in Weimar Culture*, edited by Katharina von Ankum, 89–105. Berkeley: University of California Press.

Maase, Kaspar. 1992. *BRAVO Amerika. Erkundungen zur Jugendkultur der Bundesrepublik in den fünziger Jahren*. Hamburg: Junius Verlag.

——. 1999. 'Americanization,' 'Americanness,' and 'Americanisms': Time for a Change in Perspective? Unpublished paper, German Historical Institute, Washington D.C., 25–7 March. <www.ghi-dc.org/conpotweb/westernpapers/maase. pdf>

MacCannell, Dean. 1976. *The Tourist: A New Theory of the Leisure Class*. New York: Schocken.

——. 1992. *Empty Meeting Grounds: The Tourist Papers*. London: Routledge.

Mackaman, Douglas Peter. 1998. *Leisure Settings: Bourgeois Culture, Medicine, and the Spa in Modern France*. Chicago: University of Chicago Press.

Mandel, Birgit. 1996. 'Amore ist heißer als Liebe.' Das Italien-Urlaubsimage der Westdeutschen in den 50er und 60er Jahren. In *Goldstrand und Teutonengrill: Kultur- und Sozialgeschichte des Tourismus in Deutschland 1945 bis 1989*, edited by Hasso Spode, 147–62. Berlin: Verlag für universitäre Kommunikation.

Mariotti, Angelo. 1932. Die Statistik des Fremdenverkehrs in Italien. *Archiv für den Fremdenverkehr* 4:108–11.

Mason, Tim. 1972. The Primacy of Politics: Politics and Economics in National Socialist Germany. In *Nazism and the Third Reich*, edited by Henry A. Turner, 175–200. New York: Quadrangle.

Maurer, Mechtild. 1998. Tourismus im Visier der 'Gender'-Debatte. Ein Forschungsbericht. *Voyage* 2:153–60.

Mendelson, Edward. 1985. Baedeker's Universe. *Yale Review* 74:386–403.

Menges, Günter. 1959. *Wachstum und Konjunktur des deutschen Fremdenverkehrs 1913 bis 1956*. Frankfurt am Main: Kommissionsverlag Waldemar Kramer.

Merritt, Richard L. 1995. *Democracy Imposed: U.S. Occupation Policy and the German Public, 1945–1949*. New Haven: Yale University Press.

Meyer, Henry Cord. 1955. *Mitteleuropa in German Thought and Action 1815–1945*. The Hague: Martinus Nijhoff.

Mills, Sara. 1991. *Discourses of Difference: An Analysis of Women's Travel Writing and Colonialism*. London: Routledge.

Mitscherlich, Alexander, and Margarete Mitscherlich. 1975. *The Inability to Mourn: Principles of Collective Behavior*. New York: Grove Press.

Mommsen, Hans, and Manfred Grieger. 1996. *Das Volkswagenwerk und seine Arbeiter im Dritten Reich*. Düsseldorf: ECON Verlag.

Mommsen, Wolfgang. 1993. Kaisermacht und Bürgerstolz: Berlin als Hauptstadt des Kaiserreiches. In *Die Hauptstädte der Deutschen: Von der Kaiserpfalz in Aachen zum Regierungssitz Berlin*, edited by Uwe Schultz, 181–93. Munich: C.H. Beck.

——. 1995. *Imperial Germany 1867–1918: Politics, Culture, and Society in an Authoritarian State*. London: Arnold.

Monaco, Paul. 1990. Stereotypes of Germans in American Culture: Observations from an Interdisciplinary Perspective. In *Amerikanisches Deutschlandbild und deutsches Amerikabild*, edited by Frank Krampikowski, 159–76. Baltmannsweiler: Pädagogischer Verlag/Burgbücherei Schneider.

Moreck, Curt. 1926. *Sittengeschichte des Kinos*. Dresden: Paul Aretz Verlag.

Moret, Fédéric. 1992. Images de Paris dans les guides touristiques vers 1900. *Le Mouvement Social* 160:79–98. July–September.

Morgan, Susan. 1996. *Place Matters: Gendered Geography in Victorian Women's Travel Books about Southeast Asia*. New Brunswick: Rutgers University Press.

Möser, Kurt. 1998. World War I and the Creation of Desire for Automobiles in Germany. In *Getting and Spending: European and American Consumer Societies in the Twentieth Century*, edited by Susan Strasser, Charles McGovern, and Matthias Judt, 195–222. Cambridge: Cambridge University Press.

Mosse, George. 1964. *The Crisis of German Ideology: Intellectual Origins of the Third Reich*. New York: Grosset & Dunlop.

——. 1966. *Nazi Culture. A Documentary History*. New York: Schocken.

——. 1985. *Nationalism and Sexuality: Middle-Class Morality and Sexual Norms in Europe*. Madison: University of Wisconsin Press.

——. 1990. *Fallen Soldiers: Reshaping the Memory of the World Wars*. New York: Oxford University Press.

Nagler, Jörg. 1997. From Culture to *Kultur*: Changing American Perceptions of Imperial Germany, 1870–1914. In *Transatlantic Images and Perceptions: Germany and America since 1776*, edited by David Barclay and Elisabeth Glaser-Schmidt, 131–54. Cambridge: Cambridge University Press.

Nave, Georg. 1932. Fremdenverkehr in Notzeiten. *Archiv für den Fremdenverkehr* 1:12–15. April, May, June.

Nelson, Walter Henry. 1965. *Small Wonder: The Amazing Story of the Volkswagen*. Boston: Little, Brown and Co.

Niethammer, Lutz. 1983. Privat-Wirtschaft: Erinnerungsfragmente einer anderen Umerziehung. In *'Hinterher merkt man, daß es richtig war, daß es schiefgegangen ist': Nachkriegs-Erfahrungen im Ruhrgebiet*, Vol. 2 of *Lebensgeschichte und Sozialkultur im Ruhrgebiet 1930 bis 1960*, edited by Lutz Niethammer, 17–105. Bonn: Verlag J.W.H. Dietz Nachf.

Nipperdey, Thomas. 1993. *Deutsche Geschichte 1866–1918*, Vol. 1, *Arbeitswelt und Bürgergeist*. 3rd edn. Munich: C.H. Beck.

Nolan, Mary. 1994. *Visions of Modernity: American Business and the Modernization of Germany*. New York: Oxford University Press.

Nora, Pierre, ed. 1996–8. *Realms of Memory: Rethinking the French Past*. 3 vols. New York: Columbia University Press.

Office national du tourisme, Paris. 1930. *Archiv für den Fremdenverkehr* 1:37–41. April.

Öhlberger, Reinhard. 1987. Berlin im Spiegel des Baedeker 1842–1940. In *Die Reise nach Berlin*, edited by Berliner Festspiele, 286–95. Berlin: Siedler Verlag.

Oppenheimer, Franz. 1932. Zur Soziologie des Fremdenverkehrs. *Archiv für den Fremdenverkehr* 2:33–6. July, August, September.

Organization for European Economic Co-operation, ed. 1951. *Tourism and European Recovery: An OEEC Report*. Paris: OEEC.

Ortlinghaus, Dirk. 1996. Die 'Massenmotorisierung' in der NS-Zeit. Eine sozial-wissenschaftliche Analyse der Motorisierung, des Strassenbaus und der Verkehrspolitik in der Zeit von 1932–1938. Diplomarbeit, Fachbereich Sozialwissenschaften, Universität Osnabrück.

Ousby, Ian. 1990. *The Englishman's England: Taste, Travel and the Rise of Tourism.* Cambridge: Cambridge University Press.

Pells, Richard. 1997. *Not Like Us: How Europeans have Loved, Hated, and Transformed American Culture since World War II.* New York: Basic Books.

Pelz, Annegret. 1993. *Reisen durch die eigene Fremde: Reiseliteratur von Frauen als autogeographische Schriften.* Cologne: Böhlau Verlag.

Pemble, John. 1987. *The Mediterranean Passion: Victorians and Edwardians in the South.* Oxford: Clarendon.

Pence, Katherine. 1998. From Rations to Fashions: The Gendered Politics of East and West German Consumption, 1945–1961. Dissertation, University of Michigan.

Peters, Gerhard. 1987. Redakteur an Baedekers Reisehandbüchern 1925–1934. *Reisen und Leben* 15:3–10. December.

Petersen, Jens. 1988. Vorspiel zu 'Stahlpakt' und Kriegsallianz: Das Deutsch-Italienische Kulturabkommen vom 23. November 1938. *Vierteljahreshefte für Zeitgeschichte* 36: 41–77.

Petro, Patrice. 1997. Perceptions of Difference: Women as Spectator and Spectacle. In *Women in the Metropolis: Gender and Modernity in Weimar Culture*, edited by Katharina von Ankum, 41–66. Berkeley: University of California Press.

Petzina, Dietmar, Werner Abelshauser, Anselm Faust, eds. 1978. *Sozialgeschichtliches Arbeitsbuch III: Materialien zur Statistik des Deutschen Reiches 1914–1945.* Munich: C.H. Beck.

Peukert, Detlev J.K. 1982. *Inside Nazi Germany: Conformity, Opposition and Racism in Everyday Life.* New Haven: Yale University Press.

Pile, Steven. 1996. *The Body and the City: Psychoanalysis, Space, and Subjectivity.* London: Routledge.

Plonien, Klaus. 1995. Re-Mapping the World: Travel Literature of Weimar Germany. Dissertation, University of Minnesota.

Podic, Baldo. 1986. TCI—der italienische Baedeker. *Reiseleben* 13:6–8. December.

Poock-Feller, Ulrika and Andrea Krausch. 1996. 'Berlin lebt—Berlin ruft.' Die Fremdenverkehrswerbung Ost- und West-Berlins in den Nachkriegszeit. In *Goldstrand und Teutonengrill: Kultur- und Sozialgeschichte des Tourismus in Deutschland 1945 bis 1989*, edited by Hasso Spode, 105–16. Berlin: Verlag für universitäre Kommunikation.

Prahl, Hans-Werner. 1979. *Der Millionen-Urlaub: Von der Bildungsreise zur totalen Freizeit.* Darmstadt: Luchterhand.

Pratt, Mary Louise. 1992. *Imperial Eyes: Travel Writing and Transculturation.* London: Routledge.

Pretzel, Ulrike. 1995. *Die Literaturform Reiseführer im 19. und 20. Jahrhundert. Untersuchungen am Beispiel des Rheins.* Frankfurt am Main: Peter Lang.

Putschögl, Monika. 1999. Am Anfang stand Ruhpolding. *Die Zeit* 27:49–50. 1 July.

Puvogel, Ulrike. 1987. *Gedenkstätten für die Opfer des Nationalsozialismus: Eine Dokumentation.* Bonn: Bundeszentrale für politische Bildung.

Raabe, Paul. 1985. *Die Autoren und Bücher des literarischen Expressionismus.* Stuttgart: J.B. Metzlersche Verlagsbuchhandlung.

Relph, Edward. 1987. *The Modern Urban Landscape.* Baltimore: The Johns Hopkins University Press.

# Bibliography

Roberts, Robert. 1971. *The Classic Slum: Salford Life in the First Quarter of the Century*. Harmondsworth: Penguin.

Rosenhaft, Eve. 1983. *Beating the Fascists? The German Communists and Political Violence, 1929-1933*. Cambridge: Cambridge University Press.

Sachs, Wolfgang. 1984. *For Love of the Automobile: Looking Back into the History of our Desires*. Berkeley: University of California Press.

Sauermann, Dietmar. 1992. Das Bürgertum im Spiegel von Gästebüchern des Sauerlandes. In *Reisen und Alltag: Beiträge zur kulturwissenschaftlichen Tourismusforschung*, edited by Dieter Kramer and Ronald Lutz, 81–99. Frankfurt am Main: Institut für Kultur-anthropologie und Europäische Ethnologie der Universität.

Schama, Simon. 1995. *Landscape and Memory*. New York: Alfred A. Knopf.

Schildt, Axel. 1995. *Moderne Zeiten: Freizeit, Massenmedien und 'Zeitgeist' in der Bundesrepublik der 50er Jahre*. Hamburg: Christians.

———. 1996. 'Die kostbarsten Wochen des Jahres.' Urlaubstourismus der Westdeutschen (1945–1970). In *Goldstrand und Teutonengrill: Kultur- und Sozialgeschichte des Tourismus in Deutschland 1945 bis 1989*, edited by Hasso Spode, 69–85. Berlin: Verlag für universitäre Kommunikation.

Schivelbusch, Wolfgang. 1986. *The Railway Journey: Trains and Travel in the Nineteenth Century*. Oxford: Blackwell.

Schlör, Joachim. 1991. *Nachts in der großen Stadt: Paris, Berlin, London 1840–1930*. Munich: Artemis & Winkler.

Schmidt, Alexander. 1997. *Reisen in die Moderne: Der Amerika-Diskurs des deutschen Bürgertums vor dem Ersten Weltkrieg im europäischen Vergleich*. Berlin: Akademie Verlag.

Schütz, Erhard, and Eckhard Gruber. 1996. *Mythos Reichsautobahn: Bau und Inszenierung der 'Straßen des Führers' 1933–1941*. Berlin: Ch. Links Verlag.

Schwarz, Angela. 1993a. Image and Reality: British Visitors to National Socialist Germany. *European History Quarterly* 23:381–405.

———. 1993b. *Die Reise ins Dritte Reich: Britische Augenzeugen im nationalsozialistischen Deutschland (1933–1939)*. Göttingen: Vandenhoeck & Ruprecht.

Sears, David. 1989. *Sacred Places: American Tourist Attractions in the Nineteenth Century*. New York: Oxford University Press.

Selwyn, Tom, ed. 1996. *The Tourist Image: Myths and Myth Making in Tourism*. Chichester: John Wiley & Sons.

Shaffer, Marguerite S. 1999. *See America First: Tourism and National Identity, 1880-1940*. Washington D.C.: Smithsonian Institution Press.

Sheehan, James. 1978. *German Liberalism in the Nineteenth Century*. Chicago: University of Chicago Press.

Siebert, Ulla. 1996. Reise. Nation. Text. Repräsentationen von 'Nationalität' in Reisetexten deutscher Frauen, 1871 bis 1914. In *Frauen und Nation*, edited by Frauen and Geschichte, Baden Württemberg, 49–65. Tübingen: Silberburg Verlag.

Simmel, Georg. 1971 [1903]. The Metropolis and Mental Life. In *On Individuality and Social Forms: Selected Writings*, edited by Donald N. Levine, 325–39. Chicago: University of Chicago Press.

Simpson, David. 1999. Tourism and Titanomania. *Critical Inquiry* 25:680–95.

Smith, Valene L. 1977. *Hosts and Guests: The Anthropology of Tourism*. Philadelphia: University of Pennsylvania Press.

Sombart, Werner. 1967 [1913]. *Luxury and Capitalism*. Ann Arbor: University of Michigan Press.

Speitkamp, Wilfried. 1997. Denkmalsturz und Symbolkonflikt in der modernen Geschichte: Eine Einleitung. In *Denkmalsturz: Zur Konfliktgeschichte politischer Symbolik*, edited by Winfried Speitkamp, 5–21. Göttingen: Vandenhoeck & Ruprecht.

Spode, Hasso. 1980. 'Der deutsche Arbeiter reist': Massentourismus im Dritten Reich. In *Sozialgeschichte der Freizeit. Untersuchungen zum Wandel der Alltagskultur in Deutschland*, edited by Gerhard Huck, 281–306. Wuppertal: Peter Hammer Verlag.

———. 1982. Arbeiterurlaub im Dritten Reich. In *Angst, Belohnung, Zucht und Ordnung: Herrschaftsmechanismen im Nationalsozialismus*, edited by Carola Sachse, Tilla Siegel, Hasso Spode, and Wolfgang Spohn, 275–328. Opladen: Westdeutscher Verlag.

———. 1987. *Zur Geschichte des Tourismus: Eine Skizze der Entwicklung der touristischen Reisen in der Moderne*. Starnberg: Studienkreis für Tourismus.

———. ed. 1996. *Goldstrand und Teutonengrill. Kultur- und Sozialgeschichte des Tourismus in Deutschland 1945 bis 1989*. Berlin: Verlag für universitäre Kommunikation.

Spode, Hasso, and Matthias Gutbier, eds. 1987. Berlin-Reise als Berlin-Geschichte. In *Die Reise nach Berlin*, edited by Berliner Festspiele, 25–41. Berlin: Siedler Verlag.

Statistisches Bundesamt. 1954. *Statistisches Jahrbuch für die Bundesrepublik Deutschland*. Stuttgart: W. Kohlhammer.

———. 1956. *Statistisches Jahrbuch für die Bundesrepublik Deutschland*. Stuttgart: W. Kohlhammer.

Statistisches Reichsamt. 1934. *Statistisches Jahrbuch für das Deutsche Reich*. Berlin: Verlag der Reimar Hobbing.

———. 1938. *Statistisches Jahrbuch für das Deutsche Reich*. Berlin: Verlag für Sozialpolitik, Wirtschaft und Statistik.

Sternberger, Dolf. 1977. *Panorama of the Nineteenth Century*. New York: Urizen.

Sweezy, Paul M. 1946. Germany from the Ruins. *The New Republic* 144:586. 22 April.

Swett, Pamela. 1998. Denunziation und (Selbst-)Disziplinierung: Straßenzellen der Berliner KPD, 1929–1932. *Sowi: 'Sozialwissenschaftliche Informationen'* 2:126–31. April–June.

Taylor, Charles. 1989. *Sources of the Self: The Making of Modern Identity*. Cambridge, Massachusetts: Harvard University Press.

Teichler, Hans-Joachim. 1976. Berlin 1936—Ein Sieg der NS-Propaganda? *Stadion* 2:265–306.

Thamer, Hans-Ulrich. 1998. Geschichte und Propaganda. Kulturhistorische Ausstellungen in der NS-Zeit. *Geschichte und Gesellschaft* 3:349–81. July–September.

Theweleit, Klaus. 1977–8. *Männerphantasien*, 2 vols. Frankfurt am Main: Verlag Roter Stern.

Tissot, Laurent. 1995. How did the British Conquer Switzerland? Guidebooks, Railways, Travel Agencies, 1850–1914. *The Journal of Transport History*, 3rd series, 16:21–54. March.

Titzhoff, Peter. 1959. Deutschland-Reiseland. In *Deutschland Heute*, edited by Presse- und Informationsamt der Bundesregierung. 5th edn. Bonn: Presse- und Informationsamt der Bundesregierung.

Towner, John. 1996. *An Historical Geography of Recreation and Tourism in the Western World 1540–1940*. New York: Wiley 1996.

Treue, Wilhelm. 1953. Zum Thema der Auslandsreisen im 18. und 19. Jahrhundert. *Archiv für Kulturgeschichte* 35:328–33.

Trommler, Frank. 1998. The Historical Invention and Modern Reinvention of Two National Identities. In *Identity and Intolerance: Nationalism, Racism, and Xenophobia in Germany and the United States*, edited by Norbert Finzsch and Dietmar Schirmer, 21–42. Washington, D.C.: German Historical Institute and Cambridge University Press.

# Bibliography

Trova, Assunta. 1993. Alle origini dell'Ente nazionale industrie turistiche e alberghiere (1939–1941). *Risorgimento* 45:265–77.

Tümmers, Horst Johannes. 1994. *Der Rhein. Ein europäischer Fluß und seine Geschichte.* Munich: C.H. Beck.

Urbain, Jean-Didier. 1994. *Sur la Plage: Moeurs et Coutumes Balnéaires.* Paris: Payot.

Urry, John. 1990. *The Tourist Gaze: Leisure and Travel in Contemporary Societies.* London: Sage Publications.

———. 1995. *Consuming Places.* London: Routledge.

Vaughan, John. 1974. *The English Guide Book 1780–1870: An Illustrated History.* Newton Abbot: David & Charles.

Veblen, Thorstein. 1953 [1899]. *The Theory of the Leisure Class. An Economic Study of Institutions.* New York: New American Library.

Vogel, Jakob. 1997. *Nationen im Gleichschritt: Der Kult der 'Nation in Waffen' in Deutschland und Frankreich, 1871–1914.* Göttingen: Vandenhoeck & Ruprecht.

Volksbund Deutsche Kriegsgräberfürsorge, ed. 1983. *Atlas deutscher Kriegsgräberstätten des 1. und 2. Weltkrieges in Europa und Übersee.* Munich: JRO-Kartografische Verlagsgesellschaft.

Vorsteher, Dieter. 1991. Bildungsreisen unter Dampf. In *Reisekultur. Von der Pilgerfahrt zum modernen Tourismus,* edited by Hermann Bausinger, Klaus Beyrer, and Gottfried Korff, 304–11. Munich: C.H. Beck.

Wallace, Anne D. 1993. *Walking, Literature, and English Culture: The Origins and Uses of Peripatetic in the Nineteenth Century.* Oxford: Clarendon Press.

Walton, John K. 1983. *The English Seaside Resort: A Social History 1750–1914.* New York: St. Martin's.

———. 1997. Taking the History of Tourism Seriously. *European History Quarterly* 27:563–71.

Weber, Hermann, and F. Parkes Weber. 1898. *The Mineral Waters and Health Resorts of Europe.* London: Smith, Elder, & Co.

Wehler, Hans-Ulrich. 1995. *Deutsche Gesellschaftsgeschichte,* Vol. 3, *Von der 'Deutschen Doppelrevolution' bis zum Beginn des Ersten Weltkrieges 1849–1914.* Munich: C.H. Beck.

Wildt, Michael. 1994. *Am Beginn der 'Konsumgesellschaft': Mangelerfahrung, Lebenshaltung, Wohlstandshoffnung in Westdeutschland in den fünfziger Jahren.* Hamburg: Ergebnisse Verlag.

———. 1996. *Vom kleinen Wohlstand: Eine Konsumgeschichte der fünfziger Jahre.* Frankfurt am Main: Fischer Taschenbuch Verlag.

Willett, Ralph. 1989. *The Americanization of Germany, 1945–1949.* London: Routledge.

Williams, Raymond. 1977. *Marxism and Literature.* Oxford: Oxford University Press.

Williams, Rosalind H. 1982. *Dream Worlds: Mass Consumption in Late Nineteenth Century France.* Berkeley: University of California Press.

Winter, Hans-Gert. 1935. Deutschland wirbt im Ausland. In *Deutsche Werbung* 10:1070–2, 1082–3.

Withey, Lynne. 1997. *Grand Tours and Cook's Tours: A History of Leisure Travel, 1750 to 1915.* New York: William Morrow and Co.

Wolbring, Barbara. 1996. 'Auch ich in Arkadien!' Die bürgerliche Kunst- und Bildungsreise im 19. Jahrhundert. In *Bürgerkultur im 19. Jahrhundert: Bildung, Kunst und Lebenswelt,* edited by Dieter Hein and Andreas Schulz, 82–101. Munich: C.H. Beck.

Young, James E. 1993. *The Texture of Memory: Holocaust Memorials and Meaning.* New Haven: Yale University Press.

Zannier, Italo. 1997. *Le Grand Tour in the Photographs of Travelers of the 19th Century.* Venice: Canal & Stamperia Editrice.

Zimmer, Jochen, ed. 1984. *Mit uns zieht die neue Zeit: Die Naturfreunde. Zur Geschichte eines alternativen Arbeiterkulturbewegung.* Cologne: Pahl-Rugenstein.

# Index